T0272417

Lean on Me

Lean on Me

A Politics of Radical Care

Lynne Segal

VERSO

London • New York

First published by Verso 2023
© Lynne Segal 2023

All rights reserved

The moral rights of the author have been asserted

Excerpt from 'We Don't Need the Men'
Words and music by Malvina Reynolds
© 1959 by Schroder Music Co. (ASCAP). All rights reserved.
Used with permission.

1 3 5 7 9 10 8 6 4 2

Verso
UK: 6 Meard Street, London W1F 0EG
US: 388 Atlantic Avenue, Brooklyn, NY 11217
versobooks.com

Verso is the imprint of New Left Books

ISBN-13: 978-1-80429-294-5
ISBN-13: 978-1-80429-295-2 (UK EBK)
ISBN-13: 978-1-80429-296-9 (US EBK)

British Library Cataloguing in Publication Data
A catalogue record for this book is available from the British Library

Library of Congress Cataloging-in-Publication Data
A catalog record for this book is available from the Library of Congress

Typeset in Sabon by MJ & N Gavan, Truro, Cornwall
Printed and bound by CPI Group (UK) Ltd, Croydon, CR0 4YY

For Andreas, Catherine, Éamonn, and Zim

Contents

Acknowledgements

This book has been evolving for a very long time, in my desire to celebrate our human ties and lifelong need to care for one another and the world around us. Its title, *Lean on Me*, has hovered around me for years, waiting for the words to give it life. Two of my dearest friends, Andreas Chatzidakis and Catherine Rottenberg, decided to join me in pondering the topic of care. Soon joined by Jo Littler and Jamie Hakim, we quickly formed the Care Collective, and together wrote our popular *The Care Manifesto*, which appeared in 2020. So, first up, I am profoundly grateful to our small collective, as together we expanded our thoughts on care, while taking such good care of each other. Secondly, I am extremely grateful to my editor Leo Hollis, at Verso, who not only commissioned this book but was firmly determined to ensure it would be written to reach the widest possible audience. That task was enhanced by my final copy editor, Lorna Scott Fox. I would also like to thank my agent, Eleanor Birne, from Pew Literary Agency, for her encouragement and securing my contract, and again Catherine Rottenberg, for her generous editing skills.

Along the way, I always had the support of wise and generous friends, who help me in such differing ways that I find it impossible to single them out – although I can't not mention just a few: Éamonn McKeown, Maria Brock, Misha Rudnev, Rachel Moore, Denise Riley and Tanya Skillen who visited me throughout lockdown, along with my lovely neighbours Julian Lousada, Jonathan Gore, Neve Gordon, Tony Graham, and Kim Longinotto. Political comrades in Highbury have helped me through what proved very troubling times, as have my Jewish friends around the world, including in Israel. They know that criticizing Israel's continued brutal occupation and denial of Palestinian rights has by default become the very essence of our Jewishness.

What I know is that it is the warmth and care of friends that makes life worthwhile, the more so as they expand across the generations to keep me attached to the new challenges faced by younger people nowadays. My original feminist writing group – Sally Alexander, Catherine Hall, Cora Kaplan, and Barbara Taylor – have always encouraged my writing, and shared their own. I now have the benefit of a most supportive household, Nick Davidson and I having recently been joined by Steve Skaith and Claudia Diaz, along with their son Danny. My own family, Barbara, Graeme, and Zimri Segal, Bill Tuck and Marina Warner, are always as warm and helpful as they can be, while my partner Agnes Bolsø keeps me daily aware of the possibility of closeness across distance.

Introduction

The Kindness of Strangers

'I've always depended on the kindness of strangers' is the famous last line spoken by that tragic figure Blanche DuBois in Tennessee Williams's *A Streetcar Named Desire*. I recently enjoyed a revelation from another Blanche, the theatre critic Blanche Marvin, about the origins of that remark. Once thought to be based on the fate of Williams's older sister, Rose, who spent much of her life in mental hospitals, those words, Marvin revealed, were actually her words, uttered to reassure her good friend, Tennessee, when he complained about always living in hotel rooms, surrounded by strangers. Marvin had responded: 'I've only known kindness from strangers and so can you.'[1]

It's true, we all depend upon the kindness of strangers. And yet we usually take for granted the extent to which our sense of independence relies upon care and respect from others. There is no life without care. We all care and are cared for in multiple ways if we are to stay alive – although some will receive more care than others. Many people in the UK now suffer from a serious lack of care, evident in the widening inequalities in illness and mortality rates, closely correlated with class status and social disadvantage. It is often assumed that what we give and what we receive, along with our sense of autonomy or dependence, shift considerably over a lifetime. Not just from my own experience, however, but from close observation of those around me, I suspect that in any long life our dependence

on others fluctuates less than we think, at least once past
infancy and before very old age.

At every stage of life, we lean upon others for recognition
and sustenance; indeed, we have no other choice. As feminist thinkers have always stressed, we depend upon support
throughout our lives, both interpersonal and public, in the
process of becoming our unique selves, gaining a sense of our
place in the world and how to surmount its constant challenges. What's more, not only do we depend upon assistance
and respect from others to appreciate ourselves, but if we are
not to fade into varieties of paranoid solipsism, we need to be
able to care for and about others. Especially as we age, what
remains most significant in our lives is likely to come from the
ways in which we have been able to help others to flourish.

That long-cherished Victorian children's writer known as
Lewis Carroll may have been a high-church conservative, but
among the insights he shared with his friend, the actress Ellen
Terry, was 'one of the deep secrets of Life – that all that is really
worth the doing, is what we do for others'.[2] The idea that we
flourish not simply through personal ambition, but as much – if
not more – through attending to others, is a recurring reflection
from those most attentive to the human condition.

Writing about the art of living well, the psychoanalyst Eric
Fromm argued that we thrive only in and through our relationships with others, and the responsibilities this generates.
In 1976, a few years before he died, he summed up his lifelong
clinical observations by suggesting that 'the frequency and
intensity of the desire to share, to give, and to sacrifice are not
surprising if we consider the conditions of existence of the
human species'. However, he quickly added: 'What is surprising is that this need could be so repressed as to make acts of
selfishness the rule in industrial (and many other) societies and
acts of solidarity the exception.'[3]

Contempt for anyone stigmatized as 'dependent', targeting primarily those seen as requiring direct financial assistance or other provision from the state, has kept pace with market deregulation and the curtailment of welfare supports over the last four decades. Such practices have generated rising inequality worldwide. It all resonates with the ongoing veneration for the 'self-made man' – who nowadays just might be a high-achieving woman – the triumphant neoliberal subject, the 'winner', with little time and no patience for what is dismissed as the whingeing of 'losers'.

Such battles between exaltation of individual independence, on the one hand, and acknowledgement of human dependency, on the other, are hardly new. As many have noted, the stress on complete autonomy in adulthood was central to the thinking of that Enlightenment philosopher known as the father of liberalism, John Locke. In his writing Locke laid down the conditions for individual liberty, seeing it as 'a state of perfect freedom [for men] to order their actions, and dispose of their possessions and persons, as they think fit, within the bounds of the law of nature, without asking leave, or depending upon the will of any other man'.[4]

A century later, another key thinker of Western philosophy, Immanuel Kant, echoed Locke's thoughts, insisting that men must emerge from their childhood immaturity with 'the courage to use their *own* understanding', proving themselves capable of rational thought 'without the guidance of another'.[5] This constant refrain lauding the wholly self-reliant individual ties in with notions of private property and modern citizenship.

However, through most of my own adult life I have encountered very different views. They were most clearly expressed by feminist philosophers who over the years have forcefully questioned this attachment to notions of the sovereign self. These scholars built upon alternative philosophical traditions, founded on a recognition of our lifelong fragility.

In one of the more recent feminist critiques of the Kantian tradition, the Italian philosopher and feminist thinker Adriana Cavarero describes the model of the self in play here as that of 'homo erectus', upright manhood. Women, with their supposedly softer, more caring 'inclinations', are always a threat to these men's principled autonomy and independence, stoking their fear of any return to what they see as childhood states of dependency and submission. The etymological root of 'inclination', Cavarero notes, comes from Greek philosophy, where to incline is to lean down, to *lower* oneself.

Being overwhelmingly male, philosophers historically have viewed any such need for others with a certain apprehension, including – perhaps especially – their own need to express and receive love and desire. Acknowledging any need for others, Cavarero observes, undermines men's 'egocentric verticality'. Furthermore, it is women, traditionally seen as less rational than men, who have been historically framed as potentially hazardous, challenging men's symbolic repudiations of dependency. And if women were generally viewed as the dangerous sex, it was mothers in particular who personified the original or primal threat to mature manhood.

Descending from philosophical abstraction to the highly concrete, Cavarero also comments: 'Kant did not love mothers, children, or nannies, and, like most male philosophers, he was an unrepentant bachelor, easily bothered by crying children.'[6] He was hardly alone in this, as we have heard from men down the ages: 'There is no more sombre enemy of good art than the pram in the hall', Cyril Connolly warned in 1938, already knowing he would never be the writer he had longed to be.[7]

It is the affirmation of relationality and fragility, not the claim to autonomy and power, that should be seen as what is most basic to the human condition. Cavarero follows other feminist thinkers, if rather more flamboyantly, in highlighting the maternal bond as the model for the significance of valuing relationality overall: 'Maternal inclination could work as a module for a different, more disruptive, and revolutionary geometry whose aim is to rethink the very core of community.'[8]

Inclinations was published just over a decade after an essay collection by that other much revered (when not enviously reviled) feminist philosopher, Judith Butler. In *Precarious Life*, she argued that in the face of mounting global violence we must always begin from the recognition of our 'inevitable interdependency'.[9] Butler suggests that acknowledgement of our shared vulnerability tells us that what we have in common is not so much our capacity to reason as our potential for suffering. Hence, we are all in need of care and protection, not just those traditionally identified as weak and defenceless – women and children.

Butler, and to a lesser extent Cavarero, connects with voices such as that of the messianic Jewish philosopher, Emmanuel Levinas. For Levinas, we are born into relationality, which means we must always take some *responsibility* for others, especially the suffering other. It is the face of need, of suffering, that always demands our intervention.[10] This is why many feminist philosophers today argue for a renewed form of humanism, whose norms of personhood would be grounded in an acceptance of the universality of our vulnerability.

Then again, we might turn to psychoanalysis for a similar assessment of the perpetual struggle between dependency and autonomy. Here, not only are humans all born into states of dependency, but our conscious self, that supposedly rational side of ourselves, is never really sovereign at all. As Freud memorably put it at the start of the twentieth century, 'the ego is not master in its own house'.[11] For Freud, of course, this was because of the significant role of the unconscious in determining our thoughts, feeling, and actions, which ensures that our childhood need for and reliance upon others is never entirely left behind.

An astute French psychoanalyst, the late Jean Laplanche, elaborated further on the lifelong effects of our earliest forms of dependence. He proposed that the messages we received from those who first cared for us, usually our mothers, linger all the more forcefully and compellingly throughout our lives because they could never be decoded or understood when we first received them. Such unprocessed communications always remain as 'enigmatic signifiers' that become triggered by subsequent events and situations, right up to our very last moments, meaning that psychic life is never simply linear. At any time some incident might suddenly loop us back to childhood events that are unexpectedly revived or re-experienced, if no doubt differently, through this recurrence in later life.[12]

However, for every psychoanalytic theorist, the child always starts out in a state of absolute dependence upon and erotic attachment towards its first caretaker, still usually the mother. This tends to become especially troubling for the boy child, who must somehow manage to repress or disavow his early states of dependency once he embarks, as he is firmly directed to do, on the journey towards 'normal' masculinity.

These differing ways of emphasizing our lifelong dependencies and shared vulnerability should all help to destabilize our presumptions of the rational, autonomous subject historically informing law and politics. Indeed, some may feel we hardly need the detour through philosophical abstraction or psychoanalytic reflection to confirm what seems easy enough to grasp from simple introspection, or careful scrutiny of those around us: we depend upon one another. Sadly, it's not so simple.

'I am nothing without you' is a thought rarely articulated except in moments of romantic passion. We remain largely unaware that we ground our sense of self only in and through our continuing ties to other people – family, friends, strangers, even enemies – who are themselves products of broader social belongings. First breath to last gasp, we rely upon those around us to stay human.

Although we may rarely discuss it, our sense of who and what we are – the confidence or insecurity we expose or try to conceal, how we portray our lives or what we try to bury, as

6

well as much that we fail to register or seem so easily to forget – all of these result from encounters we have, and have had, with others. Their memory shapes our memory, their perspicacity our vision, their blindness our amnesia. This need for others is the bottom line of being alive. Even after death, we 'live on' in the minds of others.

Our webs of interdependence place questions of care, and the lack of it, at the heart of everything, certainly at the heart of any seriously progressive thought. They extend beyond, but always include, human collaboration, given our global dependence upon a sustainable world favourable to human survival. It begins with all that we can count upon (or are denied) for our health, welfare, and protection. The situation has been dramatically deteriorating for too many thanks to the growth of inequality, especially in Britain and the United States, evidenced by the ten-year longevity gap between the richest and the poorest citizens.

Given this, one question I will be returning to throughout this book is why the notion of 'dependency', by which I mean our reliance upon others and on our basic infrastructures of care, continues to be perceived as weakness, facilitating the disparagement if not pathologization of those who are labelled 'dependent'. This includes widespread fear of disability and old age, with at best an attitude of condescension towards those living with physical or mental frailties, at any age.

We are all dependent, as I keep affirming, but there are differences: the richer a person is, the more dependent they are on the daily assistance of numerous others. Nowadays those who service the rich are less likely to be labelled 'servants', even though an entourage of low-paid workers still functions as an obvious sign of status. My point is that while the rich are utterly dependent on those who look after them, they nevertheless retain in full their sense of agency and entitlement. They can always sack the people who support them, or simply decide to dispense with them from one moment to the next.

However, those who should be most entitled to care, such as the chronically ill, regularly report having to accept high levels of humiliation when making any claims at all on the state. One seriously disabled friend of mine, Sarah Benton, has written about her repeated mortification when she first applied for what was then called the disability living allowance from the Department for Work and Pensions (DWP): 'There is an atmosphere of reproach and grudge in the department's communications', as though claimants 'must be made to feel bad on some pretext or another'. Being assessed for the renamed 'Personal Independence Payment' (PIP) some years later, she was asked when she 'planned to return to work', despite her assessor knowing that she was sixty-seven, suffering from progressive multiple sclerosis, and barely able to walk, her condition having forced her to leave a job she loved.[13]

This is why it's crucial to realize that we don't achieve autonomy without our basic dependency needs being met. The notion of care must expand to incorporate all the resources necessary for promoting the capabilities of both carers and cared for. At the same time, it's important to appreciate the mutual, relational empathy evident in good caring practices, however hard they may be to sustain given the lack of time or resources, often creating pressures, or, worse, in caring relations – wherever they occur. We all need both to give and to receive care, but we also need time, support, and resources, for this to be done well. Care can turn into forms of control, abuse, even cruelty, from care giver or receiver, if there is no mutual recognition or the potential for compassionate empathy within the relationship.

Never in my lifetime has life itself felt so threatened, or thoughts on care and vulnerability become so prominent, than with the impact of the COVID-19 pandemic from early 2020. It is why, for a while, questions of care were suddenly pushed to the centre of public debate. Hitherto, the mainstream media was primarily in a moral panic over the plight of 'latchkey children', for which 'working' mothers were blamed, and there were scandals over failing care homes. Today, however, we constantly hear that all our caring institutions are on the point of collapse, with many countries scarred by the disappearance of basic amenities and rising inequality on all fronts, resulting in flagrant lack of care for so many in need. This is especially true in the UK, where at the height of the pandemic hospitals were overwhelmed, and their workers routinely exhausted. Carers at home, especially mothers, were left barely coping when juggling jobs and caring responsibilities. But the lessons of COVID go far deeper than this, even if they seem to be easily forgotten.

First up, the pandemic illuminated the extent to which we live in a shared world. No borders can protect us fully, if at all, from disasters elsewhere. One way or another they impact on everyone. The pandemic was so clearly a global calamity, but our failures to deal with it globally prolonged its duration. One instance is the refusal of richer countries, and in particular their massively profitable pharmaceutical companies, to share the COVID vaccine with poorer nations.

Moreover, although COVID affected us all, it also highlighted extreme inequalities in health, mortality, security, and well-being. In Britain, as in the United States, residents of more deprived areas immediately had almost four times the average levels of mortality from COVID-19, due to their poorer living conditions and more hazardous forms of employment.[14] Black and ethnic minority (BAME) groups also experienced far higher rates of mortality from COVID-19, related to their disproportionate experience of high-risk living and working conditions, as well as reflecting the continuing effects of discrimination and exclusion resulting from systemic racism.

There was the added factor that BAME workers, so often employed in the caring professions, were rarely protected by adequate PPE (personal protective equipment) and other safety measures. Yet, though clearly dramatized by COVID fatalities, these differential health outcomes had been recorded long before the pandemic. Thus, the British epidemiologist and public health researcher Michael Marmot, for one, had been exposing health inequalities for decades, in particular recording the radically widening health and longevity gaps between different regions and diverse ethnic groups in England over the ten years prior to the pandemic.[15]

This explains why Britain early on had the worst COVID death rates in Europe, its decade of cuts in public health provision combining with the highest levels of inequality. Ideologically driven austerity policies post-2010 had slashed health provision by nearly 25 per cent in the years preceding COVID, resulting in a drastic shortage of doctors, nurses, and most other care workers. Government carelessness and increased profiteering from mass misery continued throughout the first two years of the pandemic. There were dramatic stories of medical staff and care workers having to wear bin-liners for aprons and garden-wear for gloves, while coping with a lack of ventilators for resuscitation and, at first, a refusal to follow the World Health Organization's instructions to keep testing. As the liberal journalist Jonathan Freedland concluded after the first three months of the pandemic, 'the failures of the UK's response to Covid-19 ranks as one of the severest failures of public administration in the country's long history'.[16]

One would hope that, even belatedly, the COVID calamity might have prompted governments to embark on rebuilding national caring infrastructures. However, in the UK we have seen the exact reverse. Instead of investing in health and social care, the British government has poured billions of pounds into global corporations, without scrutiny or tender, many of them already notorious for their failures. In England, at least, it is clear that the pandemic was used by government to deepen the role of the global corporate sector in further weakening the public sector. As then British prime minister

Boris Johnson announced at the Tory party conference in 2020: 'We must be clear that there comes a moment when the state must stand back and let the private sector get on with it.' This stance created a corrupt bonanza for many Tory Party donors, as companies they were linked to – often unconnected to the goods they were suddenly offering to supply – 'queue-jumped' the normal procurement process. Indeed, so much corruption has since been revealed that it almost defies belief.[17]

Unsurprisingly, the COVID pandemic has resulted in a deepening of inequality globally, both within and between countries. Billionaires have seen their wealth soar, while many others have become further trapped in poverty, neglect, and ill health. Data from the World Bank suggests that any progress towards equality has been reversed, and inequality now threatens to become even further entrenched. What we are seeing is the increased suffering of all vulnerable groups: low-income people, youth, women, and informal workers, who have all faced radical job and income losses.[18]

It is not only the World Bank that is troubled by such gloomy and enraging government and corporate failures. The UK has seen a surge in protest, with trade unions and a swathe of campaign groups taking to the streets to denounce rising inequality and injustice. Just prior to the pandemic, I joined with a few friends to publish *The Care Manifesto* (2020), addressing ways of tackling the already widespread crisis of care that long predated COVID-19. It immediately struck a chord. Many others are now making similar arguments, while noting that the left has never been good enough at prioritizing care, or promoting the consistent feminist calls for care-based economies which have grown louder over the last half century. As feminist economists in the Women's Budget Group have also declared: 'A caring economy is an idea whose time has come.'[19]

Elsewhere, *The Leap Manifesto*, headed up by Naomi Klein, calls for a Canada based upon care, opposing all trade deals that interfere with attempts to rebuild local economies, while demanding regulation of commercial corporations and rejection of damaging extractive projects.[20] Across Europe, the Foundation for European Progressive Studies (FEPS) entered 2020 with a new EU gender strategy that asks the question 'Does Europe care for care?' while seeking ways of improving both gender equality and care.[21] Women from Latin America, Asia, and sub-Saharan Africa (FEMNET) have produced their own *Care Manifesto* (2021), insisting that 'a bold rethink of the care economy is needed to build a feminist, sustainable, resilient, inclusive and caring economy and future'.[22]

In the United States, which still likes to think of itself as the world's richest (albeit most unequal) society, Joan Tronto is only one of the most prominent public figures among a swathe of contemporary feminist care theorists, including Eva Kittay, Nancy Folbre, and Daniel Engster, who contend that the systemic failures of care undermine democracy itself. Tronto calls for people to work together to ensure adequate care for all, rightly proposing that everyone should play some part in its provision – there should be no 'caring exemptions'. Finally, Tronto agrees that since 'dependence is a fact of all our lives', true freedom lies in 'our capacity to care and to make commitments to what we care about'.[23] Others, such as the political theorist Nancy Fraser or the anthropologist Laura Briggs, have been pointing out for years that the crisis of care is now the key calamity of contemporary capitalism.[24]

The pandemic has expanded people's caring commitments in practical ways as well. From the start, a host of what were quicky labelled 'mutual aid' groups mushroomed across the UK – the name derived from a concept developed around 1900 by the Russian anarchist Peter Kropotkin. In the very first month of the virus, volunteers from all walks of life signed up to help elderly people who were self-isolating. When the NHS called for 250,000 volunteers to assist their work, more than three times that number responded. Mutual aid groups continued to deploy vast numbers of volunteers determined to service and deliver goods, tied in with the tens of thousands of food banks appearing around Britain, but also attempting to engage in other forms of support work. This included visiting people known to be feeling isolated or anxious at home, especially the elderly, or donating phones for people in hospital and laptops for children to access home learning.

Within a year it was estimated that there were three million volunteers in different local communities in Britain, not only offering basic support and home deliveries, but trying to tackle more complex issues such as homelessness, debt, and mental health problems. As two researchers from the London School of Economics (LSE), Anne Power and Ellie Benton, noted in their work on mutual aid groups, volunteering gave people a sense of purpose as well as keeping them busy under lockdown. However, in their view, for such groups to survive and remain useful after the pandemic, 'more supportive social infrastructure would be necessary to help mutual aid groups themselves to thrive'.[25]

Certainly, democratically run neighbourhood forums and caring hubs had been springing up around the UK throughout the previous decade, helping communities to resist and survive austerity regimes. Using her experience as a 'community councillor' in what became known as London's first 'Community Council', founded and run by residents of Queen's Park, north-west London, the journalist Susanna Rustin underlines the significance of this form of 'redistributive neighbourliness'. Partially echoing the forms of community politics that I myself had been involved with back in the 1970s, Rustin suggests that such community participation could both help people survive difficult times and also encourage greater democratic engagement: 'I think we have built a bulwark against some of the most brutalizing and antisocial effects of austerity.'[26]

The pandemic also strengthened interest in more formal attempts at municipal socialism, with the 'Preston model', launched in one of the poorer councils in north-west England, seen as exemplary. After its welfare budget was slashed by central government, Preston Council had begun encouraging localism and workers' co-operatives, switching its public sector priorities towards investment in local providers and worker-owned co-operatives. Other councils, including my own in Islington, were soon attempting similar moves, again hoping to bring outsourced public provision back 'in-house', though harsh funding cuts from central government have always limited such possibilities.

There had already been far more ambitious efforts at radical municipalism abroad – most prominently in Barcelona, where Ada Colau was elected mayor in 2015, after her previous work in community activism. Similar patterns in local government emerged in one of the poorest areas of the United States with Ohio's Cleveland Model, where state departments tried to support community economic developments and encourage employee ownership via workers' co-operatives.[27]

Indeed, it is in the United States – with its daunting levels of inequality, racism, police brutality, and incarceration, added to extreme suspicion of politicians – that grassroots activism has always been most pronounced. When COVID-19 arrived in March 2020, widespread networking immediately began in most major cities, mobilizing armies of volunteers to address people's needs facing the pandemic. In Colorado, librarians put together kits of essentials for the elderly and for children who wouldn't be getting their usual meals at school. In California, disabled people in the Bay Area organized mutual care assistance, while in Seattle, one large network began helping undocumented queer, Black, Indigenous, and other minorities, along with the elderly and the disabled who they knew would be the first affected by the crisis.

In New York City, tens of thousands of volunteers were quickly busy delivering medicines and groceries, offering childcare and pet care, even helping to raise money for food and rent. Relief funds were raised for those working in the entertainment industry, and for sex workers and street vendors. A new Service Workers Coalition was formed just before the closure of cinemas and theatres, which raised more than $25,000 to distribute to workers, a move that spread to the whole country. Just as widely, prison abolitionists attempted to raise extra funds to support the growing needs of inmates.

Researching these initiatives for her 2020 *New Yorker* essay, 'Can I Help You? What Mutual Aid Can Do during a Pandemic', staff reporter Jia Tolentino pondered the long-term significance of this extraordinary burst of solidarity and support.[28] Tolentino herself was quickly active in mutual aid networks on her doorstep in Brooklyn, supporting out-of-work freelancers, and early on visiting Liam Elkind who had just co-founded the Invisible Hands organization in Harlem.

Within days Invisible Hands had gathered 1,200 volunteers, providing free groceries for the sick and elderly, and soon spreading to other areas: 'Not to be trite,' Elkind told Tolentino, 'but I feel like this is spreading faster than the virus.' Before long, these efforts gained support in the mainstream, not just from left Democrats such as Alexandria Ocasio-Cortez, but in the *New York Times*, under the headline 'Feeling Powerless about Coronavirus? Join a Mutual-Aid Network'. However, knowing that feel-good stories are always leveraged by conservatives eager to champion voluntarism over state welfare programmes, Tolentino stressed that such projects would only continue beyond the emergency if backed by public support. The researchers at LSE in London came to similar conclusions: volunteering and mutual aid would need some form of public funding to survive in the long run. Moreover, as this book goes to press in 2023, I read that volunteering is indeed now at an all-time low in England.[29]

Nevertheless, the activist, writer, and perennial optimist Rebecca Solnit, covering the rise of mutual aid practices for the *Guardian* in May 2020, suggested that radical collective moments do sometimes manage to endure, and can even generate permanent forms of networking and activism. For example, she noted that the Common Ground Health Clinic, formed in response to the devastation of Hurricane Katrina in New Orleans in 2005, has continued to deliver free medical care for over fifteen years.[30]

With no foreseeable end to job losses from the pandemic, Solnit thinks that this sudden spread of generosity and solidarity foreshadows what is possible, and certainly necessary, for our future survival. Many volunteers may return to 'normal life', but some will retain a new awareness of who they are, or might be; of their ties to others; and of what matters most. We can renew our attachment to life by embracing its sorrows as well as its joys, which often feel far larger than our own concerns. Moreover, coming together in moments of collective fear and despair to work on common ground also enables moments of collective joy, even with quite small victories.

More targeted and practical advice comes from the radical trans lawyer and activist Dean Spade, in Seattle, who offers a kind of manual for organizing mutual aid programmes, from delivering groceries, planting gardens, or changing diapers, to combating police violence and protecting communities from all manner of assaults. Over the course of his book, *Mutual Aid* (2020), Spade assesses both the possibilities and the pitfalls involved in building solidarity. He addresses 'burnout' and also the inevitability of group conflicts. Pointing in particular to the crucial mobilizations against police brutality from Black Lives Matter, among other transformative justice projects, Spade concludes: 'Mutual Aid work plays an immediate role in helping us get through crises, but it also has the potential to build the skills and capacities we need for an entirely new way of living at a moment when we must transform our society or face intensive, uneven suffering, followed by species extinction.'[31]

There is indeed a certain energy that comes with envisioning a more equitable, peaceful, and fairer world, at least when sharing such imaginings. Some psychologists have also reported links between political activism and feelings of well-being. For instance, when Tim Kasser and Malte Klar interviewed hundreds of German college students about their levels of political engagement, optimism, and overall happiness, they found that the activists consistently showed greater signs of well-being than other college students. Their joint political work gave them a sense of the purpose, meaning, and pleasure of life.[32]

Such findings do not surprise me. I came of age when dreaming of better lives for all in a peaceful world was the common sense of the '60s radicals I knew. This soon folded into the collective hopes of second-wave feminists, with our desire – however difficult in practice – for kinship with women everywhere, while also seeking men's involvement in care and domestic maintenance. Hence, in the pages ahead, I will be revisiting my own personal and shared history, while invoking those powers of collectivity which provide the energy that keeps hope alive, however grim and alarming our times may seem.

Who can we lean on, if not each other? I know that I have always depended on the kindness of strangers and often sought to turn those strangers into friends and comrades, when chance encounters proved recurring. However, in the beginning, the very first stranger we meet will usually be the person who brought us into the world – our mother.

1

Call That a Mother?

'Blood everywhere!' my mother said, describing her day's activities – something she did if and when she had time to sit down to an evening meal with her three children, Graeme, Barbara, and me. This time, she was telling us about the emergency caesarean section she had performed, her skilful hands apparently saving the day and bringing forth a healthy baby at the very last minute. Almost from the moment I was born, my mother spent her days away from our shared home. As a hard-working gynaecologist, she returned only at the close of the day, with little time left for her own children.

Before long she'd be off again, pleased to be summoned by a call from elsewhere, as another of her patients 'went into labour' (the interesting phrase for a woman giving birth). On the way out she would scoop up whatever we kids had not yet eaten. Often, she did not sit down at all, hovering by the phone, hoping for the summons, which was even more exciting if it was 'an emergency'. Rush! Rush!

Call that a mother? Well, we did, and had almost no criticisms of her, although I think it was me who pined most for her fleeting presence. As a severely asthmatic child, I was the 'weakling' of the family, and it was she who was always the first to visit when I ended up in hospital. Certainly, I loved her, and only in early adulthood saw some of her undeniable flaws, at least in providing that constant presence that is usually expected from a maternal caregiver. Her chronic absence stemmed from an intense resentment towards our reputedly philandering and habitually irritable father, who was also a doctor. She welcomed any escape from our family home.

Up to a point, I think Virginia Woolf was right to say, as she did in *A Room of One's Own* (1929): 'We think back through our mothers if we are women.' But the mother Woolf had in mind in her own, early-twentieth-century, upper-middle-class world, and whom she depicted in her novels and diaries, was the beautiful, altruistic, bourgeois wife, Mrs Julia Stephen. This mother had firm views on the role of women, seeing them as equal to men, but nevertheless belonging to a separate, domestic sphere.

Yet Julia Stephen, although the most attentive of wives, was equally, or perhaps a little more, devoted to her charity work. Attending to the needs of the poor, the sick or otherwise afflicted left her little time for seeing to her own seven children. In a family where husband always came first, and then sons, neither Virginia nor her sister Vanessa received much attention from their mother. According to biographers, both daughters yearned for maternal care and suffered from its lack. Woolf confided in her diaries that she could not recall being alone with her mother for more than a few minutes, except in child-hood illness, which she partly welcomed as a chance to enjoy some motherly concern. But Woolf always adored this altruistic woman, who is best portrayed in the form of Mrs Ramsay in one of her most autobiographical and popular novels, *To the Lighthouse*.

However, for me there was no such angel in the house, to think through, or to figuratively murder. This may help to explain my extreme apprehension when I found myself acci-dentally pregnant at the age of twenty-five. It happened when I was completing my doctoral studies at the University of Sydney, in a relationship with a local Sydney artist, James Clifford, who would soon decide that he was exclusively gay.

I had not the faintest idea what mothering involved and found the prospect rather terrifying, besides suspecting that the relationship I was in could not last. I was right on all counts, but soon found myself the mother of a beautiful, healthy baby boy, embarking upon the lifelong task of learning how best to handle the pleasures and perils of parenting. I'm still learning, and it has never been easy. And what I have learned from the difficulties I faced, and which I increasingly observe all around me, is that our ability to care well for others – whatever our relation to them – requires help and support from those close to us, while we also need to feel cared for ourselves.

Given that actual women's lives have changed so dramatically over the centuries, what is it that has preserved the mythic image of motherhood as the universal archetype for caring? Why is it that women as mothers have remained uniquely responsible for nurturing, supporting, and affirming life? This fantasy of selfless motherhood survives as the cornerstone of womanhood, despite all we know about the inevitabilities of maternal absence, the pathologies of maternal neglect, the regularity of maternal hardship, and the constancy, seemingly from time immemorial, of a cultural hum of mother-blaming.

Women's Place

Yet there has never been a shortage of tracts eager to instruct women about mothering. Those who know their Bible might recall its praise for the good wife: 'She gets up while it is still dark … She watches over the affairs of her household and does not eat the bread of idleness.' Modern times brought ever more specific advice for wives regarding childcare, health, and hygiene. Middle-class Victorian women were expected to follow both medical and lay guidance on good housekeeping and dedicated wifely duties, as illustrated in the pages of physician Sir Shirley Forster Murphy's influential *Our Homes and How to Make Them Healthy* (1883), or *Mrs Beeton's Book of Household Management*, whose popularity endures.

The same or similar texts flooded the United States in the nineteenth century, aimed at women seen as needing cultural instruction on how best to express their natural instincts. There was no advice or help for working-class mothers, however, whether in Victorian Britain or North America. As the feminist historian Ellen Ross argues, these mothers were commonly disparaged as 'lazy, feckless and ignorant', and held responsible for 'race deterioration', especially after one in five British men recruited for the Boer War (from 1899) proved too weak to serve.[1]

Whatever the period, it has always required some form of feminist imagination to challenge the dominant male opinion that idealizes and castigates mothers in equal measure. In Britain it began with that once derided 'hyena in petticoats', Mary Wollstonecraft, daring to speak of the rights of women back in the 1790s. Her *Vindication of the Rights of Woman* (1792) argued that women, as wives and mothers, needed to be educated and strong in order to be able to instill in their children 'the love of mankind, from which an orderly train of virtues spring'.[2] But her passionate wish that motherhood should not prevent women's civic involvement collided with the firm rock of patriarchal opinion, both conservative and radical.

It would take another hundred years, and the rise of what became known as first-wave feminism, before that thought was once more aired: for women to be primarily confined to their individual domestic spaces was good neither for women nor for creating healthy societies generally. It was forcefully voiced by thinkers in the United States writing on motherhood, such as Charlotte Perkins Gilman. In one of her many utopian texts, 'Moving the Mountain' (1911), Gilman described what a truly caring home might look like, where housework was shared, enabling women to be financially independent, with cultural lives, crafts, and beauty brought into the household.[3]

Between that time and the emergence of second-wave feminism, women reformers fought for over half a century trying to validate and improve the lives of women, and the care they were able to offer. Yet this struggle was still seen as inevitably entwined with motherhood. Motherhood certainly proved especially gruelling for working-class women, while also impacting upon their children's opportunities. As the suffragist and trade union organizer Ada Nield Chew argued in 'The Problem of the Married Working Woman' in 1914, public nurseries were needed, which could 'provide a new and glorious field of work to women'.[4] Elsewhere the British social campaigner and independent MP Eleanor Rathbone spent decades arguing for a national endowment for motherhood to be paid directly to women, in order to alleviate their near total dependence on men. More radical thinkers, such as the writer Dora Russell in her book *The Right to Be Happy* (1927), argued for shared parenting, wanting to see 'the "fusion" of paternal and maternal "feeling"'.[5]

Why then has it been so hard to shift our traditional expectations and practices of mothering? Each generation seems to be forced to refight the battles of those that went before them. Women's appeals for solidarity and equality are now over a century old, but have to be refreshed whenever it comes to motherhood or the nature of care. The unique burdens still placed upon mothers nowadays lead more women to reject motherhood altogether. It's as if nothing has changed since Simone de Beauvoir recalled, over sixty years ago, that she could only achieve autonomy and creative fulfilment by deliberately turning her back on motherhood and domesticity: 'I was spared the curse that weighs upon most women, that of dependence ... to earn one's living is not an end in itself, but it is the only way to achieve securely based inner independence.'[6]

During the postwar period when I was growing up, women were still expected to keep themselves busy with newly escalating household consumption, to help boost economic growth after the disruptions of war. Government priorities worked in tandem with suddenly influential psychoanalytic thinking to focus attention on the necessity for full-time mothering, with clinicians such as John Bowlby and Donald Winnicott given a freshly significant role in public life.

This type of thinking fostered a 'new maternalism' that for a while supported the mid-century expansion of the welfare state. Today there is a resurgence of interest in Winnicott's ideas; his emphasis on the needs and vulnerabilities of mothers and children is recognized as helping to secure the increased postwar provision of child benefits, along with healthcare and education reforms, which undoubtedly benefited mothers and their children.

Yet, as most feminists decried in the heyday of feminism, such improvements were all framed around the 'male breadwinner' logic of welfare, which saw a woman's place as primarily in the home, dependent on her husband. John Bowlby darkly warned that any interruption of maternal care was likely to cause a child permanent psychological harm, leading to subsequent antisocial behaviour, as outlined in his authoritative book written for the World Health Organization, *Maternal Care and Mental Health* (1951). Thus, while concern for the lives of mothers did, for a short time, connect with expanding welfare, it was also shadowed by increased alarm over maternal failures, especially given the growing awareness of high levels of distress among full-time housewives.

The prevalence of post-natal depression, known as the 'baby blues', along with other forms of maternal melancholy and anxiety were judged and treated as signs of individual pathology. The postwar years therefore saw rampant prescription of benzodiazepine tranquillizers and other mood-altering drugs for housebound mothers. The aggressive marketing practices of pharmaceutical companies meant that the number of women on psychiatric drugs spiralled from the 1950s, with twice as many women as men on medication. Meanwhile another tranquillizer, Valium, emerged as the most widely prescribed drug in the world by 1970, nicknamed 'Mother's Little Helper'.[7]

However, mothers were lined up for blame, whatever they did. Bowlby's Maternal Deprivation hypothesis suggested that even short-term maternal absence could result in long-term cognitive, social, and emotional damage, perhaps leading to adult delinquency or affectless psychopathy. A mother's constant monitoring was indispensable, not just for the child but supposedly for the well-being of society in general.

A mere decade later, R. D. Laing and other radical clinicians turned Bowlby on his head, broadcasting the malign effects of just those obedient full-time housewives. The dutiful mothers who thought they should be constantly present and monitoring their offspring, as instructed, now found themselves accused of 'suffocating' them, perhaps even driving them mad – especially daughters. Moreover, like Bowlby, in his best-selling books throughout the 1960s, Laing expanded his ideas on the failings of now 'over-possessive' mothers to explain the troubles of the world at large.

In *The Politics of the Family*, we learned that the love which parents (always and only mothers in Laing's case studies) lavish on their children is a form of violence, since it is not freely given but an attempt to induce in the child whatever the parent wishes to see. In sum, 'families, schools, churches are the slaughterhouses of our children'.[8] What Laing never addressed, any more than other men of his time, radical or otherwise, was how childcare, love, or caring work in general might be organized differently.

Thus, in a pincer movement, from opposite ends of male expertise, Bowlby and Laing converged in an outlook that feminists later identified as an orthodox clinical manoeuvre: the tactic of mother-blaming. Whether for any maternal absence or for constant maternal presence, 'women are ineluctably set up to fail', as the British child psychotherapist Adam Phillips noted.[9]

My own mother may have been far distant from the idealized fantasy of that selfless, cheerful '50s housewife: the housebound woman with her floral aprons, spotless floors, and home-baked cookies. She was rarely around, devoted to her busy surgery and hospital work. However, we now know that more conventional mothers also remained somewhat at odds with their supposed vocation – brought low by lethargy, guilt, frustration, and depression, which apparently required women to be sedated. Indeed, as women's liberation burst forth at the close of the 1960s, the young women who first began eagerly meeting together were often in flight from their own dissatisfied mothers, whom they had seen struggling to suppress resentment at their lot, when not full of rancour and complaint.

I was one of those young women. For though my mother steered clear of the Valium, she was nevertheless permanently embittered by my father's sense of male entitlement. This involved not just his apparent sexual betrayals, but his complete detachment from any household responsibilities, expecting his wife to ensure that all his domestic needs were always met, even though as a doctor she was better qualified than him and worked longer hours. She was constantly trying to placate his outbursts of irritation and fault-finding, while we children soaked up her ensuing resentment, often bordering on loathing. Beauvoir's insight was not mistaken: 'The great danger which threatens the infant in our culture lies in the fact that the mother to whom it is confined in all its helplessness is almost always a discontented woman.'[10]

Spilling the Beans

Such was the background to the emergence of second-wave feminism, when earlier battles over women's place in the world finally exploded again into the public domain. This time the consequences would be persistent, never less than challenging, and sometimes unpredictable.

It is hardly surprising that questions of motherhood and care lay at the heart of this movement, wherever it arose. Indeed, two of the initial four demands of the British Liberation Movement addressed issues of motherhood. They combined insistence upon support for women's reproductive choices with the affirmation that women should not have to choose between work and family. 'If the undervaluation of women in society is to end, we must begin at the beginning, by a more equitable distribution of labour around the child-rearing function and the home', announced the visiting American psychologist Sheli Wortis – to huge applause – at the first ever women's liberation conference in Britain.[11]

This would soon be music to my ears, although I missed that opening conference. I was still in Sydney, sinking under the weight of unintended motherhood, in a relationship that was failing and with no social support at all for mothers in my situation.

That conference, held over fifty years ago at Ruskin College in Oxford, in February 1970, changed many women's lives forever. None were more transformed than the young mothers who attended with their children safely elsewhere, in a crèche run by men, sometimes the children's fathers – like the rather bemused Stuart Hall, captured in an iconic photo of the event. It was all a concrete illustration of Wortis's call. Her words echoed those of her compatriot, the New Yorker Alix Kates Shulman, who caused huge controversy in 1969 with her essay 'A Marriage Agreement'.[12] Demanding that her then husband share equally in the household chores and the care of their two young children, and detailing the tasks involved, it was published widely: in *Life*, *Redbook*, *Up from Under*, and *Ms*.

Other mothers at the Ruskin conference were equally forceful in demanding change. Those attending from the newly established Peckham Rye Women's Group in London were mostly full-time, home-based mothers. They had prepared a document that dramatically stated: 'Our window on the world is looked through with our hands in the sink and we've begun to *hate that sink and all it implies – so begins our consciousness.*'[13]

These feminists were not so much responsible for stirring discontent among mothers as for refusing to stay silent about it. Hiding in broad daylight, what we swiftly illuminated was the existence of widespread maternal anguish, hitherto always pathologized, when not entirely disregarded. It quickly surfaced in feminist consciousness-raising groups, whether expressed by young mothers themselves or by women recalling the complaints of our own mothers. It was discussed in all the early newsletters and magazines of second-wave feminism, including *Shrew* and *Spare Rib* in the UK, *Off Our Backs* and *Ms.* in the States. Feminist researchers were also collecting data on women's domestic lives. The picture was far from pretty.

One of the subject's first and most influential researchers in Britain was the budding British sociologist Ann Oakley, who conducted hitherto unthinkable empirical research on the experiences of housewives in the early 1970s. Oakley herself had suffered a period of serious post-natal depression following the birth of her second child in 1968, when she felt her life was 'simply devoid of meaning'. Her doctors prescribed a variety of drugs, including the powerful anti-psychotic Stelazine, which she dutifully swallowed. The drugs enabled her to function, though in a very mechanical way, rather like the iconic figures from Ira Levin's thriller, *The Stepford Wives* (1972), soon to be immortalized on screen and television.

Oakley was only genuinely cured when she commenced her doctoral studies, choosing housework as her theme, much to the dismay of supervisors at LSE. Searching for the root of her own post-natal distress, Oakley now suspected that it expressed the radical mismatch between young housebound mothers' sense of isolation and irrelevance, and their earlier desires for greater participation in the wider world.

Sure enough, in her book *Housewife* (1974), Oakley recorded how very common were the feelings of maternal loneliness, tedium, and dejection. Dissatisfaction was the single main response from 70 per cent of the forty full-time housewives she interviewed – half of them working-class, half middle-class. Making connections between the personal and the political, Oakley's findings resonated with what was fast emerging as the feminist common sense of the early 1970s. It meant challenging the nature of the traditional nuclear family and establishing forms of intimacy in 'more open and variable relationships'.[14]

I was soon part of these new moves, arriving in London in 1970 as a rather disoriented and lonesome single mother, with an infant son to raise. Everything started to improve when I joined forces with other women who were also enthusiastically creating alternative forms of living, in more open and collective households. We took for granted that the men we cohabited with would do their full share of domestic duties – childcare, cooking, and cleaning.

This was, indeed, the unquestioned practice in the large home I owned (then, as now) and soon shared with two other single mothers, and always a few men, through most of the 1970s. Our carefully planned household rotas were never the source of any contention, not once, even though squabbles arose over other matters, worst of all when jealousy over erotic attachments undid domestic harmony. For much of the decade this arrangement seemed to work well, enabling us three mothers to care for our children while also engaging fully in the world at large. Simultaneously, we were campaigning to improve the lives of anyone involved in parenting work, insisting that 'mothering' was not limited to birth-givers, nor necessarily defined by gender. It meant exposing both the common isolation and frustrations of full-time mothering, as well as the extra burdens placed upon so-called 'working' mothers. It also required continued community struggles for more nurseries, youth clubs, and other public resources (which feminists often helped to set up and maintain).

This accompanied an insistence upon the multiple benefits of men sharing domestic and caring responsibilities, to which most of them readily agreed. However, as some of us knew, especially socialist feminists, there were many reasons why it was harder for working-class and poorer families to alter the conditions of their working lives to enable men's greater sharing of domestic roles. Through one means or another, the men we lived with mostly managed to have more flexible working arrangements.

We knew that the double burden of mothers in the workplace was also especially arduous for working-class and ethnic minority women, whose low wages often compelled them to work especially long hours. Moreover, despite the prevalence of full-time housewives, many mothers were actually already seeking employment during the postwar expansion of part-time work.[15] As the historian Sarah Crook notes, in 1971 half a million mothers with children under five could be found in the paid workforce.[16] It was not feminism alone that was driving them into work.

However, as these women's jobs mirrored their unpaid domestic activities, their labour was regarded as devoid of skill or expertise. Hence, most employed women remained consistently undervalued and poorly paid, their jobs offering little chance for advancement and barely more status than that attributed to the 'housewife'. Once home from the workplace, most women still shouldered the overwhelming bulk of responsibility for housework and childcare.

Clearly, any widespread change had to involve an extensive political agenda. However, working on all fronts and supported by male friends and comrades, the feminists I knew set out enthusiastically to obtain their goals. Second-wave feminists were not just mapping the diverse difficulties women faced as the subordinate sex, primarily responsible for all forms of domestic intimacy, care, and household maintenance. We were also determined to cast off former constraints and lead campaigns for social renewal overall, as well as to exemplify the changes we wanted to see in our daily lives.

In my own collective household, when not fulfilling domestic rotas, we were all busily engaged in social and political life. In addition to full-time paid jobs, we were helping to open and run a women's centre on Essex Road in Islington, which flourished for a few years from 1973. I also joined other feminists in visiting schools and nurseries, encouraging nursery workers in particular to improve their pay and conditions through unionization. Indeed, I cemented an enduring friendship with Sheila Rowbotham when we both spent the day travelling by train to Harlow New Town. While we both recall the journey very well, neither of us has the slightest memory of who we met, or what we said – other than to each other.

Feminist activists sometimes lived in squats, taking possession of empty houses which often belonged to the council and might later evolve into housing associations, or else in large, shared, rented or perhaps privately owned accommodation. This was a time when the cost of housing in places like inner London was not yet totally prohibitive. As Sheila records: 'During the 1970s most big cities spawned a network of community nurseries, food co-ops, squatters' groups, housing co-ops, tenants' organizations, Law Centres and Claimants Unions, as well as Women's Aid Centres and Rape Crisis Centres.'[17]

These community endeavours enabled people to find better ways of caring for each other, and especially for those women in most need who were often victims of domestic violence or sexual abuse. Our living arrangements and other collective projects also aimed to build more resilient forms of mutual interdependence, while promoting the solidarity needed in struggling for better lives for all.

Such forms of care and solidarity clearly require time and effort to sustain, conditions that were more available to activists in the 1970s, when social welfare was less squeezed and most jobs less pressurized. Political engagements were also sustained by the blossoming of creative work across all cultural genres, from women's theatres and bands, to writing, poetry, and innumerable other collective activities. People from my collective household, including Jill Hughes and Chris Whitbread, helped set up the Hackney and Islington Music Workshop, writing and performing their own songs and producing several collections of songbooks between 1976 and 1981. Chris's 'Squatter's Rant' and 'Dole Queue Shuffle' were popular, with Leon Rosselson's 'Don't Get Married, Girls' especially applauded.

Feminist writers' groups also sprang up to foster talent and provide care and support for women's creative efforts, which often first appeared as collaborative productions of short stories or poems. One such writing collective in London, including Zoe Fairbairns, Sara Maitland, Valerie Miner, Michèle Roberts, Michelene Wandor, and Alison Fell (who was then living in my household), produced a number of publications together, beginning with the collection *Tales I Tell My Mother* (1978). They all soon became recognized feminist writers.

Looking back, the decades of communal living had suited me, despite certain instabilities, occasional conflicts, and somewhat austere comforts. Indeed, I still live more collectively than most people. As I wrote in my memoir *Making Trouble* (2007), having been an apprehensive, accidental mother, I gained confidence and much-needed support through sharing my household. Both my son and I seemed to flourish throughout the years of his childhood, living in an environment that was the antithesis of the wrangling and bitterness of the home where I was raised. My son still speaks of his 'wonderful' childhood.

Today I would certainly question aspects of my own mothering, considering that the laid-back, uncompetitive, extremely permissive atmosphere hardly prepared my son for the driven, competitive world he would enter in adulthood. I know I made mistakes, perhaps involved in too many things, not offering my son the overriding personal focus which might have been helpful. And yet the open inclusiveness of our domestic life in those years remains something I still value, and he recalls with pleasure. Today, however, our appalling housing crisis, with its extortionate property and rental prices, makes finding the kind of living spaces we shared almost impossible for most people.

Various publications, including my own edited collection, *What Is to Be Done about the Family?* (1983), were analysing what we saw as the paternalistic, exclusionary, and regressive role of traditional households, kinship, and sexual relations in contemporary societies. As Michèle Barrett and Mary McIntosh spelled out in *The Anti-Social Family*, we will never be able to establish alternative models that truly enable gender equality, sexual diversity, and, above all, more flexible and responsive forms of social support and care, until we move beyond our obeisance to the traditional family. Alternative social institutions are undermined as a result: 'The family sucks the juice out of everything around it, leaving other institutions stunted and distorted.' Barrett and McIntosh conclude that 'caring, sharing and loving would be more widespread if the family did not claim them for its own'. They also agree with Oakley that 'being a housewife can drive women mad'.[18]

We hoped that these reflections might stimulate cultural shifts, moving beyond, or setting aside, traditional conceptions of motherhood as the unique archetype for care itself. Yet it was precisely this aspiration that would trigger much of the backlash against feminism in the years to come. Given the age-old equation between childbearing and female fulfilment – although only within the sanctioned confines of married life – tackling the myths of motherhood was widely resisted in mainstream culture, not least by many women themselves. However, more happily, we did succeed in helping to eradicate the shame and discrimination that had always injured unmarried mothers and their children, designed to prevent women from choosing to mother outside wedlock, and punish those who did. By the close of the 1970s, the practice had become too widespread for the stigma to endure. But the allure of motherhood as symbolic of women's personal fulfilment was harder to displace.

Celebrating the Maternal

Women's liberation strove to emancipate women in the home from the isolation and disregard many had faced, especially as full-time mothers. But within a few years, feminists had started paying more attention to the complex joys, ambivalences, and confusions surrounding experiences of mothering. Emblematic of this shift was Adrienne Rich's now legendary *Of Woman Born: Motherhood as Experience and Institution* (1976), which was read by feminists of every stripe.

Before writing that book, Rich was already a popular public figure in the US, renowned as a commanding poet and essayist. *Of Woman Born* drew upon her own maternal experiences, arguing that mothering *could* be a rich and empowering experience for women, but *only* outside male-dominated households, only when all women were able to decide for themselves if, when, and how to mother. In particular, Rich celebrated the enduring mother–daughter bond, in her view hitherto distorted within patriarchal institutions, which left mothers overworked and isolated: 'The worker can unionize, go out on strike; mothers are divided from each other in homes, tied to their children by compassionate bonds; our wildcat strikes have most often taken the form of physical or mental breakdown.'

At the close of that book Rich celebrates what could emerge with 'women's repossession of their bodies', free from patriarchal control, suggesting it could prove more important than 'the seizing of the means of production by workers': 'In such a world women will truly create new life, bringing forth not only children (if and as we choose) but the visions, and the thinking, necessary to sustain, console, and alter human existence – a new relationship to the universe ... thinking itself will be transformed. This is where we have to begin.'[19] It remains a glorious vision.

At much the same time, feminist writing also began stressing the importance of engaged fatherhood, or shared parenting, in the child's early years. In her classic text, *The Reproduction of Mothering* (1978), Nancy Chodorow saw the role of fathers as crucial, not just to relieve the burdens of mothers, but also to overturn existing gender inequality and produce more caring societies. She argued that it was women's unique role in parenting that produced such polarized and unequal gender identities: boys who are fearful of intimacy; girls who define themselves only in relation to others. Chodorow wanted to see a transformation, not a celebration, of existing patterns of parenting.[20]

However, the mothering themes of Rich and Chodorow did help to inspire a new, relatively more traditional celebration of 'maternal thinking' and 'maternal practices'. This was quickly evident in much feminist writing the following decade. The best-known and most influential works were Carol Gilligan's *In a Different Voice: Psychological Theory and Women's Development* and Sara Ruddick's *Maternal Thinking: Toward a Politics of Peace*. Gilligan argued that girls' early identification with their mothers meant that women in general think more relationally than men. Meanwhile Ruddick suggested that women's actual engagement in maternal practices led to mothers' greater awareness of vulnerability and the need for patient, attentive love for others. These writers were theorizing a new ethics of care, which could be traced back to engagement in maternal practices, but if properly appreciated could help create a more caring world.[21]

By the 1980s, therefore, more women were emphasizing that their experiences of motherhood not only highlighted the ways society undervalued care, but also helped inspire demands for a kinder, more caring, and peaceful world. Indeed, as Oakley herself reflected in 1983, feminists like her had at first fore-grounded the difficulties of motherhood, but now saw more positive sides. She realized it could also give women a certain power and fulfil women's desire 'to create this unparalleled intimacy'.[22]

Black feminists, including Toni Morrison, Alice Walker, and Patricia Hill Collins, argue even more powerfully for a recognition of the fundamental importance of motherhood which, like any awareness of ancestry, they see as a site of power for black women.[23] Also from the USA, the late Black cultural critic bell hooks criticized white feminism, suggesting, in the early 1980s, that 'had Black women voiced their views on motherhood, it would not have been named a serious obstacle to our freedom as women'.[24] By this time, however, many white feminists were also celebrating the importance of motherhood, seeing it as the basis for desiring a more caring world.

Fresh Snares and Traps

However, we need to tread carefully when applauding this new era of maternal celebration. During the 1980s, with the political right in power in Britain and the States, deregulating markets and reducing government spending, my brand of socialist feminism was fast receding into the historical wilderness. We had fought for democratically run, social provision for all, but were now facing a decline in even the most essential public resources. The consequences are that so many mothers today face long and exhausting days in paid work to ensure their economic survival, but with much of their wages simply disappearing into spiralling childcare costs. It has led some people, even erstwhile feminists such as Maureen Freely and Madeleine Bunting, to lament that 'we were betrayed by feminism'.[25]

It is a common enough view, implying that it was the impact of feminism itself that led women to start prioritizing their working lives, leaving us all with an ongoing care deficit. Yet most people seem somewhat confused by the situation. I later heard Bunting comment, with greater accuracy, when speaking about her book *Labours of Love*: 'In fact, it is more a case of our generation betraying feminism.' I would not myself put it that way.

Rather, in these tough times, many women's options have simply kept on shrinking. And feminism has nothing to do with it. Blaming feminism is a diversion deployed by the right, and markets themselves, to pretend that women's long hours in both paid and unpaid work can be seen as 'lifestyle choices', ignoring the context of welfare cuts, dwindling public resources, and greater financial need. It is sad to see some feminists falling for it.

In illustration, by the late 1990s, a wide-ranging poll in the US found 81 per cent of women reporting that it was harder to be a mother now than it had been twenty or thirty years ago. Meanwhile, 56 per cent felt mothers were doing a worse job today than they once had.[26] In much of the Western world, the situation has only worsened further under the heightened austerity regimes in Britain and elsewhere over the last decade and more. It is why in both Britain and the States, the headlines frequently inform us that the pressures new mothers face are greater than ever.

Marianne Levy's *Don't Forget to Scream* is just one of the most recent books on the lonely, alienating experiences of pregnancy and motherhood today. It graphically depicts the near-impossible social and economic challenges endured by so many mothers nowadays, even as research reveals that mothers are working more and sleeping less than a generation ago. There is now an official medical label for the problem in the US: 'Depleted Mother Syndrome' (DMS), to describe the physical and emotional exhaustion of mothers as demands on them increase and resources decrease.[27]

It is all hardly news, when there has been a deluge of books about the tough and treacherous terrain of mothering throughout the twenty-first century. Whether in humorous or heart-breaking tones, it is a sense of fear, failure, frustration, or foreboding that these books largely convey, overshadowing any attendant feelings of fulfilled desire, delight, or celebration. This degree of apprehension is not something I recall from my own days of mothering, once we were sharing the childcare, while campaigning to improve women's lot in their caring roles.

Enduring Maternal Matters

'Apologies all round' is how the eminent Irish novelist Anne Enright begins her own reflections on the matter, in *Making Babies: Stumbling into Motherhood* (2004). Although Enright is a high-achieving writer, the success of that book was due to it being thick with apology, self-mockery, and confusion. Like most literary mothers nowadays, Enright rejects the myth of the selfless mother; in her experience, a woman's all-consuming love for baby and family can vanish with a 'single crying jag'. Indeed, she recalls wondering at times whom she hated the most: 'her baby, her husband or herself'.[28]

Any reported enjoyment of caring, or the sharing of parenting responsibilities, is scarce in the recent surge of 'Mums-lit' books, written and consumed by mothers themselves. Overall, they elaborate on feelings of guilt at the lack of time, energy, or capacity for pleasure that can be mustered for childcare and family life. Those studying this genre, such as Roberta Garrett, find that the writing exposes anxious, envious sentiments, with other mothers often the targets of satire, even though the authors ostensibly reject notions of maternal perfectionism.[29] The books illustrate what Angela McRobbie and other cultural commentators describe as the 'intensification of mothering'. This genre highlights insecure but aspiring and sexually confident middle-class mothers, consistently pitched against a contrasting, abject image of the slovenly, benefits-dependent 'underclass' of single mothers. The latter is the UK equivalent of the US 'welfare queen'.[30]

Maternal anxieties seem almost inevitable in an economic climate increasingly at odds with motherhood and most forms of caring work, viewed as the pitiful antithesis of autonomy, productivity, and success. As Catherine Rottenberg stresses in her book *The Rise of Neoliberal Feminism*, today we are rarely able to escape market metrics. We are encouraged to be relentlessly self-monitoring, always upping our personal value in the race to be winners and, if mothers, seeking to raise only 'perfect' children so they, too, can compete in this zeitgeist. It's another manifestation of the disavowal of fragility, dependency, or any patient and persisting engagement in the work of care – unless that work serves our own immediate interests or that of our children.[31]

This is the reason why so much caring work is outsourced to others as paid labour, why it is precisely this low-waged, precarious care sector that has been mushrooming for decades. Meanwhile, the startling media vilification of mothers on benefits persists, as if they were responsible for rather than victims of austerity regimes and our wider social failings. Such stories exemplify how easily mothers can become targets of public condemnation. In the UK, the current Conservative government has continued to shame single parents and increase the financial pressure on them. This was highlighted in a damning report from the UN in 2019, charging that not only had single parents been hardest hit by benefit cuts, but it seemed that 'women, particularly poorer women, have been intentionally targeted'.[32]

Yet, at the other end of our extreme class divisions in income and assets, we also find heightened levels of anxiety and resentment. In her book *Heading Home: Motherhood, Work, and the Failed Promise of Equality*, the feminist media scholar Shani Orgad interviewed a group of professional women who had 'chosen' to leave their former well-paid jobs for full-time mothering. Despite their access to private resources, Orgad found these home-bound mothers suffering from the very same symptoms as those 1950s housewives my generation of feminists had so determinedly refused to imitate.

Orgad's group of 'privileged' women insist that they had made the 'right decision', though expressing unease at finding themselves dependent on their husbands, and now feeling subordinate to them, whatever their previous career. They admitted to experiences of loneliness and isolation similar to those which women's liberationists uncovered in 'housewives' half a century ago. 'It's quite lonely for a woman to be at home all the time', these latest housebound mothers confess to Orgad; one of them speaks openly of the 'emotional and psychological trauma' of 'leaving her life behind'.

Even while these mothers extolled the virtues of their choice, underneath lay anger and resentment. They intuited something they barely dared to confront: that it was the huge demands of their former working lives, combined with the inflexibilities of their husbands' careers, that prompted their 'heading home'.[33] Unsurprisingly, these relatively affluent homemakers were mostly cynical and sarcastic about any possibilities for overcoming gender inequality, which their own choices were helping to preserve. Rather than oppose toxic employment conditions demanding long hours and permanent availability, these mothers had decided instead to facilitate their husband's career, and now pleaded the impossibility of challenging the underlying structural conditions of gender inequality.

The urgent need for some form of release or escapism, whether for housebound mothers or exhausted 'working' ones, is evident in the recent surge of popular media depictions of motherhood. They all satirize the impossible demands of mothering today. As another British media scholar, Jo Littler, comments, recent TV comedies such as *Bad Moms* or *Motherland* depict primarily middle-class mothers resorting to alcohol or other reckless bursts of hedonism to relieve the daily chaos and trauma of trying to cope with the combined pressures of work and home life.

Sadly absent is any direct assault on our contemporary culture of overwork, or any critique of the welfare cuts and lack of affordable community resources which leave all mothers struggling to parent adequately, and most fathers unwilling, or largely unable, to co-parent fully. Nor do we find much media attention given to those single or working-class mothers who are hit hardest of all, perhaps because the extreme precarity and hardship of their lives leave little space for comedy.[34]

The upshot is yet another victory for neoliberal rationality, upholding the idea of mothers making individual 'choices', and thereby veiling a reality in which many women find it impossible to believe, or even imagine, that there might be alternatives to the existing dysfunctional patterns of domestic responsibility underpinning gender inequality. As the American sociologist Arlie Hochschild suggested in 2014, motherhood remains 'a magnet for the strains of the stalled revolution'.[35] For, as feminists once proclaimed, that revolution requires a massive struggle to transform workplaces, as well as commitments to genuine equality within the home.

All the same, such a revolution should not be so very hard to envisage, when for many decades we have observed something like it operating in Nordic countries, particularly Denmark, Norway, and Sweden. In their different ways these countries have invested heavily in the creation of generous state-funded family policies that allow for more genuine choices in patterns of childcare: longer paid parental leave, fully subsidized pre-school nurseries, and, most important, policies requiring men to take time off work for childcare duties. These policies are pursued in the name of both gender equality and the best interests of children.[36]

Repoliticizing Mothering

Here in the UK, campaigners speak of the 'Motherhood Penalty' – the social and financial losses faced by women when they have children. This contrasts with the 'Fatherhood Bonus': what men gain from parenthood. The Fawcett Society notes that 'parenthood has a distinct wage "penalty" for women, and a wage "bonus" for men'.[37]

Likewise discussing the 'unfinished business' of feminism, in her *Motherhood: A Manifesto*, Eliane Glaser suggests that 'in too many areas, the clock has run backwards'. Her figures are chilling. Half of all mothers develop a mental health problem before or after giving birth; 50 per cent of new mothers feel lonely all or most of the time; suicide is the leading cause of death for mothers during their baby's first year. Glaser herself confesses that despite being a well-resourced feminist, and within a caring relation, 'I have felt as if I am failing every single day since my son was born 11 years ago'.[38]

Such thoughts could lead many to the resigned conclusion that motherhood necessarily involves sacrifice and loss, which is no doubt why the birth rate has been plummeting in Britain, as in the United States, and has now hit record lows. Indeed, today nearly half of women born in the late twentieth century remain childless by their thirtieth birthday, compared with just over 20 per cent of those born in the mid-twentieth century.

Interestingly, though, feminist demands that fathers should get more involved in childcare has met with some success. Nowadays fathers are far more engaged with their children than was the case with my generation of boomers. They are often seen playing with and cuddling them, even changing nappies. But this does not extend to housework: apparently, less than 7 per cent of fathers share the chores equally with women in the household. Even more alarmingly, it remains the case, as midwives have reported for years, that domestic abuse often starts or worsens when women are pregnant.

The enduring reason why so many mothers end up being reproached or disdained, however, returns us to one key theme of this book: the dread of dependency. Many of us, but especially men, remain uneasy before their oldest attachment, to a mother, with its memories of helplessness and need. This can be displaced onto a stubborn avoidance of any engagement with the maternal – clinging to the illusion that in adulthood our dependence on others has long been superseded. As Adam Phillips notes, discouragingly, 'the male child [has] to turn the trauma of having been mothered into the triumphalism of male potency. In this set-up *vulnerability is masculinity's dirty secret*, leaving men with a haunting and haunted sense of impotence that only becoming a bully can assuage.'[39]

This is one reason why the encomium of women's 'sacred calling' is shadowed by recurrent hostility towards actual mothers. The British literary scholar Jacqueline Rose agrees. In her powerful text *Mothers: An Essay on Love and Cruelty*, she argues that mothers remain 'the ultimate scapegoat for our personal and political failings, for everything that is wrong with the world'. We are still demanding that mothers perform the impossible, that they rescue us from all our personal and political weaknesses, and then we blame them for failing at this hopeless task.[40]

In Rose's view, what society does to mothers is 'licensed cruelty', and, what's more, it is getting worse. This is evident, for instance, in the 77 per cent of pregnant women and mothers now reporting discrimination in the workplace, up from 45 per cent a decade earlier, with double the number of pregnant women now losing their jobs. Rose notes that it is crucial to recognize that the idea of maternal virtue is a myth that serves no one. This is even clearer when we reflect that it is frequently migrants who actually perform much of the daily grind of childcare, partly replacing biological mothers – even those who might well want to spend more time with their children if their jobs permitted.

From 2016, the British government did offer subsidies (now under threat) for thirty hours of childcare when children turn three. However, since this help is only available for parents working full-time, it is a policy that has largely benefited professional women. Poorer parents find it hard to make up the deficit, having to work thirty-five hours or more a week. These state subsidies are usually paid via childcare vouchers or tax breaks for working parents, which translate into huge profits annually for corporate childcare providers. Such an approach is inimical to feminism's earlier vision of a publicly funded, universal childcare system.[41]

The arrival of the COVID-19 pandemic aggravated the dilemmas of mothers everywhere. In line with reports from around the world, Maddy Savage announced on the BBC that COVID-19 was damaging women's lives across the board: 'As working mums perform more childcare and face increased job insecurity, there are fears COVID-19 has undone decades of advancement.'[42]

But the pandemic was not solely responsible. Maude Perrier, another British sociologist who specializes in motherhood and parenting today, has tracked the continuing deterioration of childcare provision over the last twenty years. There has been a dramatic decline in publicly funded provision, directing vast profits into the corporate markets now providing it. In her latest book, *Childcare Struggles, Maternal Workers and Social Reproduction*, Perrier notes that while the media occasionally reported on the new threats faced by professional mothers trying to juggle jobs and caring responsibilities during lockdowns, they paid little or no attention to waged childcare workers, who remain among the lowest paid and most vulnerable, as well as being disproportionately working-class, migrant, and ethnic minority women.[43]

Nothing is more damning of our failures to care about our carers than the fact that the majority of women under sixty-five who died from COVID-19 in the first year of the pandemic were social care and domestic employees. Globally, as Perrier notes, some nannies faced increased risks when employers refused, as often happened, to adhere to lockdown rules. Others lost their jobs, with some becoming homeless and stranded, at the mercy of their former employers. The applause we heard for some key workers during the pandemic thus coincided with the continuing economic and symbolic devaluation of paid childcare workers everywhere. It led Perrier, herself a working mother, to join others in calling for unity between all maternal workers, paid or unpaid, hard as this has traditionally been to achieve. Today, however, she is far from alone in making this call.

There is now an exciting movement of Black, ethnic minority, and queer women, especially visible in the United States. They are presenting their own radical vision of motherhood as an essential part of their struggle for better lives and a more caring world. In her important book *We Live for the We: The Political Power of Black Motherhood*, the journalist Dani McClain, for instance, writes that Black mothers must fight for liberation, if they are not to participate in their own and their children's destruction.[44]

The Washington-based Black writer Angela Garbes, in her book *Essential Labor: Mothering as Social Change*, connects mothering to the poorly paid care work which Black and ethnic minority women have historically always performed, if habitually for others. Now is the time, she writes, to celebrate all the creating, nurturing, and life affirmation Black women are doing for their own families and their own communities.

Crucially, she emphasizes that caring for children is not simply a private affair, but 'requires robust community support'. With others, Garbes is eager to proclaim that 'mothering' is a verb, and should be less of a gendered identity, considering that the work of raising children, of *mothering*, 'includes people of all genders and non-parents alike'.

Once we see it like this, it's clear what is so wrong with our current reality, where raising children is so often a 'lonely, bankrupting, and exhausting' affair, rather than what it could and should be, all about celebrating and building upon our interdependence.[45] Put this way, mothering once more becomes a crucial vehicle for social change: not only a place for resisting individual loneliness but also a revolutionary vehicle of wider rebellion, once mothers have joined care workers everywhere in fighting to rebuild caring communities.

Reviewing *Essential Labor*, the *New Yorker* journalist Jia Tolentino, like Garbes of Filipino descent, asks 'Can Motherhood Be a Mode of Rebellion?' She reflects upon her own experiences as a young mother during the pandemic, before suggesting that Garbes 'signals a way out of a prominent contemporary narrative in which women – usually white women – are portrayed as intellectually and creatively stifled by childbearing, and motherhood is characterized as an inherent threat to individual possibility'. In contrast, Tolentino writes that becoming a mother made her feel 'more civically capable and existentially malleable than [she'd] ever felt before'.[46]

Thus, rethinking all aspects of mothering and care work is once more becoming a widespread feminist goal, essential for our vision of social well-being overall. It's why another US feminist scholar and historian of reproductive politics, Laura Briggs, titled one of her recent works *How All Politics Became Reproductive Politics*. Similarly, the Boston-based psychoanalytic theorist Lynne Layton maintains that since many more people are noticing the ways in which neoliberalism has produced the systematic failure of any caretaking environment, it is surely not beyond our imaginations to see how it *might* be otherwise.[47]

Marching in step with Layton, Sarah Knott, the much-acclaimed young historian of motherhood, writes of her own sense of maternal affinity with the silenced voices of mothers over the centuries in *Mother: An Unconventional History*. She joins Rose, Glaser, Perrier, McClain, Garbes, and Tolentino in an urgent call to action: 'A defence of caring under late capitalism, uttered by caregivers of every persuasion – adoptive, biological and employed; female, male, lesbian, gay, trans and the rest – could be a wide coalition indeed.'[48]

For an ageing feminist like me, it is wonderful to hear all these new voices stressing our interdependence and asserting once more that care work should be public and universal. They speak of the need to keep building the widest possible coalition so we can begin tackling the failures of care. It is also clear that without a caring environment some mothers will *not* manage to muddle through at all, which is why the number of children taken away from their mothers and into 'care' has increased year on year since 2010, now mounting to over 100,000 cases annually.

Feminists once hoped that creating better conditions for mothering might inspire demands for a kinder, more caring world. Despite facing formidably greater obstacles, that thought has returned for many young women activists today, now joining campaigning groups arguing for a reduced working week, along with the reversal of welfare cuts and increased public funding for childcare provision. In my day, before austerity and extreme job pressures, those household rotas and shared parenting meant that some of us did succeed in making significant changes in our domestic lives. Indeed, it was those less-demanding domestic lives that enabled more of us to forge different lives in the workplace.

2

Valuing Education

When I was a young child, my education was constantly interrupted by sojourns in hospital for asthma. But something about my fragility and status, as the skinny daughter of very respectable parents, meant that I often felt warmth and occasionally attentive care from some of my teachers. I was able to enjoy most of my time in school, and later university, developing frequent crushes on teachers, older girls, or other mentors. In my family, academic prowess was really all that mattered, which is often seen as characteristic of Jewish families. Both my mother and my brother had been high achievers, each celebrated as 'top of the state', with the highest exam results across New South Wales in their final year of school.

Long before public metrics of 'achievement' became paramount in ranking all aspects of education, I imbibed an outlook where exam results were of overriding importance, the sole indicator of worth. Both my sister and I rebelled against this myopic view, though we were less sure about what was important instead.

Today, however, it is more obvious than ever that we should value education purely for its own sake, crucial for helping us understand how to build a more peaceful, caring, and inclusive world. For me, pondering the purpose of education has become more significant as the years pass.

Classrooms and Care

The North American philosopher Martha Nussbaum draws upon the classic *Émile* by her French forebear Jean-Jacques Rousseau in analysing the function of education. Crucially, she is persuasive about the need to educate our emotions so as to develop a respect for humanity, and curb 'the excesses of the greedy self'. Indeed, she is certain that this is the only way to create caring citizens:

> An education in common human weakness and vulnerability should be a very profound part of the education of all children ... they should be able to decode the suffering of others, and this decoding should deliberately lead them into lives both near and far, including the lives of distant humans and the lives of animals.[1]

Before her, the celebrated Brazilian educator and Christian Marxist Paulo Freire published over twenty books on how to build a new, interactive relationship between teachers, learners, and society. Always on the side of the disadvantaged, his most influential book, *Pedagogy of the Oppressed* (1968), drew upon his personal experience teaching Brazilian adults and Chilean peasants to read and write. He argued that education was necessary to help the exploited fight back against their dehumanization, to consolidate a stronger sense of identity, and to participate in the social transformation of their world.[2]

Many others were influenced by Freire, though some feminists, like the Black American bell hooks, otherwise an admirer, noted the sexism in his language. She also felt that Freire's prioritizing of class led to forms of gender and race blindness. In her own book *Teaching to Transgress: Education as the Practice of Freedom*, hooks joins the call for a new kind of education, one now known as 'critical pedagogy', designed to help build multicultural communities and encourage people to resist injustice and work for change. Drawing on her own experience as a teacher, hooks does admit that transgressive teaching practices, rewarding as they are, will never be easy. She concludes *Teaching to Transgress* with this thought:

> The classroom, with all its limitations, remains a location of possibility. In that field of possibility we have the opportunity to labor for freedom, to demand of ourselves and our comrades an openness of mind and heart that allows us to face reality even as we collectively imagine ways to move beyond boundaries, to transgress. This is education as the practice of freedom.[3]

It should be clear that only inclusive and supportive educational practices can help build a strong sense of agency and connection to others in classrooms, whatever people's distinct abilities. Unresponsive or indifferent modes of teaching, attentive only to instrumental goals, are more likely to have the opposite effect, either stigmatizing or alienating those who feel neglected or inadequate. Sadly, as I am forced to conclude from the changes I've observed over the half century I spent in education, such inclusive and enabling teaching is almost the reverse of dominant trends in all educational institutions today. As a result, we have been witnessing an ever fiercer attack on the very idea of education for its own sake, with curricula increasingly geared to external goals and job markets.

As those interested in its history know, there have always been deep political divisions surrounding education, impacting upon people's experiences of it at all levels of learning. The battles began as soon as a minimum level of education became compulsory for children in industrialized countries by the close of the nineteenth century. Britain, in particular, is notorious for the lifelong privileges conferred upon those attending its elite private schools, bizarrely known as 'public schools'. In the genuinely public sector, wrangles over selective versus all-inclusive public education accompanied the very start of universal free secondary education, from 1944, with 80 per cent of children assigned to secondary moderns and only around 20 per cent going to grammar schools – those who scored well in the 11-plus exam at the end of primary school. Grammar schools received four times more money per pupil than secondary moderns.

To this day the myth persists that this system provided upward mobility for intelligent working-class children, despite all studies revealing that the overwhelming majority of grammar-school students came from middle-class backgrounds. The minority of working-class youth attending grammars rarely went on to university, while those who did nevertheless often recalled that they had felt out of place and hated their school experience. One of them, the British cultural theorist Annette Kuhn, described feeling 'conspicuously out of place' in her grammar school in the 1950s, in her moving memoir *Family Secrets: Acts of Memory and Imagination* (1995). Meanwhile, those children 'left behind' at secondary moderns often described a sense of feeling already labelled as failures.

Meditating on the limits of the British education system, during his first ever job as a secondary-modern teacher in the late 1950s, the young Stuart Hall reflected that instead of teaching students to think critically, schools were primarily engines of propaganda for 'making students familiar ... with the social and class barriers to education and culture which the society has already imposed'. Struggling with crowded class-rooms and poor equipment, he found that most of his fellow teachers were all too aware that their schools were considered inferior; they despised the homes from which their students mainly came, and sought to keep 'a safe distance between themselves and the school'.[4] Call this a caring environment?

In stark contrast, Chris Searle became one of the most famous radical teachers in Britain. Searle was arguing, over fifty years ago, that schools should care about all their students, especially the most disadvantaged, to enable pupils to challenge society's established values and existing hierarchies. It was a belief he first put into practice, publicly, when teaching English in one of the lower-stream classes at Sir John Cass and Redcote Secondary Modern, in an impoverished area of Stepney, East London. To encourage their writing, Searle compiled a book of poetry written by his pupils, those children who had hitherto viewed themselves as their school's rejects. However, the school governors rejected the collection as 'too gloomy', since the children had written about their difficult home lives in East End slums.

Searle found a way to publish the collection, *Stepney Words* (1971), anyway, and was duly sacked. It led to a walk-out by 500 pupils, rapidly joined by others from three neighbouring schools, and the protest culminated in a large rally in Trafalgar Square calling, without success, to have Searle reinstated. However, *Stepney Words* made its mark, and Searle was soon successfully pursuing his ideas in other schools. A third edition of *Stepney Words* appeared a few years ago, its launch attended by some of the original young poets, almost five decades later.

It would later be widely acknowledged that the impact of racism on schooling in the 1960s and 1970s created the most abysmal and uncaring situations for some pupils. This was a time when hundreds of Black children were incorrectly labelled as 'educationally subnormal' across Britain, and wrongly assigned to ESN schools for children of low intelligence. The London teacher Bernard Coard, who later became notorious for a failed coup against his own socialist government in Grenada, most powerfully denounced this practice in his searing polemic *How the West Indian Child Is Made Educationally Sub-normal in the British School System* (1971).[5] Indeed, racism was prevalent throughout the educational system, impeding the success of non-white children at any school. Little has changed since. In its latest comprehensive report in 2020, the World Economic Forum found that almost all Black British children have experienced racism at school.

Selina Todd is another well-known educational historian emphasizing the failures of British schools, whether in terms of race or class. Her extensive research confirms that grammar schools never met even their own dubious meritocratic aims, serving more to exacerbate divisions and convince working-class children of their unworthiness.[6] In fact, the golden age for upward mobility arrived only with the widespread abolition of grammar schools and the establishment of the comprehensive system.

It was the rise of comprehensive education that actually enabled more working-class children to enter further or higher education from the 1970s, whatever their gender or ethnicity. However, any golden age for comprehensives was short-lived. Teachers overall attribute this to government imposition of ever more stringent regimes of testing, inspections, and the monitoring of teaching staff.

In recent years, new forms of school managerialism have accompanied the enshrinement of extensive commercialized competitiveness. The public ranking of schools which began in 1988 led to increasing segregation, as more affluent parents could select supposedly 'better' schools. These moves paved the way for the growth of independent or academy schools, no longer run by or even accountable to local communities. Meanwhile, the ever narrower national curriculum imposed on comprehensives from 2014 determinedly sidelined the arts to focus on English, maths, and science, the so-called STEM subjects.

Melissa Benn confirms this predicament in her challenging book *Life Lessons: The Case for a National Education Service* (2018): she reports that creativity and play are being squeezed out even in nursery settings, where testing is already beginning. The impact of market-style competition, endless testing, and a skeleton curriculum has ensured 'a harmful narrowing of the educational experience from the early years through to university'.

Sadly, these forces have combined to leave British schools near the bottom of the European rankings for creative learning.

There is little space for any form of critical pedagogy that might attempt to tackle inequality and teach the value of care, compassion, and other life skills. Unsurprisingly, we now hear complaints from teachers daily, while a National Education Union survey from 2021 discovered that an extraordinary one in three teachers was planning to quit within five years.

Although I am most familiar with the changes in the British education system, they largely mimic the process in the United States. Diane Ravitch, a leading educationalist and former government adviser in Washington, published a highly influential book called *The Death and Life of the Great American School System: How Testing and Choice Are Undermining Education*. Although Ravitch herself had once supported testing and choice, she came to see that the imposition of testing, accountability, markets, and so-called choice had ended up undermining American schools. She concluded that these shifts had in fact been shrinking the intellectual capacity and creativity of schoolchildren, whether headed for university or not.[7]

Since then, numerous reports have continued to map the various ways in which the educational system is deteriorating in the States. Six years after Ravitch's report, in 2016, measures of children's reading skills from around the world found that ten-year-old Americans possessed far lower reading skills than they had a decade earlier. This was a signal that the country was slipping even further behind on global ratings overall. Researchers link this decline to a lack of care on all fronts, inside and outside the classroom. However competent and caring the teachers, they are facing growing numbers of extremely poor students, trying to learn to read and think clearly while coping with hunger, homelessness, and other upheavals at home.

The classroom can certainly strive to be a caring space, when children are able and willing to attend. However, the situation of poor or disadvantaged students was dramatically worsened by the closure of schools for almost a year during the recent

COVID pandemic. Of course, theirs is a situation that has been evident globally, as the United Nations emphasizes in its numerous education reports. The higher the levels of inequality in any society, the less under-resourced schools have been able to reach poorer students across expanding digital divides. In the UK, the Department for Education noted in 2022 that the gap in grades between poorer pupils and their peers in English secondary schools is the widest in a decade, and certain to increase if there are more spending cuts.

The Purpose of Education

Grades for some may be slipping, but a university degree is still the goal of a large percentage of young people and their families everywhere. In the UK, the Institute of Education found that 97 per cent of parents wanted their children to go to university, obviously including many who had no higher education themselves. Indeed, by 2017 some 50 per cent of young people were taking part in higher education in the UK, although that figure had dropped 5 per cent by 2022.[8] The fall is hardly surprising when many universities are themselves in serious crisis, due to government funding cuts. Weakened further by the shrinking number of international students during the pandemic, many British universities are reported to be on the point of collapse, with talk of between fourteen and forty institutions seriously threatened.

We need to understand just what has gone so wrong. For whatever the situation, education will always remain worth fighting for, and fighting over, as a fundamental part of any vision of a healthy and caring world.

First, we must acknowledge the consequences of commodification for our places of learning.

Globally, those who have raised the loudest alarm about the threat to higher education have also conveyed the clearest vision of its fundamental significance as a public good. Reject-ing any idea that the purpose of universities is to encourage commercial reasoning, they insist that the crucial function of higher education has always been to promote critical thinking and autonomous research, both essential for their own sake. As the British literary critic Stefan Collini contends, universi-ties must be places where 'pushing at the boundaries of present understanding is ... the very rationale of those institutions themselves'.[9]

This is also why higher education needs to be made as accessible as possible to everyone, something that cannot be achieved by tinkering with university entrance requirements. Rather, it depends upon first-rate support and schooling for everybody from the very start of life.

Recently, the gains and losses of university life were mov-ingly sketched in Les Back's reflective ethnography of his three decades of teaching, chiefly in the sociology depart-ment at London's Goldsmiths College. Back's *Academic Diary* celebrates the satisfying aspects of his work, despite all the managerial time-wasting, current student indebtedness, marketization of degrees, and increasing anxieties of his peers.

The real reward, he affirms, is the knowledge that teachers really can make a difference to student lives, even now. This is what matters, and he cherishes it. It returns him to the best moments of his own experiences as a working-class boy at school, encouraged and supported by one radical teacher. A similar sentiment is expressed in an elegant essay by the soci-ologist Rosalind Gill, now also teaching sociology in London, at City University. After being expelled from school as a mis-erable, troubled child, she was rescued by two remarkable sociology teachers at an FE college: 'I am forever indebted to them for all the conversations, possibilities and perspectives they opened up.'[10]

What is most important and also most rewarding about teaching, Back suggests, is holding students' interest in the things they care about, as well as leaving time to themselves to keep thinking, researching, or writing about such things. Fulfilling teaching is caring teaching. This begins, as Back notes, with listening to students and assuring them that they matter, but, above all, conveying a sense of the importance of ideas: 'Universities are at their best when they are places where minds are allowed to wander, be it through the labyrinth of high theory or [echoing Stuart Hall] the lowly task of making the familiar strange.'[11] Or perhaps, even more importantly, making the strange familiar.

Contemplating her twenty years in academia, Jo Littler echoes these sentiments. Expressing the thoughts of so many workers in higher education almost everywhere today, but especially in the UK (excluding Scotland with its different, less commercialized, free university system, and Wales which offers more generous student support), Littler confesses she feels demoralized to see how bureaucratic micro-management is competitively dividing and infantilizing academics, and also exhausting them through overwork. Yet certain rewards persist: 'At the same time, it is also a privilege and a pleasure: it is a privilege to work in a university, a pleasure to be able to hear and to learn with others; and both bring with them a responsibility to work towards any forms of democratization we might be able to visualize.'[12]

This was certainly evident throughout most of my own educational journey. I began my career in higher education reluctantly, qualified as I was only to teach in what I viewed as largely uninspiring departments of psychology. Indeed, in 1968 I signed off my doctorate with Wittgenstein's provocative words regarding the confusions and barrenness of that discipline: 'For in psychology, there are experimental methods and conceptual confusion.'[13]

Like many others, especially young women, I had wanted to study psychology to understand more about human actions and emotions. Frustratingly, our chief research projects at the time entirely precluded this, involving instead the study of rats running mazes to collect food. This taught us nothing even about the everyday behaviour of rats, let alone about the complexities of human thought and behaviour. My doctorate, obtained in 1969, was a critique of such disciplinary folly, with psychology's 'science envy' forcing it to distance itself from the humanities, forgoing all interest in the joys and miseries of the human condition.

'How absurd is that?' I asked, repeatedly. This meant exhaustively criticizing the misconceptions of the then hegemonic school of behaviourist psychology, which eschewed engagement with thoughts or emotions for an exclusive focus on 'observable behaviour'. Yet by rejecting any notion of goals or intentions, experimental psychology could never provide anything like an adequate description of the nuances of the behaviour it fetishized – was that cough a sign of COVID, or a bid to gain attention? The behaviourist could not tell us.

Naturally, Sydney's few traditional psychology departments refused even to consider employing me. On the other hand, the two eminent North American professors who had marked my doctorate, Sigmund Koch and William Rozeboom, each immediately offered me a job in their departments, in Texas and Alberta. Knowing no one in those locations, I departed for London where I did have a few contacts, arriving in September 1970 with my fourteen-month-old son.

The expansion of higher education in Britain in the 1960s ensured that academic openings were thick on the ground for recent doctoral graduates, even graduates from abroad who were cynical about their discipline. I immediately accepted one of the first jobs I heard about, at Enfield College of Technology. For a single mother, the working conditions were perfect: I was able to fit classroom hours around everyday childcare, with additional help from friends, alongside local free community-run playgroups and the nurseries we had fought for or helped to establish.

The pressurizing sense that one should always be trying to improve one's market value by switching jobs was then almost unthinkable, certainly to political activists. So, I stayed put for almost thirty years. In 1972 Enfield College of Technology became Middlesex Polytechnic, and then Middlesex University two decades later. Meanwhile, each decade brought exciting new possibilities in higher education, enabling me to draw upon my own engaged, left-feminist politics throughout.

The Nature of Knowledge

Predictably, at work, my energies went into critiquing psychology's narrow theoretical framing and disciplinary boundaries, while broadening its potential for engagement with contemporary social issues.

Officially, I was teaching 'social psychology', but I spent little time discussing the classic experiments then seen as fundamental in that branch of psychology. These included the eyeblink test, training a subject not to blink at a puff of air; or conformity experiments, observing how one person could affect the behaviour of others through insisting upon false information. They did involve human subjects rather than rats, although, in line with existing practices, data was collected in conditions wiped clean of the socio-historical particulars of the subjects' lives outside the lab. In textbooks the prominent figures included the US-based Solomon Asch, or the Oxford academic Michael Argyle, with their detailed measurements of tightly controlled behaviour in laboratory settings (irrespective of class, race, gender, or any other distinctive trait). How this related to behaviour in the world at large remained mere speculation.[14]

The idea that we are social beings from the outset, embedded in language, culture, and diverse webs of power, was disavowed in mainstream psychology. However, it was bedrock in the left-feminist, anti-racist, Marxist milieu I now occupied, and I tried to communicate it in class. Such teaching was popular with most students since it morphed into whatever issues most engaged me, and often them, at the time. Politically reframed, for instance, and updating R. D. Laing, the concept of 'mental illness' could easily encompass women's startlingly higher rates of depression, while questioning their routine treatment with addictive benzodiazepines, marketed as 'Mother's Little Helper'.[15]

Understandings of 'prejudice' shifted dramatically once no longer framed and measured as individual 'attitudes' but placed in the context of the still-entrenched outcome of various histories of white colonialism, racism, and discrimination, drawing in particular upon Frantz Fanon and Stuart Hall.[16] From Fanon's classic *Black Skin, White Masks*, written in 1952, it was possible to think about the white world's perpetual debasement of the Black world, woven into language itself. More complexly again, Stuart Hall introduced a cultural focus on raced identities as always situated, imagined, and multiple. These broader understandings of our distinct sense of ourselves as inevitably affected by class, ethnicity, and gender entailed moving across disciplines, vastly enriching our understandings of people's place in the world.

Similar structural forces provided fresh comprehension of 'delinquent behaviour' as conceptualized by the 'new criminologists', including Jock Young, John Lea, and Roger Matthews, who were, happily, my colleagues and friends at Middlesex.[17] They pointed to the crucial role of marginalization and relative deprivation in working-class crime, as well as the importance of caring community programmes in reducing or controlling such crime.

Each topic was framed at every turn by the newly emerging landscapes of gender, still ludicrously reduced in my discipline to putative individual attributes known as 'sex differences', and tirelessly fought over by 'nature' versus 'nurture' brigades.

The problems of that depressed housewife, for instance, looked very different in the light of research by Ann Oakley or the American sociologist Jessie Bernard. Both of them explored the isolation and loss of status experienced by the majority of women who described themselves as 'just' a housewife, an occupation often at odds with their earlier hopes for greater engagement with the wider world.

Gender relations could now be shown to intersect with all areas of human thought and action, from which they had hitherto been largely excluded. Women's subjectivity, in particular, was rendered more complex by the use of critical psychoanalytic perspectives, be it those of Juliet Mitchell, Janet Sayers, or Nancy Chodorow. Every week saw the emergence of fresh research and debate addressing every aspect of women's lives, from issues of violence, sexuality, parenting, and family life to media representations, and even fashion.

Although I was tolerated as an oddball in my otherwise orthodox psychology department at Middlesex, there were no attempts to interfere with anyone's teaching practices or curriculum.

I did feel that most staff were committed and helpful with the students, although I was only directly supported by, and close to, a handful of my colleagues. For the most part, I gained my confidence and backing from relevant engagements outside the college, which then fed into a certain sense of purpose in my teaching work.

It was the heyday of political sociology which, combined with the critical thinking coming from radical philosophy and the burgeoning field of cultural studies and media theory, enabled progressive teachers to find a scholarly footing in academia. This happened especially in the newer redbrick universities and polytechnics, where young radicals could be quite as iconoclastic as we liked – even inside my own conservative discipline.

In the polytechnics of the 1970s, mostly created and funded by local authorities, there seemed little to curb our creativity should we wish to develop it. This was in contrast to the older, elite universities, under the control of central government. Our departments were autonomous, and we had few dealings with bureaucracy of any sort.

Unless one was unlucky, academic life remained relatively relaxed for several decades as student numbers were steadily rising and still largely underpinned by government spending. Thus, while only just over 5 per cent of young people attended British universities at the start of the 1970s, this had increased almost threefold, to 14 per cent, by the end of the decade. Moreover, our working conditions were such that we had the luxury of time for developing engaged and caring relations with all our students, should we so choose.

We soon found ourselves satirized in the mainstream media, such as in Malcolm Bradbury's best-selling fiction *The History Man*, written in the mid-1970s and aired as a TV mini-series the following decade, starring Anthony Sher. Its formerly working-class protagonist, Howard Kirk, is an ardently left-wing academic, using his radical politics in self-serving and manipulative ways to sleep with students and neglect his wife.

Nevertheless, with intellectual life back then still favouring progressive thought, the blossoming of movement politics in the 1970s and '80s did mean that some of our 'radical' ideas began appearing in the mainstream cultural vernacular, and not just as satire or ridicule. Once there, however, they were always liable to mutate and be disputed afresh. This was especially true in relation to gender and race issues. The leading liberal broadsheet the *Guardian* had caught up with women's liberation by the mid-1970s, as evident in Jill Tweedie's colourful feminist columns. There was widespread coverage of the 100,000 people at the Rock against Racism concert in Victoria Park in 1978. Black novelists, playwrights, and poets, including Darcus Howe, Linton Kwesi Johnson, and Hanif Kureishi, started to be mentioned in the British press in the wake of a multitude of well-established North American artists, beginning with Richard Wright, James Baldwin, Maya Angelou, Toni Morrison, and Alice Walker.

Meanwhile, the popular expansion of the humanities and social sciences meant that, within a few decades, many former outsiders were suddenly being snapped up by the old universities. Those of us who had been busy trying to highlight the theoretical oversights, historical exclusions, and conceptual and methodological rigidities of our own distinct areas of knowledge since the 1970s were, twenty years later, being absorbed into the older, more traditional sector of higher education.

Regrettably, however, this occurred just when the institutions that had perhaps reluctantly sustained our radical pedagogic transformations were themselves becoming starved of cash and declared to be failing. As Jo Littler recalls about obtaining her first job, at Middlesex University in 2000: 'Ex-polys were where to me the interesting work was happening, in the late '90s and early 2000s ... I liked their openness to working with organizations and communities outside the university in the days before such activity was put through the unnecessary time-consuming sausage mincer of audit otherwise known as *the impact case study*.'[18] That mincer was set to grow ever hungrier.

I had little awareness of education policy when I started my teaching career in 1970 amid the repercussions of the progressive Robbins Report (1963), itself part of a general expansion of welfare provision. Its recommendations had triggered a huge expansion in higher education, with the opening of many new universities; it also firmly emphasized the value of learning for its own sake, and for the good of society as a whole. Crucially, Robbins stressed the democratic, social value of higher education, arguing that this should be recognized with government funding, thus giving everyone with the ability and desire to attend university the chance to do so.

Teaching and Engagement

Not only was higher education gratis in the 1970s, but maintenance grants were available for many students, leaving most of them free from student loans, bank overdrafts, or even credit card debts. In my experience, teaching was almost always rewarding in the more relaxed schedules of the 1970s and '80s.

However, things began to change across the public sector under Margaret Thatcher. Class sizes were growing, yet funding for higher education was shrinking, as good jobs in both industry and the public sector increasingly required evidence of post-school certificates. With this came a ruthless harping on individual choice, with its pretence that anyone could be a high achiever whatever their schooling or background, so long as they worked hard enough.

A second major educational report was produced in 1997, the Dearing Report, which laid the groundwork for the troubles ahead. It recommended the introduction of tuition fees for undergraduate students, and the replacement of maintenance grants with repayable loans, for all but the very poorest. However, although it was certainly a turning point, the Dearing Report did still maintain that the purpose of higher education was not only to enable individuals to achieve their highest potential and equip them for work, but also 'to increase knowledge and understanding for their own sake' and to play a major role in shaping a 'democratic, civilised, inclusive society'.

That report appeared just two months after the Labour leader Tony Blair became prime minister. Blair had pledged to expand higher education to enable at least half the population to benefit from it, and student numbers did rapidly increase in the late 1990s. However, this was also when free education ended, with the imposition of an annual 'top-up' fee of £1,000 in 1998. That fee was tripled to £3,000 in 2006, then tripled yet again to an alarming £9,000 under the new Coalition/Tory government in 2010, instituting fees that by some measures exceed those at any comparable public universities elsewhere in the world. Turning the Robbins Report on its head, Conservative politicians were determined to introduce market principles, having always seen higher education as a personal investment rather than a social good or national asset.

At Middlesex in the late 1990s, we sometimes saw several hundred eager young faces in a single classroom. This trend had begun a little earlier in the United States and around Europe, partly driven by rising female participation in higher education: indeed, my own classes shifted from being gender-balanced to a clear majority of women studying psychology. Nevertheless, class sizes still seemed manageable, and there was usually some provision for teaching assistants. Always start with a joke, I decided, especially when introducing topics, such as psychoanalysis, which students of psychology were typically taught to disdain: 'Here's to the happiest years of our lives / Spent in the arms of other men's wives ... Here's to ... our mothers!'

In 1992, polytechnics were rebranded as universities, which was ironic since funding was falling at the time, and the hierarchy between universities growing. This relabelling magically tripled the number of working-class youth studying in universities. However, given the new policy of ranking universities, instead of eliminating inequality in higher education it entrenched it. I recall our best-known Trotskyist lecturer, Ian Birchall, joking: 'It's like giving people a medal to wear as you evict them onto the streets.'

Incorporation into the unitary national system also diminished the extent to which the old polytechnics, now new universities, could respond to local communities. It was all part of the increased centralization of authority in Westminster, deliberately undermining the role of municipal government and local councils. The management of these brand-new universities, including Middlesex, immediately felt compelled to play catch-up with the old universities: where were our professors? Our doctoral students? Oh dear, where were our publications?

This piled much more pressure on teaching staff across the board, as universities were forced into constant competition to attract more students.

Fortunately for me, I had been publishing ever since the 1980s, always in relation to conflicting debates and differing strategies in feminist and left politics. My writing was very much an offshoot of my activism. I was eager to enter feminist debates to affirm a socialist perspective, as in *Is the Future Female? Troubled Thoughts on Contemporary Feminism*, and conversely to engage in disputes on the left to assert feminist positions, as in *Beyond the Fragments: Feminism and the Making of Socialism*. That was my very first book, written with Hilary Wainwright and Sheila Rowbotham, its hugely encouraging lead author.[19] The popularity of that publication – a collective project, originally self-published as a pamphlet in 1979 by the Islington Community Press, where I worked unwaged part-time – generated a large conference in Leeds the following year.

The confidence and support I gained in my political work assisted my academic career, enabling me to publish regularly, each book in the series written as a sequel to address, as best I could, the gender-inflected politics of their time.[20] Because of this, I was made a professor in 1994, two years after Middlesex became a university, despite never having submitted a single article to any psychology journal. Today, when what counts as successful publication is judged primarily by the parochial prestige conferred by a hierarchy of elite journals in distinct disciplines, individual academics inevitably feel much more pressurized, as well as less cared for and supported by either their colleagues or their readers.

At the close of the 1990s I was encouraged to apply for an Anniversary Professorship at Birkbeck, which unlike most universities was established 'to educate the working people of London', and was one of the first colleges to admit women, in 1830. Birkbeck has retained a certain patina of progressivism ever since, becoming part of the University of London in 1920 on the condition that it continued to offer evening study, as it does to this day.

In celebration of its origins, 175 years earlier, what Birkbeck was looking for then was not so much disciplinary experts as a few scholars who had gained a broader audience from their participation in public affairs, alongside their academic life. It meant that these particular professorships were not restricted to what was officially rated as one's disciplinary field in the new competition for funding that had been created between, and even within, universities. This was very lucky for me.

Looking back, I realize that I always enjoyed teaching because it was so completely entwined with my political engagements, and the sense of belonging to a supportive, if contentious, left-feminist milieu. I was far from alone in this at the time, at least within some of the outlets of women's liberation, where theory and engagement still existed hand in glove. Undeniably, there was often tension between some feminist activists and others seen as 'over-invested' in theory and less involved in grassroots struggles. As a result, feminist solidarities were somewhat fraying by the close of the 1970s.

Yet feminists were still able to develop accessible magazines that attempted to weave together scholarship and practice. For instance, *Feminist Review*, which I joined for a decade a few years after its launch in 1979, was a journal as committed to diverse feminist research as to debates over political perspectives and strategy. It aimed explicitly 'to bridge the gap between academic and political work'. Of course, this mission never proved easy, least of all when addressing complex tensions around matters of race and ethnicity, then or now. In its opening issue the topics ranged from assessing the impact of Britain's Equal Pay and Sex Discrimination Acts within the job market, to the place of female sexuality in Italian fascist ideology, alongside – remarkable as it seems today – interviews with Yemeni women who had been affected by the creation of the People's Democratic Republic of Yemen.

For me, the election of Margaret Thatcher as British prime minister in 1979 meant that the ties between teaching and politics simply intensified. It required keeping abreast of the resistance and defeats of left and feminist struggles throughout the 1980s, always trying to encourage greater understanding of the world around us and broaden our concern for others in those harsher times. There was so much to discuss, from race uprisings and union struggles exploding onto the streets, to the Greenham Common women's peace camp set up in 1981 to oppose the British deployment of US nuclear missiles at Greenham. Sometimes I might be addressing the effects of Britain's imperial legacy in the classroom, while also busy expressing solidarity with Black resistance to police violence and harassment on the streets. Other times I might be connecting the importance of community ties on mental health with the widespread support for miners holding out against pit closures (before Thatcher's brutal and finally successful confrontation with the National Union of Miners in 1984–85). There were also days of action at the women's peace camp at Greenham Common, accompanying scholarly discussions about the 'feminine' and its possible links to non-violence.

Renewed Theoretical Combat

Sadly, by the time Thatcher was elected for the third successive time in 1987, political resistance to the now seemingly unbeatable Conservative hegemony was waning everywhere, ushering in the most quiescent decade of my lifetime. Yet, even as street activism declined – apart from the women's occupation at Greenham Common, and periodic protests led by gay men demanding more assistance for victims of HIV/AIDS – the 1980s and '90s were vibrant and combative decades within higher education.

The growth of women's studies around the globe, for example, helped to support and inspire some of the young women now entering higher education in droves. It was an exciting time, animated by heated debates around how to affirm and care for *all* women, with a deeper understanding of difference and diversity between women.

In the States, fierce battles broke out between feminists at the 'Politics of Sexuality' conference at New York's Barnard College in 1982, inaugurating the so-called Feminist Sex Wars over issues of censorship and explicit sexual representation, which continue to this day. Under the banner of 'Women against Pornography', some radical feminists – including the forceful Robin Morgan, following in the footsteps of Andrea Dworkin and Catharine MacKinnon – declared that 'pornography' was the cause of men's violence against women, and there should be laws to ban it. In the opposite camp were the conference organizers and participants, critical of calls to censor any sexual image that could be deemed 'degrading' without allowing time for discussion of the potential hazards of state censorship. The organizers also worried that it was reductive to equate men's violence against women with pornography, rather than with the whole edifice of male power. In the heat of the moment, the conference organizers were denounced by radical feminist critics who lodged complaints with university employers – in some cases putting academic careers in permanent jeopardy.

Further conflict arose when critical theory, or what was loosely labelled 'postmodernism' – a focus on the role of language in creating 'truth' or certainties – came to dominate the writing of leading feminist thinkers throughout the 1990s. Dissenters objected that this scholarly focus on subjectivity and representation entailed the neglect of socio-economic or class concerns.

In particular, Judith Butler's philosophical questioning of any genuinely secure base for gender identity, other than 'as an ongoing *discursive* practice', was seen as an attack on possibilities for shared feminist agency and concrete struggle. This was despite her insistence that 'gender', conceived as highly regulated, repeated performances that congeal over time, was nevertheless always open to intervention and resignification. Moreover, Butler suggested that her analysis might actually expand the possibilities for feminist resistance, given that the very identity categories often seen as foundational in feminist politics can also work to limit and constrain certain cultural possibilities that feminism might otherwise open up. Thus, as she confidently concluded in her iconic text *Gender Trouble*, the deconstruction of identity is not the deconstruction of politics, but rather 'establishes as political the very terms through which identity is constructed'.[21]

However, this is not always easy to grasp, even when carefully expounded, since it is usually some form of collective identity struggle that leads us into politics, *as* women, *as* mothers, *as* teachers, and so on. Although, very much in line with Butler's thinking, the form that struggle takes usually involves us *objecting* to how we have been seen and treated within those identity positions. For instance, it was as a woman that I questioned what a 'woman' is supposed to be; it was as a mother that I rejected the mythologies of motherhood; it was as a psychologist that I queried the job of the psychologist. Yet, *Gender Trouble* has remained as notorious as it was influential.

At the same time, race studies, anti-colonial thought, and queer studies were joining feminist scholarship on university curricula, in principle enabling more students from increasingly diverse backgrounds to feel recognized and addressed in certain courses. As I had found in my own teaching, what was most interesting about the growth of the new forms of scholarship from the 1970s, beyond their concern with the burning issues of the day, was their embrace of 'transdisciplinarity', which encouraged a desire to listen to and learn from each other across borders of all kinds. Transdisciplinarity recognized the interdependence of knowledge, foregrounding what could be learned from differing academic traditions as well as from attending more closely to everyday habits and opinions outside the academy.

This was expressed in the growth of new methodologies, consciously outlined in 'feminist methodology'. Such practices of enquiry aimed to be both self-reflexive, with researchers pondering their own impact on what they investigated, and empowering for those being studied, who were encouraged to provide feedback and discuss the effects of being objects of study.

However, by the late 1990s the initial excitement of introducing new programmes and ideas into teaching practices, or prioritizing caring relations in classrooms and research interactions, was being steadily undermined by budget cuts and the commercialization of higher education globally. Academics were now forced into competitive assessments, with individual career-building and personal recognition essential for teachers to survive in their jobs, while students braced themselves for more streamlined job markets. As we'll see, the resulting atmosphere in higher education has continued to impoverish interactive, caring engagements, whether in classroom teaching, creative research, or intellectual exchanges generally.

Shrinking Budgets, Accelerating Commodification

On reaching retirement age, well over a decade ago, I was fortunately able to secure part-time contracts from 2008, which meant escaping some of the worsening conditions at work. It had been clear for some time that universities were undergoing profound change, both in the UK and globally. Yet Britain has always been internationally renowned for its prestigious seats of learning, attracting students from every corner of the globe. This was what spurred Tony Blair to embark upon his massive expansion of higher education in the late 1990s. The 350,000 students enrolled at the start of the decade jumped to over 2 million at its close.

However, in keeping with neoliberal tenet – the curtailment of state provision in favour of commercial arrangements – the costs of higher education in Britain had been shifted from the state onto the students, via student loans. Yet, as Stefan Collini points out, such effective privatization of the sector went ahead without any type of mandate, or evidence concerning its likely effects.

Indeed, government savings from the debt burden now imposed on students, often stretching into later life, is minimal in relation to overall spending. The new regime has no obvious benefit for either the economy or society generally, let alone encouraging caring teaching practices. Collini concludes that the overriding aim has been purely to change the character of universities, as symbolized by the absurdly high salaries vice chancellors now pay themselves in Britain, frequently over half a million pounds.

The result is that universities are now forced to conform to market dogma, whereas once they offered an alternative ethic, even an antidote, to the commercial world by insisting upon the value of pursuing learning entirely for its own sake – in the process producing more knowledgeable people and societies. The disastrous outcome, Collini suggests, has been to 'turn some first-rate universities into third-rate companies'.[22]

Collini is not alone in describing this steady erosion of university life via the denial of funds and imposition of managerialism since 2010. The process has been so comprehensive that another academic witness, the astute British sociologist Will Davies, describes it as a species of 'state vendetta' against higher education.[23] The maddening paradox is that the government's withdrawal of subsidies has accompanied an ever greater intrusion into higher education. There is a blatant contradiction between neoliberal rhetoric railing against *old* bureaucratic constraints and the imposition of *new* bureaucratic managerialism, surveillance, and control over public institutions, enforcing a specious hierarchical competitiveness.

In the crusade to conjoin pedagogy with market logics, universities must provide data on the outcomes of graduating students, *not* in terms of the knowledge, personal satisfaction, or confidence acquired, but in terms of expected subsequent incomes. Universities are advised to develop courses that can be shown to be related to market matters. Hence, they have been encouraged to close down highly respected departments of English and history, replacing them with tailor-made courses more appropriate for business.

Business-oriented courses tend to have a far narrower focus than the more traditional subjects. In line with this process the British government recently approved a further 50 per cent cut to art and design to be diverted into STEM subjects. This is in response to further calls to defund the humanities coming from conservative British media and reactionary voices in government, leading several UK universities to begin shedding some of their traditional courses. Sheffield Hallam suspended its teaching in English literature, causing one lecturer to tweet despairingly that the humanities were being subjected to 'cultural vandalism'. Before the close of 2022, Roehampton announced that it would be drastically cutting its humanities departments, while other new universities, including Wolverhampton, proposed shedding courses in the visual and performing arts.[24]

Meanwhile, the constant pressure to publish and pursue (disappearing) research grants, increased administrative responsibilities, and the competitive practices of monitoring, assessment, and accreditation at every level of university life drain time away from teaching or shared creative engagement except with specialized elite journals, which tend to have a tiny readership. This sorry situation has led the eminent British cultural figure Marina Warner, who only recently was publicly honoured for her services to the humanities, to mourn that 'the model for higher education [now] mimics supermarkets' competition on the high street; the need for external funding pits one institution against another – and even one colleague against another, and young scholars waste their best energies writing grant proposals'.[25]

A decade ago, in 2012, some of the most renowned scholars based in Britain came together to form the Council for the Defence of British Universities. Rowan Williams, then archbishop of Canterbury, headed up its board of trustees, and he has remained outspoken ever since in his passionate denunciations of 'the barbarity and incoherence' of higher education policy.[26] This is a battle that will not go away.

Although with little success so far, the main British body representing university teachers, the University and College Union, has published several white papers against privatization and supported ongoing strike actions from the early 2020s, which raised a host of crucial issues. As well as protesting against shrinking pensions, strikers demanded pay increases for all staff, meaningful action to tackle unmanageable workloads, and an end to casualized contracts, along with the elimination of race, gender, and disability pay gaps.

Of course, Britain is not alone in this commodification of higher education, although it's interesting to note that in much of Europe (as in Scotland) public universities are still free, if sometimes under-resourced. However, in my birthplace, Australia, a reform package called 'Job-Ready Graduates' plans to more than double the cost of courses in the humanities, while significantly lowering them for maths and science.[27] In the States, apart from the problem of skyrocketing student debt, Joy Connolly – current president of the American Council of Learned Societies – warns of an ongoing assault on the humanities and social sciences, with various states, including Florida and Iowa, introducing legislation designed to dictate what can be discussed and taught on publicly funded campuses.[28]

Yet, despite all these hurdles, many students still desire to study the humanities as much as they ever did, although the fee hikes obviously discriminate against poorer candidates. And there is not the slightest evidence that a degree in humanities makes you less employable, as a recent study by the British Academy shows, underlining the sheer philistinism behind these moves.[29]

Whatever the course of study, the escalating pressures in higher education, amplified by the growing prevalence of underpaid casualized staff (between 25 and 30 per cent in many institutions), means that universities are fostering cultures that are less and less caring. There is insecurity among students and staff alike, generating declining mental health and routine anxiety, especially for young academics.[30] This also amplifies generational divides, increasing the envy and resentment some young academics may well feel towards more privileged older folk, such as me, first for our luck in having studied and taught in the good old days before all the current constraints arose, and now for finding it easier to dodge them or increasingly escape them entirely.

What Remains?

Although times are certainly getting tougher in academia, I still found it hard to leave at the close of 2020, only returning for guest lectures every now and then. We seldom know what students might have gained from our presence, when we leave our mark, if at all, in such diverse ways. Yet some reports flow back. Most recently I received an email from a middle-aged man in the Gambia, hoping I might remember him, because some thirty years ago my teaching had somehow changed his life. I always respond, though sadly can rarely remember the names, having taught some 5,000 students over the decades.

I may not recall them, but I miss them. How lucky my generation was to have worked in an era when it was easier to have an impact in the classroom, when there was less competitive pressure on staff, less resentment and internal strife. So, for as long as I can, and in one way and another, I hope to keep studying and trying to communicate the ideas that I find important, leaning upon those who now educate me with their latest thoughts and conceptual framings. Across the generations, we surely still have something to offer one another.

Moreover, we certainly need one another if we are to build and maintain strong coalitions that help us reimagine and fight for properly funded, truly caring education systems. It means returning to ideas of education as a fundamental social good, rejecting the introduction of market logics that are always distinct from logics of care, and opposing the new managerialism whose instrumental goals are inherently at odds with the cultivation of care.

For a caring education not only involves listening to and encouraging all learners, enriching whatever capabilities they possess; it also means conveying awareness of our shared vulnerabilities and interdependence on one another and the world at large. Those who are trained to be self-sufficient above all and to deny fear and weakness, which is often the case with boys and men, tend to lack an adequate language even for understanding themselves, let alone others. It's why, as we saw earlier, Martha Nussbaum argued that instilling compassion for shared human weakness, suffering, and vulnerability should be at the heart of education from the beginning, along with developing a capacity for understanding the potential suffering of all living creatures.[31]

More cheerfully, a caring education can engage pupils and students in discussing people's reliance on love, care, solidarity, and justice, as essential for the preservation of inclusive democracies and sustainable environments. Caring educational practices should also allow for and encourage lifelong learning for everyone, a process that has for many years been stalled in the UK; although the University of the Third Age (U3A), launched in France in 1973, is now an international movement aiming to engage retired people in diverse forms of educational activity. Despite relying upon voluntary teachers and having few formal links to educational institutions, in the UK it now consists of over 1,000 different groups, with a membership of nearly half a million. Its success not only tells us that all people, of any age, can be interested in the sharing of knowledge; it also highlights the importance of well-resourced, local provision to sustain lifelong learning.

In the meantime, there remain numerous other forums connected to community activism or more organized progressive political forums that draw people together for sharing knowledge and community bonding. For those who know where to look, the educational resources on virtual podcasts, games, and other platforms continue to expand and flourish, even though one can rightly deplore the internet's role in spreading misinformation. However, there are certainly endless possibilities for bringing people together in interactive, educational exchanges that build on affiliations already established by progressive forms of belonging.

Globally, struggles to build or sustain more caring, critical education practices at all levels are without doubt essential for upholding any sort of well-informed and caring world, as well as for spreading consciousness of the planetary crisis now potentially threatening us all. Feminists like me once hoped that creating better, more caring conditions for everyone, making visible and sharing the hitherto largely invisible care performed by women at so many different levels, could help to build a new world, allowing everyone to flourish. For a short while we seemed to be headed in that direction. However, for those hopes to be rekindled we would have to resume many of feminism's old battles, or at least those of socialist feminism. I return to the successes and failures of those struggles in my next chapter.

3

A Feminist Life

After entering adulthood in the 1960s, I was eager to escape the sad and acrimonious home I was born into. I first found a form of shelter with a group of free-floating intellectuals, university lecturers, dropouts, drifters, and gamblers, known as the Sydney Libertarians, or the Push. They were anti-authoritarian, pessimistic anarchists, wedded to 'permanent protest'. They also held regular talks on politics, morality, and freedom in the philosophy department at Sydney University, where I was a student.

The talks were an occasion of much conviviality. After meetings, we all dined together in some cheap café, moving swiftly on to our favourite pub of the moment. I was attracted to their 'free-thinking' libertarian contempt for the still-rigid conservatism and hyper-conformity of life and politics in Australia's authoritarian postwar world. The Push's fulsome commitment to 'free love' also offered relief from the hypocritical double standards of the day, so blatant in my own childhood home.

A few key men dominated this small enclave, yet women's assertiveness was encouraged, making it easier for us, and certainly for me, to move on when the men's heavy drinking, gambling, and rootless lifestyle grew boring. I sidestepped into the countercultural and art scene of the '60s while completing my graduate studies at Sydney's main university, before finding myself accidentally pregnant and jobless in 1969. Unexpected motherhood cut me abruptly adrift from any clear sense of belonging anywhere. Who or what was I to lean on now?

I fled to London with my infant son the following year, in late 1970. Once there, I was quickly immersed in the emerging growth of women's liberation, then largely associated with diverse forms of radical community activism. I had missed the very first exuberant outburst at the 'Miss World' competition at London's Royal Albert Hall, in November 1970, and the excitement of calling out the outlandish sexism of Bob Hope as he welcomed his audience to 'this cattle market tonight'. Happily, I was soon friends with almost all the women involved in that protest, many of whom lived near me once I settled in Islington the following year. The rest of my younger life was spent in the warm, if sometimes contentious, embrace of feminism – socialist feminism.

Being part of this new kind of political movement, one with women at its heart, seemed to me the perfect place to be. Whatever our living arrangements, feminists no longer felt quite so dependent on men, since we were finally celebrating the fact that women could assert their independence, while also starting to depend more upon each other. The veteran American folk singer and political activist Malvina Reynolds, among others, was a great source of comfort and merriment, as we sang along to her song 'We Don't Need the Men'.

> We don't need the men,
> We don't need the men,
> We don't need to have them round.
> Except for now and then.
> They can come to see us
> When they're feeling pleasant and agreeable,
> Otherwise, they can stay at home
> And holler at the TV programs.[1]

Of course, many feminists did still fancy men, and in my own collective household, accommodating three single mothers through most of the 1970s, this was sometimes a source of tension. Nevertheless, there is no question that serious work went into finding new ways for us women to support each other, and our children, parallel to the political commitments we shared. We were active in a range of political projects. These included setting up and supporting our local women's centre, the Essex Road Women's Centre, where we gathered for meetings and to plan activities. It meant discussing and contributing to women's cultural activities, with *Spare Rib* just one of the well-thumbed magazines all feminists were reading. Much of the time, feminists were busy helping to run or raise money for any number of campaigns and struggles, whether to secure women's reproductive rights and solve broader health issues, or to demand improved community resources and access to training. We were also involved in workplace struggles. All this encouraged us to look to our history.

History Matters

Notorious in her lifetime, Mary Wollstonecraft, author of *Vindication of the Rights of Woman* (1792), eventually became the accepted 'mother' of British feminism. Today she has her own – ironically still-controversial – statue, almost on my doorstep on Newington Green in North London. But the major forebears of socialist feminism, rather tellingly, are less well known.

This began with the women involved in the utopian Owenite movement of the mid-nineteenth century, who wanted to combat all forms of social oppression and antagonism. Robert Owen was a socialist visionary who in 1800 managed to create a commercially successful model factory in New Lanark, near Glasgow. It had its own welfare and education programmes, including housing, healthcare, and free schooling for all its workers. As the feminist historian Barbara Taylor shows in her book, *Eve and the New Jerusalem*, the women who supported Owen should be seen as early socialist feminists. She cites one Owenite woman speaking out in 1839: 'Woman has been the slave of a slave ... set[ting] one half of the poor people against the other half.' However, as Taylor lamented, the feminist aspirations of Owenism were quickly forgotten, not just by historians, but in the collective memory of the left.[2]

Happily, two other forebears of British socialist feminism – Eleanor Marx and Sylvia Pankhurst – have recently been the subject of substantial investigation in vivid biographies by cultural historian Rachel Holmes. While they had distinct political pedigrees, both tried to combine gender and class analysis. Although she was the formidable, favourite daughter of Karl Marx, Eleanor Marx, if ever we recall her, is perhaps most remembered for being driven to suicide by her arrogant, dishonest, and serially cheating lover, Edward Aveling, at the early age of forty-three. It's therefore startling to read Holmes's opening claim: 'Eleanor Marx changed the world.'

She was certainly a precursor of so much that we would later try to do, though none of us could match her tireless dedication, or what was then the radical originality of everything she did. For Eleanor had to help create the labour movement she worked for, assisting in the foundation of three trade unions and joining dockers and gas workers when they went on strike for better pay and conditions. She was also part of the creation of the revolutionary Socialist League in Britain in the mid-1880s, as well as a moving spirit behind and actively involved in the Second International in the 1890s.

But this commitment to class struggle went hand in hand with Eleanor's embrace of first-wave feminism and the growth of women's activism that appeared in the late nineteenth and early twentieth centuries. In Britain it was led by middle-class women such as Emmeline Pankhurst, who founded the Women's Social and Political Union (WSPU) in Manchester in 1903, dedicated to securing women's right to vote. However, that movement had also attracted many working women, bringing to it their own class interests. This is what Eleanor addressed in her groundbreaking text 'The Woman Question:

From a Socialist Point of View', said to be published with some minor input from Aveling. In the passionate conclusion to that text, we find Eleanor's vision of a future that unites socialism and feminism. It is the sort of utopian vision we are still fighting for today, one where not only are women educated alongside men but, crucially, both will be working only a few hours a day:

> There will no longer be one law for the woman and one for the man ... Nor will there be the hideous disguise, the constant lying that makes the domestic life of almost all our English homes an organised hypocrisy ... Husband and wife will be able to do that which but few can do now – look clear through one another's eyes into one another's hearts.[3]

The personal was clearly political in this moving treatise. But in Eleanor's own life, the political itself was always deeply personal, all too personal, as she continually tried but failed to get support from her duplicitous lover. The personal was also political in the work of her good friend, Olive Schreiner, another pioneering socialist, feminist, anti-war campaigner, and political activist. She outlived Eleanor by over two decades, but also failed to find what she was looking for, whether in the political or the private sphere.

Schreiner was born in South Africa and lived most of her life there, although she became a close friend and brief lover of the British social reformer and sexologist Havelock Ellis during her time in London in the 1880s. She met other radical reformers in the pioneering discussion groups she joined at that time, including the Men and Women's Club, founded by the mathematician Karl Pearson to discuss relations between the sexes. Wherever present, Schreiner insisted upon the key importance of equality and fairness in gender relationships.

Schreiner was soon equally admired for her novels and her political tracts. Her treatise 'Woman and Labour', calling for a world in which women could be both workers and mothers, remained particularly influential after its publication in 1911.

However, today Schreiner is best known for her novels, which were often semi-autobiographical, lamenting women's domestic confinement while opposing the entrenched racism of her day. Her first and most popular novel, *The Story of an African Farm* (originally published under the male pseudonym Ralph Iron), was an immediate success, and later described as one of the first feminist novels. It dealt primarily with issues of love, marriage, and motherhood, with marriage seen as always subordinating women, while the volatility of male passion remained at odds with the greater constancy of women's devotion.

Schreiner addressed the issue of race and colonialism in her lesser-known later novels, such as *Trooper Peter Halket of Mashonaland*, which describes the brutal treatment of the Black population. At odds with many popular writers of her day, such as Henry Rider Haggard, Schreiner condemned the exploitative cruelty of the colonial mindset, knowing colonialism must end before Black people could be free.

However, it was the youngest daughter in the Pankhurst family, Sylvia, who emerged as the closest to my generation of socialist feminists, most inspirational for standing up to her family to support both the working class and the anti-imperialist, anti-fascist struggles of her day. By 1914 she had founded and regularly wrote for *The Woman's Dreadnought* (formerly the *Workers' Dreadnought*), following her expulsion from the Women's Social and Political Union (WSPU) by her mother, Emmeline, and her sister Christabel. They objected to Sylvia bringing working-class women and their struggles into the heart of the suffrage movement, and demanded she choose between the two causes. She refused. Her choice had already been made in 1913 when she moved to London's East End, where she helped to start a nursery, a toy factory, and a low-cost restaurant.

At the same time, Sylvia was busy campaigning for welfare reform, alongside her work to secure votes for women. For her, the two campaigns amounted to the same thing. This was reflected in her long and intimate relationship with the former Scottish miners' leader, Keir Hardie, who would become the first leader of the Labour Party. It was through his friendship with Sylvia that Hardie himself became a keen supporter of women's suffrage.

Despite her expulsion from the WSPU, Sylvia remained a feminist to the core. In ways that further anticipate the work we undertook decades later as feminist activists, she campaigned around motherhood, domestic labour, and violence against women. Sylvia was jailed at least thirteen times (more than any other suffragette) and experienced the repeated state torture of force-feeding. Nevertheless, once released she always immediately continued her speaking tours and political writing.

While her mother and sister moved increasingly to the right, finally joining the Conservative Party, Sylvia remained as active as ever after female suffrage was won in 1918 (initially just for women over thirty). In her pamphlet, *Save the Mothers*, she drew attention to the tens of thousands of women who died giving birth, alongside the high rates of infant mortality – over 25 per cent at that time. Her feminism accompanied endless other struggles to transform harsh and exploitative social relations. She helped to launch the British Communist Party in 1920. And when accused of sedition in 1921, Sylvia asserted forcefully in her own defence: 'I am going to fight capitalism even if it kills me. It is wrong that people like you should be comfortable and well fed while all around you people are starving.'[4]

The following decade, Sylvia petitioned the government to allow Jewish refugees to escape from Nazi Germany, while continuing with her lifelong anti-fascist, anti-colonialist, and anti-racist work. She supported Haile Selassie in his struggle for Ethiopian independence and, with her long-term lover and partner, the Italian anarchist Silvio Corio, spent the last five years of her life active in Addis Ababa, where she received a full state funeral on her death in 1960.

Whatever the situation, Sylvia fought for a better world in which everyone would have justice and equality, as she wrote in another of her many visionary essays, available in her collected papers now based in Amsterdam – 'What I Am Aiming At: A Chance for the Children of Tomorrow'. Tellingly, Sylvia remains as a largely unsung forebear of socialist feminism in Britain; it was the Dutch, not the British, who offered safekeeping for Sylvia's writings and memorabilia after her death. Some women I know have long been fundraising for a statue of Sylvia to be erected in Clerkenwell Green, at the eastern tip of Islington, but this has yet to materialize.

There would be other attempts to make the world a better place for women, and especially mothers, in the mid-twentieth century. One of the very few British female MPs, Eleanor Rathbone, campaigned for over twenty years for a welfare benefit, or family allowance, to be paid directly to mothers to improve their lot. However, when finally secured in 1945 it was, bizarrely, paid to husbands.

Remarkably, on the eve of second-wave feminism, at the very close of the 1960s, feminism itself had been officially declared a 'dead issue' throughout the Western world. This was forcefully corroborated by one of the rare women then in British broadcasting, the influential anti-war writer and journalist Marghanita Laski, niece of the economist Harold Laski and known for her dismissal of any need for feminism. According to such authorities, women were 'free' now, other than in the pages of *The Second Sex*. And even in that landmark text, Simone de Beauvoir opened with an apologetic acknowledgement of feminism's demise: 'For a long time I have hesitated to write a book on woman. The subject is irritating, especially to women ... Enough ink has been spilled in quarrelling over feminism, and perhaps we should say no more about it.'[5]

Who would have thought, then, that a mere two decades later not only would feminism rise again, with plenty new to say, but it would rise with a decisively socialist glow?

On the Move Again

Indeed, in the UK it was working-class women who kicked off women's renewed militancy. Take, for example, Lil Bilocca and other fishermen's wives in Hull who campaigned against unsafe conditions on trawlers at the start of 1968. That same year, almost 200 sewing machinists at the Ford Motor Company plant in Dagenham, Essex, downed tools to demand equal pay after their jobs were suddenly downgraded, to avoid paying them the same rates as men. The struggles of these working-class women were reported, and championed, by Sheila Rowbotham in her earliest publications, which helped launch second-wave feminism in the UK, along with her own lifelong trajectory as our first, most prolific and enduring socialist feminist.

In her initial pamphlet, 'Women's Liberation and the New Politics' (1969), Sheila tried to find words for what was then still a 'language of silence' to encompass women's own emerging hopes for a better world. Struggling to find those words, Sheila quickly produced six books and numerous articles in the opening decade of women's liberation. From the beginning, her goal was to engage with feminist thought and women's militancy to rethink socialism. Alongside her writing, in what she described as 'the hurly-burly of battle', Sheila became involved in the Night Cleaners Campaign, supporting May Hobbes, who in 1970 had begun trying to unionize women who, like Hobbes herself, worked long hours for ridiculously low pay cleaning offices at night. The campaign was initially successful, winning substantial pay rises, until within a few years new contractors were brought in who rescinded the previous agreement. That struggle continues to this day.

As is evident in her impressive memoir, *Daring to Hope: My Life in the 1970s* (2021), Sheila was present in most of the other feminist campaigns of the day, whether supporting women's full reproductive rights or the family allowance campaign to ensure it was mothers, not their husbands, who received childcare allowance, while also attempting to unionize other women workers. When not tramping around the country, talking to schools, she was heading further afield to discuss feminism, or support women's struggles internationally. For instance, with the end of the Greek military dictatorship in 1974, she travelled to Athens to speak at what would be the first public meeting of the Athenian women's movement, urged on by the passion of the Greek socialist feminist Eleni Varikas.

At home, Sheila had also found time to establish a WEA course on 'Revolutionary Thought' in inner London in 1971, which I often attended. These classes highlighted the role of female radicals alongside male militants and thinkers. Sheila was at the time a valued guide and mentor for many young feminists, including me, who quickly became a lifelong friend. She has persisted ever since, busily mapping women's evolving radical activism for over fifty years. This is despite Sheila perpetually questioning her own credentials as a middle-class white woman trying to be a rigorous historical witness. As she expressed in her memoir of the 1970s, she was always trying not just to unpick capitalism, but 'to reassert the depth and scope of what we attempted in the hope that future generations will be able to uncover these strands and go beyond them'.[6]

There were so many strands. With sweeping enthusiasm, the women's liberation movement wanted to change everything, beginning with our home lives and reproductive and sexual rights, moving on to everyday workplace struggles, and outwards to encompass transforming cultural and political life across the board. For instance, when feminists fought for more public resources, sometimes successfully, we always wanted them to be controlled by the people using them. In this way we tried to democratize the relation between the state and those using its services.

This was borne out in several local nurseries that were established at that time, such as the Dartmouth Park Children's

Community Centre in North London, opened by the Camden Women's Group in 1972.[7] Women's centres and advice groups also sprang up around Britain, including the Essex Road Women's Centre that I had helped to establish, which opened in 1974 focusing on four main issues – housing, work, child-care, and women's health. The idea was to provide women with additional, alternative forms of help to that offered by the welfare state, as well as to fight the gradual gentrification of Islington and Camden, which was driving working-class people out.

In a similar way, employment struggles, seeking to secure better conditions for working women, were always accompanied by attempts to democratize both workplaces and union practices to make them more women-friendly, while also seeking to broaden and transform union goals. When Audrey Wise, then a union organizer for shop workers in USDAW, spoke at the very first Women's Liberation Conference in Ruskin College in 1970, she argued that feminism needed to be a part of a broadly-based socialist movement: 'I don't want to be just an equal economic unit any more than I want to be a decoration or a drudge.'

She was echoing what she had outlined in the revolutionary socialist newspaper *Black Dwarf* the previous year: 'We must ask ourselves ... equality with what? People should not be valued simply as economic units.'[8] Wise later became a Labour MP, taking her feminist and labour movement experiences into Parliament, believing women's presence everywhere was a necessary step towards making connections between 'working life' and home life.[9]

Elsewhere, feminists were actively supporting the many women's strikes of the day. This included joining picket lines of women shoemakers occupying their factory against redundancy at Fakenham, in Norfolk, and supporting the successful strike for equal pay for women making windscreen wipers at Trico, in West London. Feminists also actively supported Black women workers who were being victimized by employers and white colleagues at Leicester's Imperial Typewriters factory, while demanding an end to agency nursing, and better pay and conditions for nurses. In the process, feminist activists were not only changing the face of workplace struggles, but equally building solidarity between each other, and across our differences.

In 1974, a group of British feminists from the Trotskyist group the Fourth International launched the Working Women's Charter campaign, which was quickly supported by most feminists active in trade unions and trade councils. Its ten ambitious demands covered women's pay, training, job opportunities, maternity leave, childcare, abortion rights, and minimum pay. Nursery workers who were now joining trade unions supported the campaign, which soon initiated a nationwide struggle for a thirty-five-hour week, above all to allow more caring time in the home.

The Charter was supported by the various trade unions in the London Trades Council, although it was defeated by the general Trade Union Congress (TUC) the following year, primarily over its demands for a minimum wage and abortion rights. Later, things would change again, after tireless feminist pressure resulted in the 100,000-strong march in defence of women's 'right to choose' in 1979, headed up by the TUC, under the banner: 'Keep it legal! Keep it safe!'

Not only in Britain, but almost everywhere, feminists often complained about how hard it was to make themselves heard and gain support from within the still heavily male-dominated trade union movement. Even so, tenacious solidarity between women workers would soon result in widespread historical changes within that movement, making unions friendlier places for women, even in the face of the class offensive against them from the 1980s. As employers began shifting more jobs overseas in search of cheaper labour, calls to support women's global struggles strengthened.

In her groundbreaking book *Common Fate, Common Bond: Women in the Global Economy*, the late radical Indian economist Swasti Mitter, after actively opposing the spread of low-pay sweatshops and homeworking throughout India to produce goods for Britain and the States, made the stakes clear: 'The time has now come to make explicit room for womankind ... if we are to build solidarity for employment and justice.'[10] This was the goal of several later global rights movements, mainly from the 1980s, such as the UK-based Womankind Worldwide, formed in 1989 to work in solidarity with women's movements in Africa and Asia.

My own engagement was mainly in community organizing. Despite my teaching job, I was often able to spend time at our squatted community centre in Islington, where I helped produce the local alternative paper, the *Islington Gutter Press*. I probably had most fun when travelling around delivering the paper to the great diversity of community centres at that time, building friendships and solidarities across the borough. In the evening there was often some women's meeting to plan our next intervention, as when we picketed our local paper the *Islington Gazette* for carrying pin-ups of near-naked women.

At other times I might head off with my housemates and other friends to chat and dance together at one of the many benefits to raise money for projects needing funding, usually to provide diverse forms of care or shelter for women. By the mid-1970s we had our own women's bands, one of the most popular being Jam Today, drawing from Lewis Carroll's *Through the Looking Glass* – 'The rule is, jam tomorrow and jam yesterday – but never jam today.' Many other feminist bands flowered and folded, such as the Stepney Sisters and Ova, in London alone.

There were always Black and ethnic minority women in the feminist groups I was part of at this time, but not many; two Black women's groups met for a while in Islington and Brixton. However, we engaged in significant solidarity work whenever we felt able to join in struggles against racism. There were campaigns in support of women facing deportation, or to assist them in the myriad of other ways they might be struggling with racist immigration laws. Later in the decade, as the National Front was growing stronger, many feminists, including me, helped to form the Islington Campaign against Racism and Fascism (ICARF).

This took us out onto the streets, handing out leaflets or marching, often met with violent sexist abuse from local fascists. This was especially severe whenever we ventured into Hoxton, in the neighbouring borough of Hackney, where we would invariably encounter a man called Derrick Day. He was in charge of security at the NF's headquarters in Shoreditch, and also controlled the tenants' group in one of the Hackney housing estates. Fortunately, confronting him together was more distressing than frightening. As violently sexist as he was racist, Day was described by one veteran Hackney anti-fascist, Martin Lux, as 'a fuckin' gorilla with a face covered with razor cuts'.[11]

Though typically organizing first of all in local neighbourhoods, women's liberation was always a global movement. This meant that wherever you looked, activists could be found eager to join campaigns to improve women's lives, whether in Western capitals or in early protests against men's violence against women in Delhi and Mumbai. In other existing welfare states, campaigns were usually focused, as in the UK, on securing more and better public resources locally and nationally, whether for housing, healthcare, playgrounds, or shelters for battered women. Campaigns around anything that could develop and enrich community life and provide better care for women and children globally were soon being created and led by women, all drawing upon the collective feminist energy emerging everywhere in those years.

Hence, wherever possible, feminists aligned themselves with women's struggles internationally, whether in workplaces or communities, or confronting patriarchal domination in every-day life. For some, this began with support for Irish struggles for independence. For everyone, it meant supporting anti-apartheid, anti-war, and anti-colonial causes worldwide; the Vietnam War only ended in 1975. There was so much calling us out onto the streets in those years.

Off the streets, gathering together in the small groups favoured within women's liberation, women joined consciousness-raising (CR) groups or other gatherings eager to discuss and share our personal dilemmas. 'How are you feeling, today?' was always the place to begin. In these small groups, looking inwards as well as outwards, there was a great deal to address: embarrassments still surrounding our bodies; issues of fertility and how to decide if or when to have a child; repudiation of sexist language and culture, still prevalent even in the alternative press; men's fear of women's strength and sexual autonomy; problems related to housework and childcare; fear of men's potential violence and coerciveness. As Sally Belfridge, from the very first and most enduring women's liberation group in London, the Belsize Lane group, later recalled:

> We began as fragments, guilt-ridden, inadequate as people (because mere women – no, not women, mere girls then, whatever our ages) and by bringing our depression to each other like a gift, an offering of pain, we gradually drew each other out of our isolation ... It taught me new ways to love myself, by loving all of us.[12]

Feminists recalling those years almost all agree that it was women's liberation that enabled them to make sense of the world, live with contradictory emotions, and embrace a politics that meshed their public and private lives. Above all it offered a sense of connection and an end to loneliness. We learned how to lean on each other, and this changed everything.

Nonetheless, certain issues threatened the common bonds feminists were trying to build and maintain between women.

One was the challenge of lesbian desire and relationships, as some feminists came to view lesbianism as the best and most effective way to express feminist politics, moving towards the prescriptive. It was perplexing, too, trying to tackle the depth and destructiveness of everyday racism and prejudice in a white-dominated movement, while class remained a dilemma in what was largely a middle-class movement.

A desire to preserve our 'independence' was voiced by many feminists, concerned for instance that if they moved in with their partner, of whatever gender, they risked losing it. This was never an anxiety of mine, although jealousy certainly lay at the heart of my worries in intimate relationships. I was also more sceptical than some who spoke of the empowering effects of sexual satisfaction and the imperative to obtain it, most famously in one account in *Spare Rib* that breezily reported, 'Asking my boss for a raise was easy once I'd asked my boyfriend for oral sex.'[13]

Unsurprisingly, humour was crucial in sustaining feminist work and friendships. However, it's one thing to dream up or enjoy feminist jokes and puns – 'I've never had a climax … It's the clitoral truth' – and quite another to deal with the everyday competitiveness or envy that might shadow collective engagements, even between feminists – especially since this was so discordant with our cherished principles of sisterhood.

Some women expressed more extreme forms of mental anguish or depression, leading a few of us at the Essex Road Women's Centre, including me, to start a women's counselling group to support one woman suffering from acute anxiety. It ended with us all finding a space for one-to-one 'feminist' therapy within the Women's Therapy Centre that had been founded in Islington by Susie Orbach and Luise Eichenbaum in 1976.

Throughout those early years, forms of socialist feminism were in the ascendant. The men I was closest to joined others in 'men's groups' to discuss and overcome their own sexism or fear of women, especially assertive women. As one of these groups testified in an article for *Spare Rib*: 'Fears of being devoured, possessed, weakened or contaminated by women suddenly poured out of a lot of men.'[14] Memorably, that happened in a meeting upstairs in my collective household, as I sat obliviously reading below: the men were bellowing out their fears so forcefully into the night that the police arrived, assuming someone was being murdered – probably me. 'We're just letting go of our fears and hatred', the men explained. Familiar with the house, one policeman retorted: 'Class hatred, I presume.' Still, whatever the tensions, socialist feminists were always present alongside men in militant activism in those days.

By the mid-1970s there was a regular network of visiting international feminists, and I formed a lasting friendship with the New York activist and writer Barbara Ehrenreich. I'm not sure how we first made contact, but like others I was immediately fascinated by this feisty, witty, remarkable feminist. I had invited her to visit our Islington Community Press, and while there she laughingly suggested, 'We must form an international conspiracy of feminist guerrillas.' Captivated, I soon visited my new friend in her home in Syosset, Long Island, meeting her charming daughter, Rosa, and her son, then known as Benjy, along with her second husband, Gary Stevenson. A militant teamster, Gary sent us out to support some rather scary, often armed picket lines in Long Island.

Barbara died at the age of eighty-one shortly before I finished this book. To her dying breath she remained first and foremost an archetypal socialist feminist. Like Sheila Rowbotham in the UK, Barbara helped shape the meaning of that identity as an 'internationalist, anti-racist, anti-heterosexist feminist'. In her seminal essay 'What Is Socialist Feminism?' she defined the core of socialist feminism as the simple belief that we cannot understand how sexism acts on our lives 'without putting it in the historical context of capitalism'.

However, she went on, socialist feminists are distinct from classical Marxists in aiming 'to transform not only the ownership of the means of production, but the totality of social existence ... women who seemed most peripheral [to Marxists], the housewives, are at the very heart of their class – raising children, holding together families, maintaining the cultural and social networks of the community'.[15] Marxists called this 'social reproduction', but were forever subordinating it to 'production', rather than seeing the two as always intrinsically entwined.

Dilemmas and Disputes

Feminist analysis and strategic reflection kept on moving, trying to encompass an endless array of thorny theoretical issues. We advanced from unpacking gender regimes and the effects of women's distinct position in and outside the home, to addressing the disturbing prevalence of rape, domestic violence, and sexual harassment, while grappling as best we could with the diverse crossings of gender hierarchies with other axes of subordination – class, race, ethnicity, sexual orientation, and disability – within the wider world of the women's movement itself.

From the beginning we had talked about multiple oppressions, knowing that some women were far more privileged, secure, or assertive than others. However, this did not in itself uncover the various ways in which race, class, gender, sexuality, ethnicity, nationality, education, disability, and age operate as reciprocally constructing phenomena, creating distinct experiences, ways of belonging, or exclusion. By the close of the 1980s Black feminist scholars had introduced the notion of 'intersectionality', or the 'matrix of domination', following the work of theorists such as Kimberlé Crenshaw and Patricia Hill Collins.[16] What was needed at every level was greater attentiveness to power relations and social inequalities between women.

If patriarchy normalizes men's power and hides their invisible dependence upon women, other hierarchies of domination similarly conceal the unspoken dependence of white or affluent people on those they dominate. In that sense, intersectionality can be seen as affirming our traditionally hidden and hierarchical co-dependencies. It also tells us, of course, as socialist feminists had always understood, why a purely feminist perspective could never encompass all aspects of domination, any more than a purely socialist dimension had been able to theorize all aspects of gender or race oppression.

There was also contention around women's relation to the state. Socialist feminists were quite likely to be working in welfare-related jobs of one kind or another, often part of or funded by the state. Nevertheless, we knew that from its inception the welfare state was at the service of a patriarchal capitalist system, reliant upon women's unpaid or underpaid labour, even as feminists tried to wrest more resources from it to assist us in mitigating women's particular disadvantages. It was fears of reformist 'co-option' to conventional paternalistic state traditions that made some feminists wary of accessing state funds, which is why there was such a stress on grassroots, democratic control over resources, as well as on collective 'self-help' – where we could rely upon each other, hopefully on a more equal footing.

Another perpetual source of conflict rumbling within socialist feminism emerged in 1972, when Selma James and her followers circulated a pamphlet critical of trade union struggles as divisive for women and demanding 'Wages for Housework' (WFH). They reiterated this singular call vociferously at every subsequent feminist gathering they attended, despite always meeting overwhelming opposition.

For multiple reasons, the content and style of the Wages for Housework campaign jarred with both the favoured collective practices and the dominant political goals of most feminists. It sidelined our struggle both for shorter working hours without loss of pay and for men's equal participation in domestic responsibilities. It ignored demands for affordable nurseries and other welfare benefits and resources to support anyone engaged in caring work, whatever their relation to those in need of care.

In fact, Wages for Housework showed little interest in joining any of our campaigns, although they always correctly stressed the significance of women's unwaged work, while organizing with the most stigmatized women, beginning with demands to decriminalize sex work. Most conflictual of all, however, was the vanguardist, hectoring approach of WFH activists, who had no interest in listening, but only in asserting their single answer for everything.

So, we had serious differences, but whatever our strategic priorities, working collectively for change on so many fronts meant that our feminism was never primarily a movement for women's individual rights. Indeed, we tended to downplay any personal status we might have acquired. Testifying to the public impact we made back then, several well-known men of the left, including the New Left eminence Herbert Marcuse in the US and André Gorz and Alain Touraine in France, were now announcing – just as we hoped – that it was the women's liberation movement that was showing the way forward for socialism.[17]

There were parallels in the United States. The late New York writer and journalist Ellen Willis recalled that most feminists in the early 1970s considered themselves 'leftists of one form or another', although other American friends suggest that the absence of a strong labour movement made this attachment less significant than in Britain at the time.[18]

Here, feminists could regularly be found on picket lines, especially where female workers were involved. One of my most exciting memories from that time is heading out to Brent in North London to join the Grunwick picket line. Grunwick proved to be one of the longest and most thrilling strikes of the late 1970s, initiated by largely East African and South Asian women workers in protest over low pay and degrading conditions at the Grunwick photo processing plant. Headed up by the remarkable Mrs Jayaben Desai, it gained huge support, with at times tens of thousands of feminists, trade unionists, and activists of every stripe swelling that picket line. 'The strike is not so much about pay, it is a strike about human dignity', Mrs Desai emphasized.[19]

The strikers held out for nearly two years before being finally defeated. And I recall to this day being squashed up with friends against police shields or pushed back against garden walls. Feminist friends from outside London remember waiting excitedly for buses to drive them down to Brent. These were high points of solidarity for us, but they also signified a shift in trade union priorities, supporting women who in the past they would have largely ignored.

We shared news and information through feminist magazines, such as the well-distributed *Spare Rib*, launched in 1972. These publications helped nurture self-awareness, solidarity, and, crucially, our knowledge of women's actual diversity. As my friend Marsha Rowe, one of the founders of *Spare Rib*, recalls, in her very first women's group in 1972 they read Juliet Mitchell, Sheila Rowbotham, and Toni Morrison, along with other feminist writers, but also Marx's *Capital*, Wilhelm Reich, and Frantz Fanon.

That year also saw the creation of the Marxist feminist magazine *Red Rag*, which I briefly joined, founded by women in the British Communist Party but describing itself as 'feminist first and foremost', and open to all socialist feminists. At the Essex Road Women's Centre in 1974 we organized a big meeting of socialist feminists with the nearby Arsenal Women's Group, which Sheila was part of, with the rewarding outcome of meeting feminists who arrived from over sixty different women's groups nationally. They were all eager to keep meeting, so we could learn from and assist one another.

Although the egalitarian ethos of women's liberation discouraged any form of self-promotion or search for mainstream acclaim, there were always some famous women who supported our feminist ideas and activities. Few were as colourful as the much-mourned Angela Carter. With the rise of women's liberation, she was quickly convinced that women were destined to become the stronger, more creative and joyful sex. Above all she celebrated any possibilities for expanding women's sexual pleasure, with its rich and subversive potential once freed of the constraints that hitherto had hobbled us.

Carter was an early recruit onto the editorial board of the first feminist publishing company, Virago Press, founded in London in 1973, and her daring essay, *The Sadeian Woman*, was one of its first commissioned books. She was a generous supporter of other feminist writers and activists, as I found when chairing a session that she addressed on the family at a Socialist Society conference I helped organize in 1983. But Carter also delighted in provoking the mounting tide of pessimistic, moralistic, anti-heterosexual feminists, then obsessed with pornography, which emerged towards the end of the 1970s. When one of its prime instigators, the North American Andrea Dworkin, predictably attacked *The Sadeian Woman*, Carter is reported as saying: 'If I can get up ... the Dworkin proboscis then my living has not been in vain.'

I cherished her defiance, fully attuned to her clear account of (and calls to resist) the impacts of culture on our sexual lives: 'We do not go to bed in simple pairs ... we still drag there with us the cultural impedimenta of our social class, our parents' lives, our bank balances, our sexual and emotional expectations, our unique biographies – all the bits and pieces of our unique existences.'[20]

Conferences, too, were occasions for coming together to refresh and share our understandings and priorities. There were five national socialist feminist conferences between 1973 and 1975. However, though well attended, they were riven by fierce arguments, most prominently around the intransigent economism of the vociferous Wages for Housework campaign, in which even feminist sexual politics was reduced to a monetary exchange. Other sectarian tensions emerged as women from far-left groups attempted to dominate these conferences, making unpopular calls for a central committee, or proposing their own single overriding 'transitional' demand, such as the right to abortion. This practice proved so destructive at one socialist feminist conference, in London's Mile End in 1975, that future ones were suspended for several years. Feminists were still committed to building solidarity and recognizing our mutual dependence, but sadly our gatherings could always be disrupted by other factions with their own distinct agenda.

Interestingly, Barbara Ehrenreich described similar problems in the States at much the same time, with socialist feminist conferences irreparably damaged by the antics of a few Marxist-Leninist and Maoist groups.[21] It was, of course, the success of the autonomous socialist feminist movement at that time which attracted these aggressive irruptions at national conferences, with a minority of women determined to impose the discipline of their own fringe-left grouplets on the rest of us.

It led many socialist feminists to prioritize our local activities, ranging widely from community issues to supporting global anti-imperialist struggles, especially in Northern Ireland. In Britain there were two more successful socialist feminist conferences at the very close of the 1970s, raising all the old issues, and focusing primarily on racism and violence against women, with new voices addressing old age and disability rights.

In Europe, 4,000 socialist feminists attended a conference in Paris's Vincennes University in 1977, and the following month saw a large gathering in Amsterdam, once more affirming that socialism is a precondition for women's liberation but not a guarantee of it.[22] However, the mood within the broader feminist movement was changing, reflecting overall shifts in the political context accompanying the worsening recession. Divisions within feminism were deepening just when maximum unity was required before the invigoration of conservative forces, not excluding the extreme right.

There had always been some women's liberationists who called themselves 'radical feminists' and saw 'the patriarchy' as the fundamental cause of women's oppression. This meant that they routinely prioritized issues of male dominance over any analysis of capitalist class divisions or other systemic structures of oppression. Radical feminists principally focused on issues of men's violence against women and children, or other aspects of male power in directly subordinating women. Even so, they were usually far from blind to class and other forms of oppression, which enabled feminists for the most part to muddle along with our overlapping but slightly differing priorities.

At the close of the 1970s, however, a new brand of radical feminism, in the UK calling itself 'revolutionary feminism', was creating profound unease in women's gatherings, preaching extreme antagonism towards men as 'the main enemy' (extending even to little boys), along with scorn for any women who disagreed. They were disciples of the fiery American radical Andrea Dworkin, who was fixated on men's hatred and subjugation of women and saw 'pornography' as the abiding cause and weapon of their domination.

With her academic credentials as a Harvard don, Catharine MacKinnon joined Dworkin in denouncing male violence, and between them they headed what many of us saw as a reductive, though exceedingly popular, campaign against pornography. MacKinnon condensed this one-dimensional mindset in a classic article summarizing the history of feminism in ways that negated most of it: 'Feminism is a theory of how the eroticization of dominance and submission creates gender, creates woman and man in the social form in which we know them.'[23] Here 'male sexuality' was reduced to 'male violence' and seen as the core of both masculinity and men's power over women, with 'pornography' its timeless tool.

More importantly, such thinking disregarded the work of feminists who had been busy building critical alliances with progressive activists seeking change on many fronts, especially in resisting the rising inequality and oppression emerging from the close of the 1970s. As in *Straight Sex: The Politics of Pleasure*, I have criticized the reductive reasoning of the anti-pornography movement in almost everything I have written over the years. I agree with that inspiring New York feminist and left activist, the late Ann Snitow, that for many feminists at the close of the 1970s 'pornography' became a metaphor for a sense of defeat, in the loss of confidence that our shared collective activism could remain a motor of change. As we'll see, its emphasis on timeless female victimhood was sadly a mood that fitted neatly with the gathering conservative backlash, when struggles seeking social transformation grew ever harder to win.[24]

Resolved to combat any such separatist politics, Sheila and I, soon joined by the then Newcastle-based socialist feminist Hilary Wainwright, decided to put out a general appeal to the whole of the feminist movement and the wider left – to move beyond our distinctive aspirations or sectarian frameworks and support one another against the rising forces of the right. Combining our experiences of feminist activism in grassroots movements with Sheila's critique of the vanguardist practices of far-left parties, we hoped to find a new, democratic way forward, generating maximum support and solidarity.

The resulting publication of *Beyond the Fragments: Feminism and the Making of Socialism*, first as a pamphlet from Islington Community Press in 1979, then expanded into a book the following year, printed by Merlin Press, was an instant success. It was read and debated widely within feminism and the broader left, in the UK and around the world. Yet, despite remaining influential over the years and generating a large conference in Leeds in 1981, it largely failed in its immediate mission. Many feminists remained suspicious of our calls for greater solidarity with the left, while there was little change in the sectarianism of the organized left.

Resistance in Harsher Times

Socialist feminism had thrived in days of hope, with the 1970s a decade of maximum equality following the rise in public welfare accompanying the Western postwar economic boom. However, times change, and it was not so much internal divisions but steadily harsher times that would gradually disarm socialist feminism, even though many of us who survive to this day continue to embrace the bonds we formed and the ideas we shared back then.

Profits had begun falling during the 1970s, reaching an all-time low in 1975, in response to external causes of recession plus the higher wages won by increased unionization. This fuelled a ferocious conservative reaction that would usher in far-right governments from the close of the decade, beginning with the advent of Margaret Thatcher (1979) and Ronald Reagan (1981), both committed to destroying the postwar consensus, rolling back welfare, and expanding profits by any means possible.

The 1980s launched a very different political moment. While socialist feminism never went away, and as we'll see has even had a recent resurgence, it was increasingly marginalized in narratives of feminism, and there was a gradual decline in the grassroots activities it had generated. Many activists blamed shifts in the theoretical direction of academic feminism, which had by then found a niche in higher education. The feminist academy cultivated an interest in language and the instabilities of subjectivity, especially from the close of the 1980s. This accompanied work on the pathologies of colonialism and the deep historic abuses of racism. Interesting as this work remains in questioning normative frameworks, its ties to direct political engagement were not straightforward. However, I believe such contestations of feminist theory were merely a diversion from the mounting challenges confronting any radical action at that time.

The new state of affairs orchestrated by Margaret Thatcher and her supportive media barons had a specific agenda: to change the ideological mindset from concern with equality to competitive individualism. Above all Thatcher abhorred, and set out to destroy, any discourse of collectivity and solidarity with the vulnerable or threatened – the very hallmark of socialist feminism. She recognized only individual (self-sufficient) men and women, and their families. Socialist feminists wanted to expand and democratize the welfare state and make jobs compatible with having time and space for caring work, whether at home or in sustaining community life. Thatcher wanted, and largely managed to obtain, the opposite. Similar political dynamics were soon evident in the United States, with Ronald Reagan in the White House.

It became clear that the divisions between women themselves (as between men) were deepening fast, mainly along lines of class, ethnicity, religion, disability, or any form of vulnerability. Because of its overriding emphasis on individual success, the new conservative agenda was sometimes presented in the name of women's rights. Some middle-class women did indeed benefit from a few of the doors that feminists had helped to open, moving into managerial and professional jobs. At the same time, other women, those least privileged, were pushed further to the margins, with longer hours in paid work and shrinking public resources to call upon, as welfare entitlements and benefits disappeared.

This was the inevitable outcome of Thatcher's crusade to make Britain a tougher, more competitive country, one where the rich could get richer, while anyone failing to do so had only themselves to blame. Stalling state investment in industry to promote finance capital and selling off public housing were just some of Thatcher's most destructive policies for achieving this goal. Presented with evidence of soaring unemployment and business failures two years into her first term, Thatcher spoke merely of the necessity to discipline the workforce and prune industry, concluding: 'Economics are the method; the object is to change the heart and soul.'[25]

Not unexpectedly, it was socialist feminists around the world who were especially prominent in analysing the economic costs of this process (which came to be loosely known as 'neoliberalism'), particularly in its impact on women. In the UK, this included feminist economists and political theorists such as Sue Himmelweit and Anne Phillips. Others driven to expose the harms of rising inequality sometimes found jobs in Britain's Low Pay Unit, set up in 1974 to campaign for economic and social justice, including Jenny Hurstfield. Some, like the indefatigable Ruth Lister, joined the Child Poverty Action Group, established in 1965 to collect and analyse the effects of welfare changes upon the well-being of children, families, and communities.

Focusing on women's position as second-class citizens, Lister later published books on the poverty and economic injustice many women faced because of their unpaid caring roles. Much of this thinking was spelled out by the political theorist Anne Phillips in her first work, *Hidden Hands: Women and Economic Policies* (1987). Some of these scholars and activists later established the Women's Budget Group, which has now lobbied successive governments on gender and economic issues for over thirty years, pointing out the policies that most harm women, especially in their caring roles.[26]

For a few exciting years in the 1980s a group of socialist feminists found jobs at the Greater London Council (GLC) during Ken Livingstone's first stint as Lord Mayor of London.

Feminist, anti-racist, lesbian, and gay activists were invited to work in a County Hall that backed many grassroots initiatives. Inside the GLC plans were developed to encourage workers' co-operatives, while the Women's Committee headed by Valerie Wise was eager to ensure a more open and responsive city government by holding regular public meetings with veteran socialist feminists. Sheila Rowbotham and Hilary Wainwright were recruited into the GLC's popular planning unit, working with local groups to find ways of preserving older industrial areas and creating new sustainable jobs.

Their activities were disseminated in the magazine *Jobs for a Change*, which Sheila produced together with the late John Hoyland, covering any successful projects in job creation or amplification of community resources. *Jobs for a Change* also organized two free music festivals to highlight growing unemployment and the fight to create and fund jobs during the year-long miners' strike. The first, in 1984, drew about 150,000 people to the Thames embankment, and the second, in Battersea Park, around 250,000 in 1985. Numerous illustrious musicians succeeded one another on stage; in between there were theatre performances and a range of speakers, all surrounded by stalls run by community groups and other alternative organizations.

As the hub of so much community activity and left-wing bonding, the GLC's old headquarters at County Hall represented exuberant defiance of the ideas emanating from across the Thames, in Downing Street. Indeed, it so infuriated Margaret Thatcher that she finally succeeded in eradicating this colourful site of resistance and collectivity. In 1986, she abolished the GLC and sold off County Hall to private buyers.

Other significant feminist activism in the 1980s included the women's peace camp at Greenham Common, established in 1981 to rid Britain of US nuclear missiles. Most socialist feminists, including me, joined the tens of thousands of women who visited the camp and supported its days of action. Greenham became an inspiration for the peace movement internationally and the focus for feminist anti-nuclear activism. The occupation continued for nineteen years, well after the last cruise missile was withdrawn in 1991, and included women of all ages, from teenagers to some in their seventies and eighties. As one of its original, anarchist participants, the sociologist Sasha Roseneil – now vice chancellor of Sussex University – later reflected, it was the amazing bonds established between women that helped them endure, despite being expelled by the police and even jailed many times over. The Greenham women did not give up, she suggests, because the camp became their home: 'The bonds of friendship, care and affection, and often sexual love, forged at Greenham became the life-sustaining forces that women were choosing over the families from whence they came.'[27]

Many Black and Asian women's groups flourished in the 1980s. This included the Organisation of Women of African and Asian Descent (OWAAD), founded by Beverley Bryan, Stella Dadzie, and Suzanne Scafe in 1978. An umbrella group for many different Black and Asian feminists, it campaigned on issues around immigration and deportation, domestic violence, racism in schools, support for Black women workers, and women's reproductive rights, including medical interference with Black women's fertility. Although short-lived, by the early 1980s OWAAD had helped place the experiences of Black and Asian women firmly on the feminist agenda.

Outside London, the Manchester Black Women's Co-operative and the Liverpool Black Sisters were meeting and prioritizing Black women's needs throughout the 1980s. Two key publications from these groups were *Heart of the Race* (1985) from the feminists who had founded OWAAD, exploring Black women's position in British society in the wake of slavery, colonialism, and migration, while the anthology *Charting the Journey* (1988) contained moving stories, poems, and more, from seventy-five different writers highlighting the conflicts and contradictions still faced by Black and Global Southern women in a white-dominated world.[28] Meanwhile, the journal *Feminist Review*, founded in 1979 and still going strong, has always been clearly situated on the left, exploring the challenges of race, class, age, disability, and sexuality.

Most prominently, Southall Black Sisters (SBS), founded in 1979 following race riots in Southall, survives to this day, offering care and support for victims of violence or forced marriage, as well as challenging racism and opposing religious fundamentalism. One of its founders, the solicitor Pragna Patel, who remained, intermittently, its director until 2022, was always ready to build coalitions with other feminists fighting oppression. As Patel said recently, the goal of SBS was to encourage all their supporters to feel empowered, as well as to be part of wider social movements that carry the promise of change, building solidarity across the walls that divide us. After all, 'understanding what unites us is more important than what divides us … More and more I am coming to the view that we need to come together not on the basis of identity but on the basis of need.'[29]

Ghosts at the Rebranding of Feminism

Yet, despite its persistent activism on many fronts, in the closing decades of the twentieth century socialist feminism came to be seen as tied to an earlier era: demanding more from the state, more from men, applauding women's work in trade unions, and insisting that class must never be forgotten. Looking back on contemporary feminism in the year 2000, the British journalist and writer Melissa Benn observed that 'socialist feminists in the 1980s and 1990s were suddenly considered unfashionable, dull'. Indeed, in paying homage to Sheila Rowbotham's legacy, Benn concluded that 'she had become a ghost at the feast of the politics she helped create'.[30]

In fact, many left feminists, including Sheila, were still publishing, performing, and active in many settings, but the media only cared to promote a form of liberal, aspirational feminism, ignoring any other values. 'Feminism is boring', the left-leaning liberal journalist Polly Toynbee declared in the late 1990s, summing up the position of influential women in the media, even while they stressed the continuing inequalities and difficulties women face. There was a new common assumption, as another *Guardian* journalist, Libby Brooks, reported, that '70s feminists were 'po-faced, anti-sex misandrists' beset by infighting. Brooks added that this was not a view she shared.[31]

Indeed, exactly ten years earlier, at the very end of the 1990s, Brooks had welcomed my own socialist feminist book, *Why Feminism?*, under the heading 'No Turning Back'. She also noted then that nothing sold better than 'an obituary of feminism', with the media always eager 'to dance on feminism's grave', consistently portraying it 'as anachronism or antagonist: a binary monolith pitting women against men, work against family, old against new', in the hope that 'there is no danger in a dead thing'. Yet Brooks agreed with me that 'the tempered marketplace dilution of feminism that pervades our culture cannot trump a genuinely transformative, long-term political vision'. Feminism is actually more needed than ever, she concluded, and the strength of *Why Feminism?* lay in its 'willingness to encompass the rich connections of feminism, socialism and history itself'.[32]

Unlike Brooks, sadly, the wider media remained determined to discount or despise those rich historical ties between feminism and socialism. When not dismissive, it actively sought out new ways of accommodating feminism, always suppressing its radical potential. This included praising women's superior caring virtues and values, while refusing to condemn the poor remuneration for most caring work. The media also now embraced the idea that women (especially young women) were sexually vulnerable and in need of protection. Meanwhile they routinely tarnished those girls who were actually most vulnerable to predators as 'sexual delinquents', especially those living in or just leaving 'care homes'.

However, the main way feminism was rebranded in the mainstream from the 1980s onwards was in its embrace of managerial discourses of equal opportunities, primarily for women in professional jobs, while ignoring the underlying dynamics hampering women's career patterns overall. Noting this mainstreaming of their movement in the 1980s, a few '70s feminists themselves began admitting that their collective voices might inadvertently have eased the way for new developments in capitalism, via some women moving into elite positions.

One feminist pioneer, Juliet Mitchell, noted that the new focus on differences between women had been divisive. What's more, she added, the idea that feminists should first and foremost attend to the all-embracing opposition between the sexes had collaborated in the construction of an ideology that could disregard class and sideline the economic, allowing a few women to advance while most others were further marginalized.[33]

In my view, apart from completely ignoring socialist feminism, this argument attributes far too much agency to feminism in assisting the rise of neoliberal capitalism, when the reality is the other way around: women became ensnared within market forces, especially with the failure of old patterns of resistance. However, in what is always a complicated story, many older feminists were also noting, like Mitchell, how easily a feminist-sounding rhetoric, albeit addressing individual rather than collective rights, could be twisted to fit changes that were the very opposite of the wholesale transformation feminists had once envisaged and fought for.

Needless to say, it was older feminists who were immediately in the forefront of denouncing this situation. The British playwright Caryl Churchill penned her much-admired play *Top Girls*, dramatizing how the rise of one woman was so often at the expense of another. Nevertheless, there was the further irony that many '70s feminists who remained attached to the left had often themselves acquired greater confidence and financial comfort, despite remaining deeply troubled by the growth of inequality, insecurity, and racism, and the deteriorating situation of many younger women (and men). Indeed, as in my own case, this material success had been bolstered early on by the feminist commitments we took into educational or media arenas, or in the jobs we had found within the (soon shrinking) public sector.

Before long, the American feminist Nancy Fraser was arguing even more judgmentally in *Fortunes of Feminism* that feminists had been secretly complicit with the rise of neoliberalism, claiming (falsely) that we had always stressed 'choice' over 'exploitation' and placed a politics of cultural recognition (of diverse identities) above a politics of economic redistribution.[34] I disagree, and would simply stress again that capitalism wasted no time in incorporating what it wanted from feminism while scorning its redistributive, transformative struggles, even as some of us watched in horror the harm caused by the billions slashed from welfare.

Feminists, rightly, had certainly tried to address intersectionality and exclusion, but many of us also worried about redistribution, along with the virulent racism and xenophobia routinely accompanying greater hardship. Inevitably, however, women generally were forced to adjust themselves to the ever more competitive, individualist cultural climate and the commercial reasoning that had become almost ubiquitous.

Along with other feminist scholars, in her book *The Aftermath of Feminism* Angela McRobbie noted the glamorous images of highly educated, professional women that were being widely promoted across the media by the close of the twentieth century.[35] In programmes celebrating women's apparent new freedoms and emancipation, the only real concern of the prosperous female protagonists was the search for 'Mr Right'. This was most unswervingly typified in the popular sitcom *Sex and the City*, which ran from 1998 to 2004, while the same themes highlighting successful, smart women in pursuit of marriage appeared in *Ally McBeal* (1997–2002), *Friends* (1994–2004), or almost any of the high-end media productions of the time.

The common thread was the assumption that gender equality had been achieved, via education and careers, and was now evident in women's happy embrace of consumer culture. With women portrayed as individually free to choose whatever lifestyle they wished, feminist claims of women's oppression were now presented as both obsolete and hostile to women's desire for success and excitement.

Troublingly, these same images of successful women soon served to promote an entirely new, media-driven brand of 'aspirational feminism'. This was strengthened once the most powerful of women – the likes of Hillary Clinton, Theresa May, and Michelle Obama – all claimed to be feminists, with Obama famously asserting: 'There is no limit to what we, as women, can accomplish.'

Emerging from the very heart of the neoliberal order, this was a feminism that was no longer oppositional in any general sense, but one inviting more women to join the race to be winners in a capitalist world – a world now largely eager to cater for any proliferation of identities and sexual tastes in its ruthless drive for profit. Its iconic figurehead was Sheryl Sandberg, who as chief operating officer of Facebook produced what she called 'a sort of feminist manifesto' in 2013, written to inspire men and women alike. The best-selling *Lean In: Women, Work and the Will to Lead* brought Sandberg to every major television talk show and placed her on the cover of *Time* magazine.[36]

So, here was indeed a 'new feminism', celebrating 'top girls' and disparaging other women's supposed lack of ambition, just as Caryl Churchill had foreseen back in the early 1980s. More

maddeningly for many ageing feminists, this strange mutation
of our movement arrived at a time that was tougher than ever
for countless women workers whose situation was becoming
ever more precarious and underpaid. For a former Facebook
operator, Kate Losse noted, it is a weird form of feminism that
encourages women to exploit themselves by working ever
harder, and in the name of freedom: 'Don't put on the brakes.
Accelerate. Keep your foot on the gas pedal', she describes
Sandberg continually exhorting women.[37] Before her tragically
early death, the young British journalist Dawn Foster published
her excellent riposte *Lean Out*, accusing Sandberg of 'complic-
ity in the economic structures that perpetuate inequality'.[38]

Another feminist scholar, Catherine Rottenberg, adds to
these critiques of Sandberg and her ilk in her book *The Rise
of Neoliberal Feminism*. She sees this corporate rebranding of
feminism as playing a key role in the global infusion of market
principles into all aspects of our lives – however personal and
domestic. Drawing upon other scholarly feminist works, such
as the American political theorist Wendy Brown's *Undoing the
Demos*, Rottenberg notes that whatever we do, wherever we
are, we are nagged to relentlessly increase our market value,
with women's traditional maternal and caring roles given ever
less space in the process. The pressure has caused some women
to freeze their eggs, delay having children, and then outsource
their care to other, less privileged women if and when they do
become mothers. Any such commoditized 'feminism' is thus
one that seriously deepens divisions between women, jettison-
ing feminist visions of enhancing women's lives overall.[39]

Meanwhile, people had become so unused to reading about
non-entrepreneurial, working-class lives that when that resolute
old socialist feminist Barbara Ehrenreich decided temporarily
to join poor women workers, writing up her experiences in
Nickel and Dimed, it was an instant best-seller, with a million
and a half copies bought. Aware of the capitalist juggernaut
that has rolled over so many of her dreams, Ehrenreich simply

concluded, when interviewed about the failure of her socialist vision shortly before her death: 'The idea is not that we will win in our own lifetimes and that's the measure of us, but that we will die trying. That's all I can say.'[40] And she did fight till the end.

Global Feminisms and the Resurgence of Feminist Militancy

Fortunately, there *is* always more to say, to hear, and to do, as feminists continue to learn from each other. This includes applauding the recent and continuing upsurge in women's engagement in collective resistance, noticeable for many years now. It also means taking note of something which is often harder for many in the anglophone world to register, the significance of feminist militancy in the Global South, and what it can teach the Global North.

A recent 'Green Wave' of feminist militancy (symbolized by women waving or wearing large green handkerchiefs or scarves) has swept across Argentina, Colombia, and Mexico, with huge mobilizations to end violence against women and secure their reproductive rights. Even as the US Supreme Court in 2022 succeeded in revoking legislation enshrining a woman's right to terminate an unwanted pregnancy, activists in Latin America have been successfully supporting each other to overturn the historically conservative barriers harming women in their region, knowing how many have died from botched abortions. Turning history on its head, the Colombian lawyer Catalina Martínez Coral, now regional director for Latin America and the Caribbean at the Center for Reproductive Rights, says: 'We are going to inspire people in the United States to defend the rights set out in Roe v. Wade.'[41]

The contemporary green scarves in Latin America were inspired by the white scarves worn by the earlier Mothers of the Plaza de Mayo, who came together from the early 1980s to denounce the kidnapping of their children during the Argentine military dictatorship, their scarves often embroidered with the names of those who had 'disappeared'. Feminists globally have borrowed from the memorializing practices of these Argentinian mothers, determined to force people not to forget those who were murdered.

Thus, 'Her Name Was Sarah' appeared on one of the placards at the vigil for Sarah Everard in London in 2021, after she was murdered by a serving police officer. In her book *Feminist International: How to Change Everything*, the inspiring Argentinian feminist Verónica Gago discusses the significance of Ni Una Menos (Not One Less), the powerful Latin American movement launched in Argentina against all the forms of violence 'faced by women and feminized bodies'.

After the initial demonstrations against femicide in 2015, this movement began to draw connections between different kinds of violence, from that against women and transvestites, to police violence, and what amounts to economic and financial violence. It led to the International Women's Strike in 2017, in which 800,000 women took to the streets in Argentina alone. As Gago explains, this feminist militancy had been building up for years across the continent, 'patiently woven and worked on, threading together enormous street events with everyday activism that is equally monumental in scope'.[42]

This new international wave of feminism is also evident in the huge marches to defend the right to abortion in Poland, as described by the Polish feminist philosopher Ewa Majewska in her book *Feminist Antifascism: Counterpublics of the Common*. Almost overnight, she records, in April 2016, 100,000 women, and some men, joined an ad hoc Polish social media group, Gals for Gals, using social media to protest against Poland's proposed anti-abortion legislation. Like Gago, Majewska is committed to building large-scale radical feminist coalitions, arguing that flexible, inclusive, and inventive feminist countercultures now offer a key bulwark against the rise of fascist forces globally.

Majewska believes that it is outside of the West that we can see the most promising left futures.[43] Similarly, from the southern hemisphere, the young feminist historian Rosa Campbell has reported the way global elements made a significant impact upon the women's liberation movement in Australia, starting in the second half of the twentieth century. She suggests that East Asian communism, in particular, influenced that movement, with Australian feminists visiting China and Vietnam, and vice versa. Hence, she also emphasizes that the history of feminism is not one that begins in the North and spreads to the South: 'Tactics, philosophy, ideas and techniques also move from the Global South to the Global North – from Beijing to Sydney and London – or they may not go through the centres of the Global North at all, they might spread from Bogotá to Warsaw.'[44]

Thus, we see again that feminist activism never simply disappears, even though in Britain, as in North America, there was no longer any single feminist movement from the end of the 1970s – making it easier for the media to promote its own favoured version of celebrity-endorsed 'aspirational feminism'. Yet many Western feminists remained involved in a multitude of political campaigns, especially those opposing austerity, given that the ongoing dismantling or outsourcing of much of our welfare provision always impacts hardest on women. Hence the continuing need to confront on a global scale the often devastating inadequacies of caring provision, something highlighted by the COVID pandemic with its hideously unequal outcomes.

The fact that employment conditions barely leave time for us to care for our loved ones in need, let alone help our communities survive, has prompted the revival of many earlier feminist demands, including calls for shorter working time in paid employment and the need for universal benefits. That is why today we hear more from those feminist researchers and activists who have been busy addressing these issues for decades, whether in the British Women's Budget Group, the Fawcett Society, Child Poverty Action Group, or other autonomous welfare organizations. They have kept tirelessly reaching out to media contacts, policymakers, trade unionists, and diverse community groups, presenting evidence of the difficulties faced by so many women today, especially those with significant caring responsibilities, and suggesting how best to solve them.

Although far from alone, given the struggles against gendered violence taking place in Latin America and also strengthening in the Indian women's movement, many Western feminists have continued agitating to end men's violence against women. The sudden, sometimes derided Western media interest in the #MeToo movement from 2017 was merely the celebrity end of this struggle, after the New York actress Alyssa Milano urged survivors of sexual coercion to share their experiences on social media, tweeting #MeToo. The #MeToo hashtag was rapidly trending in over eighty countries, gaining huge momentum after the prosecution of Harvey Weinstein and the apprehension of other hitherto protected, yet well-known, sexual predators.

However, 'Me Too' had initially emerged over a decade before its media uptake, as part of a grassroots US movement spearheaded by the African American activist Tarana Burke. She had herself been raped at thirteen and became involved in organizing workshops in schools, to raise young women's confidence in the face of sexual assault. She also visited rape crisis centres, discussing the links between racism, sexism, violence, and poverty.[45]

Earlier forms of collective repudiation of men's violence towards women had emerged with the vibrant appearance of SlutWalks, which burst forth globally in 2011 – originally provoked by a Toronto policeman advising women that they could avoid rape by not dressing like 'sluts'. It quickly triggered tens of thousands of people taking to the streets against any form of victim-blaming in cases of rape, with women, men, and children in over 200 cities in 40 different countries attending, often joyfully parading in luminous 'sluttish' attire, to stress that no person should ever be sexually assaulted, whoever they were and whatever they wore.[46]

Other forms of resistance to gender-based violence involve ongoing attempts to combat the routine intimidation, or worse, faced by trans women. This includes the need to address their experiences of rejection by certain older Western feminists, who have adopted trans-exclusionary positions in the name of defending women's spaces.[47] However, it is interesting to note that the more openly activist the feminist assemblies, the more trans-inclusive they usually become.

The resurgence of campaigns against racial violence, especially state violence at the hands of police, is now well known, primarily through the different incarnations of Black Lives Matter. Founded in the States in 2013, Black Lives Matter remains a decentralized social and political movement protesting police brutality and all racially motivated violence. In the UK, alongside Southall Black Sisters, we have seen the emergence of Sisters Uncut, founded in 2014, as an intersectional feminist organization against austerity and all legislation harming women, including the criminalization of prostitution that puts sex workers in greater danger. Over recent years they have drawn thousands of women into street protests, especially against cuts in facilities for victims of domestic violence, as when bridges were blocked in several British cities in 2016 to coincide with government proposals for further welfare reductions. Participants aimed to heighten public awareness of the cruelty of such cuts, which as they rightly said 'blocked bridges to safety' for domestic violence victims.

It all means that activists today are more likely to agree that there is no way to tackle rising inequality, social neglect of the vulnerable, and not least climate change, without confronting contemporary capitalism itself. Yet, though we began with just such wide-ranging resistance back in the 1970s, the task seems far more daunting in our current corporate world, making feminist militancy more essential than ever.

Strangely, one form it has taken is the resurgence of the old Wages for Housework campaign (WFH), along with its founding figureheads, Selma James and Silvia Federici. In Britain, a compilation of James's writing over six decades was published in 2012, followed by interviews in the mainstream media for the first time in four decades, in which James confidently asserted that people were finally getting interested in WFH.[48] Five years later Federici's collected writings appeared, documenting the day-to-day organizing of the US-based committee agitating for WFH from the 1970s.[49] Reviewing this publication for the *Nation*, the journalist Sara Jaffe expressed her agreement with all its basic assumptions, proclaiming that WFH was a revolutionary demand and now more relevant than ever, since if women refused to perform unwaged domestic labour it would set off a crisis in the capitalist system, exposing domestic labour as the pivot on which capitalism relied.[50]

Nevertheless, what is so peculiar about the reappearance of this demand is that paying for domestic services is now actually the norm for many people, women and men alike, while doing nothing to overturn existing gender inequalities and positively amplifying 'racial' ones. In my view, paying for domestic services is now helping to *secure*, not *disrupt*, capitalist hegemony, as neoliberal reasoning extends its economic metrics into every area of life, while giving salaried workers little time for their own housework or caring – other than what they can afford to buy. It suggests to me that WFH has lost whatever radical edge it might once have been thought to have.

Quite unlike the close of the 1960s, when women's household labour was rarely seen as 'work', politicians and economists of every stripe are now well aware that it is; the United Nations has even tried to measure its economic value, and governments are familiar with calls to include unpaid domestic labour in the overall GNP.[51] So, today we see the continuing outsourcing of domestic and care work to other women, and for the lowest possible wages. Indeed, in affluent countries everywhere, the fastest-growing job markets have for years been those for cheap domestic workers and personal care services.[52]

Rather than providing any pathway to liberation, the current wages for housework, care work, and sexual servicing are not only smoothly compatible with market rationality, but seemingly necessary for it. Meanwhile, as socialist feminists once predicted, this process is deepening old class and racialized divisions between women, with low-waged, caring jobs remaining so unpopular that there is now a shortfall of carers, with almost 100,000 vacancies in the UK alone.

However, if WFH remains a perplexing slogan for these – or any – times, the resolute group of WFH activists have worked tirelessly on behalf of poorer women, wherever they are based, always highlighting the load placed on unpaid, unassisted, women carers. Supporters of WFH also fought for the rights of sex workers and supported campaigns against racism. Moreover, while always contemptuous of those she dismisses as 'middle-class' or 'equal rights' Western feminists, like me, Selma James has always been interested in the sharp end of global women's rights movements. She and her followers early on made links with exploited women in Peru and Trinidad and Tobago, as well as rural women in India and Uganda, alongside sex workers in the Philippines – often on the move to richer countries.

Hence, while many left feminists, along with some Black and ethnic minority scholars, are now prominent in higher education where they analyse the complexities of women's overlapping identities, attending to 'intersectionality' and post-colonial subjugation, it was the very concrete organizing of IWFH (International Wages for Housework) that both noisily highlighted the deepening divisions between women and also engaged with the worldwide rise of feminist militancy. This was most visible in 2000 when, following the example of women in Iceland, and a request from the Irish playwright and activist Margaretta D'Arcy, IWFH called for a Global Women's Strike on 8 March.

As we saw with the Green Wave in Latin America, this movement has gained momentum ever since, with many new demands that are no longer contentious, such as 'Invest in Caring, Not Killing'. The Global Women's Strike also launched a petition demanding a 'living wage' for mothers and all other carers, presented as essential for undermining divisions of sex, race, age, and migrant status. The resonance and appeal of these moves is obvious, and in Europe the largest manifestation of Women's Strike action was when 5 million women took part in Spain's feminist strike on 8 March 2018. Nevertheless, the continuing centrality of wages for *individuals* over more *collective* solutions seems to me insufficient. More than ever, what we need now is a vast expansion of services to tackle the escalating inequality between households. No mere personal allowance can do that!

However, near and far, global women's militancy continues to evolve, and we should respond wholeheartedly to any calls for large-scale, open, and inclusive radical coalitions. It is undoubtedly the global feminist movement that is setting the agenda for much of what Western feminists currently need to address. Learning from the successes and defeats of our past, while paying heed to the renewal of feminist militancy around the world, provides the lessons I can draw upon when revisiting my life in politics. This is what sustains me as I reflect further on issues of human vulnerability. And as I head into what is definitely old age, they could hardly be more relevant for me, personally or politically.

4

Admitting Vulnerability

As we age, more fears emerge to haunt us – fading looks, poorer health, an awareness of our mortality. Perhaps we are also likely to be more understanding of the pain and suffering of others, which unless we swiftly turn away is greater than we can easily address, let alone remedy. Acknowledging any of this can easily generate anxiety, alarm, or, worst of all, defensive paranoia.

We often feel we must face our fears or pain alone, and not bother others with our problems. Yet the resulting sense of isolation can prove the greatest misery of all. This is what the English poet John Donne discovered when he was suddenly stricken by an unknown disease, which those around him thought might be contagious. His enforced segregation produced an agonizing loneliness that was even harder to endure than his intense physical suffering. It was reflecting upon the lessons of this unexpected isolation that led Donne to write his famous 'No Man Is an Island' the following year, asserting the natural unity of humankind, above all in suffering:

> Any man's death diminishes me
> Because I am involved in mankind.[1]

That was in 1624. Five centuries later, we are daily made aware of our ties to the rest of the world, although governments still fail to acknowledge our common humanity.

It is always easier to imagine the death of others than it is to imagine our own. Despite always wanting to compel our gaze inwards as well as outwards, Freud suggested that 'it is indeed impossible to imagine our own death ... whenever we attempt to do so we can perceive that we are in fact still present as spectators'.[2] There are a few who seem to dwell with equanimity upon death, but that is usually only when young enough for their own end to remain abstract and distant. This comes over in the words of Walt Whitman pondering the eternal cycles of life, and insisting that each age has its woes – although then he was a mere youth of twenty-one:

> So, welcome death! Whene'er the time
> That the dread summons must be met,
> I'll yield without one pang of awe,
> Or sigh, or vain regret.[3]

Maybe so, but on reaching old age, thoughts of death are usually pushed aside. Clearly this helps us to live each day as it comes, whatever our age or physical condition. However, it need hardly stop us from reflecting seriously upon our own vulnerabilities and greater frailties, nor should it prevent us paying heed to the various needs of others, near and far.

Yet, today, there is massive pressure on us individually to remain fit and robust in mind and body throughout our lives. It intensifies our own fears of impairment, often making them too scary to face. However, there are many reasons for us all to remain as responsive as we can to the pain and suffering of others. For once we admit that vulnerability and disappointment are an inevitable part of life, it is immediately clear why throughout our lives we need each other.

Vulnerability and Inclusion

We need each other. We all rely upon the shared structures and evolving social relations that protect, feed, educate, and sustain us wherever we reside. This is why vulnerability is not simply an individual or even a collective attribute, but an aspect of our shared life. Some people find themselves in constant danger, with few if any networks of support or care, while others are able to retain some sense of control over their lives, whatever their situation. Our goal should not be to surmount dependency to achieve self-sufficiency, but rather to recognize our interdependence as the basis of democracy.

The sudden emergence of the COVID-19 pandemic dramatically highlighted this reality. We were all vulnerable to this disease, yet contrasts remain between those groups who were most vulnerable, especially along lines of race, ethnicity, geography, and migration. Inequality is just one of the reasons for this, although a major one. Any one of us, at any age, may become a casualty of injury or disease. Or we may have endured or continue to endure varying degrees of neglect, derision, cruelty, abuse, or desertion from those close to us. It is why survival stories are so interesting: we sometimes see those who have been rendered most helpless in so many differing ways emerge with courage and dignity if their narratives are heeded, and assistance is offered.

The scholarly and campaigning work of disability activists, reflecting upon the lives and needs of the more physically and mentally challenged, has been especially significant in unfolding the complexities of the language of 'vulnerability', revealing why autonomy and dependence are best seen as two sides of the same coin. There are good reasons why many disability activists have rejected the idea of themselves as intrinsically vulnerable, when this has too often served as a pretext for their exclusion from public life.

I knew Jenny Morris, one of the most well-known and persistent of British disability campaigners, before and after her shift from being an active, able-bodied socialist feminist to a new life as a wheelchair-bound disability champion. Strangely, it was in her second life that Morris seemed most independent and forceful. Living a few blocks away from me in Islington, she was rendered suddenly paraplegic in 1980, at the age of thirty-three, after she climbed onto a railway ledge to protect a stranded child whom she feared might tumble down onto the tracks below. Instead, it was Morris who took the tumble. And the worst of it was, she would later say, that her physical impairment pitched her into a new experience of social exclusion, which regrettably included feeling disregarded by the women's movement itself.

Morris points out that her injury occurred just when the disabled people's movement in Britain was growing, in the early 1980s. As she describes in her book *Pride against Prejudice: Transforming Attitudes to Disability*, this proved critical in grounding her ever since, supplying a supportive network and political framework for understanding and acting upon her new situation. Becoming a feminist disability activist and trade union organizer, Morris was soon determined to confront the disabling social barriers of prejudice, discrimination, and exclusion. Indeed, she argues that the perception of disability or impairment in the traditional medical model has proved the gateway for the *denial* of basic human and civil rights for those seen as afflicted. Being categorized as 'severely disabled', for example, all too often led to people's social segregation into isolated institutional settings.

Fortunately for Morris, a new social model of disability was being developed, clearly outlined by Mike Oliver, another disability scholar and activist, in *The Politics of Disablement*. Most of the difficulties faced by people living with a disability stemmed from the failure of society to adapt to their needs, rather than from any intrinsic or inevitable attribute of the person concerned. Such an approach proved extremely empowering for activists in their own struggles against 'disablism', as Morris's friend and collaborator Liz Crow celebrated: 'Discovering this way of thinking about my experiences was the proverbial raft in stormy seas. It gave me an understanding of my life, shared with thousands, even millions, of other people around the world, and I clung to it.'[4]

Though we so often fail to notice, we are actually surrounded by disabled people everywhere. Another very close neighbour of mine, Lois Keith, was in her mid-thirties, the healthy mother of two young children, when a truck knocked her down. Wheelchair-bound ever since, Keith, too, quickly joined the disability movement, using her expertise as an English scholar to chart the negative messages surrounding impairment and disability, which she shows are unsuspectingly imbibed by children from an early age. Her book *Take Up Thy Bed and Walk* looks at many classic works of children's literature, such as *Heidi* or *The Secret Garden*, noting their depiction of disabled characters whose lives are at best pitiable, while their suffering is often seen as largely self-created and curable by force of will.[5]

The first thing all disability activists have been asking for is recognition of their human rights for social inclusion. They insist that people with impairments should cease to be 'disabled by society'. Distinct physical or psychological differences mean that some people will only be able to access their shared human rights for choice and social participation once there is adequate provision for their inclusion. On this view, the biggest hurdle faced by those who lack robust capabilities is not their personal vulnerability, but rather the political failure to ensure full and adequate social inclusion for everybody. It led Morris to conclude: 'The recognition of our difference (including our dependence), because of our impairments, can thus become a passport to the recognition of our common humanity.'[6]

Morris was for many years a government consultant on disability rights in the UK. Under a Labour government, she was a moving force behind the optimistic policy report of 2005 'Improving the Life Chances of Disabled People', aiming to give those seen as disabled greater choices in their lives. That report called for disability equality as part of an 'Independent Living Strategy', which was agreed in 2008, proposing the allocation of public money to provide services, housing adaptations, and all necessary equipment to promote choice, control, and social inclusion. If these guidelines were followed it would enable many disabled people currently incarcerated in institutions to live in the community, with similar choices to those available for the able-bodied.

This social model for addressing 'impairment', or 'debility', through a democratic insistence on shared human rights strengthened disability activists everywhere. In Britain, the grassroots Disabled People's Movement (DPM) first met in 1974 and continued into the 2000s. It was images of collective strength, not vulnerability, that fed its determined struggles for positive cultural recognition and increased social support, which for a while managed to secure improved access to education, transport, and housing for people with disabilities. Similar movements mushroomed elsewhere, with successful outcomes, including a strong Disability Rights Movement in the United States.

In the early 1970s, disability activists lobbied Congress and marched on Washington until they obtained the Rehabilitation Act, passed in 1973, recognizing the civil rights of people with disabilities. American disability activists, unsurprisingly, adopted similar approaches to British activists in emphasizing the social model of disability. They identified social and environmental obstacles, along with prejudice, as the barriers to full inclusion of differently abled people in society at large.

The election of Ronald Reagan in 1980, however, would threaten or reverse all the civil rights laws from the previous decade. Nevertheless, in certain cities there were local gains around independent living for disabled people. Cleveland opened the first Independent Living Center in 1980, and worked on legislation to grant accessible housing and public transportation for disabled people. Soon there were hundreds of independent living facilities nationwide.

One key disability activist, wheelchair user Mary Verdi-Fletcher, born with spina bifida, had helped to create that first Independent Living Center in the state of Ohio. She became the founding artistic director of the Dancing Wheels company in the same year, incorporating disabled artists into dance classes and performances. A decade later, realizing how hard it was for disabled dancers to find training, Verdi-Fletcher founded the Dancing Wheels School, which rapidly attracted students from around the globe eager to learn the techniques of disability integration in dance. At the same time, she worked to change legislation around disability, resulting in the updated Americans with Disabilities Act (ADA) of 1990, designed to protect the rights of disabled people to full and equal treatment, with access to employment opportunities and to public housing.[7]

Nevertheless, there are dangers in downplaying vulnerability to affirm only shared human rights, especially in harsh times. For example, in her book *Dangerous Discourses of Disability, Subjectivity, and Sexuality*, the British feminist scholar Margrit Shildrick applauds disability politics for stressing the significance of inclusion and dissolving the binaries between the 'disabled' and the able-bodied, while also celebrating the strength of people who were once written off as incapable. However, she worries that this approach fits too neatly with the neoliberal rhetoric that only glorifies personal self-reliance and self-management.[8]

I would add to this my more general concern that talk of individual rights and self-reliance, although at times valuable, has fostered the dangerous denunciation of dependency in social welfare policies and practices. As the psychoanalyst Tim Dartington notes in his impressive and moving book *Managing Vulnerability*, not only have we seen a distressing denigration of dependency in welfare discourses, but this has accompanied a devaluation of the importance of relationships, in favour of a more individualistic approach to human relations overall.

Dartington himself spent many years caring for his much-loved wife, Anna, after she developed early-onset Alzheimer's, always putting her needs first. He was responding almost instinctively, he reflected, to her ever greater helplessness.

Indeed, he points out that you can see any number of partners and children devoting huge amounts of time to looking after 'the most basic and intimate needs of those who apparently have nothing to give back'. Dartington agrees that the disability movement's emphasis on human rights has been useful for thinking about discrimination and disadvantage in many forms of social exclusion, not only towards the disabled, but also in relation to 'our prisons full of people with mental health problems, and asylum seekers denied the opportunity to be other than criminal'.[9] Nevertheless, it is dependency, not autonomy, that is the issue in caring for some forms of comprehensive disability.

Punitive Welfare Regimes

Other problems with the autonomy framing were soon evident in the UK. Once individualized, the 'able-disabled' can be declared fit for work, and this is just what has happened, with catastrophic consequences following the onslaught on welfare entitlements following the financial crisis of 2007–08. With the massive removal of services under the Tory-led austerity regimes of British governments from 2010, there was soon a determination to increase the productivity and financial contribution of disabled people. This resulted in the creation of the Work Capability Assessment (WCA), continually testing every individual's fitness for work, whatever their situation. The consequence was immense misery for almost all disabled people and those who cared for or about them.

WCA assessments have been shown to be grotesquely inadequate, often resulting in the withdrawal of any form of financial support from seriously vulnerable people of all ages and levels of impairment. As ever, race and ethnicity played a part in defining which cases failed this assessment. The government's own statistics reveal that almost 10 per cent more disabled people from ethnic minority groups are declared fit for work, with that gap slightly increasing, rather than decreasing, on appeals.[10]

This led to thousands of deaths every year, some by suicide, among those falsely declared 'fit to work'. The calamity was recorded in the Department for Work and Pensions' own statistics, released in 2015.[11] That same year, Jenny Morris reported that nearly half of disabled people receiving care and support from their local authority had seen their quality of life falling, *despite* major new legislation allegedly designed to boost their well-being, choice, and control.[12] There are now plans to scrap the WCA in the latest government proposals on health and disability issues in 2023, along with fears that the result could be an even more broken benefits system – again only stressing the need to get claimants off benefits and into work.[13]

Thus things have only got worse in recent years, as the disability activist Eileen Clifford described in *The War on Disabled People*.[14] In 2016 the United Nations found the UK government guilty of 'grave and systematic violations' of disabled people's rights, due to its punitive welfare regimes and lack of essential support and services, concluding that the situation was a 'human catastrophe' for many disabled people.

That human catastrophe is evident in the writings of all disability activists today, including Frances Ryan's *Crippled* and Stef Benstead's *Second Class Citizens*.[15] Both books provide harrowing accounts of government cuts destroying the lives of the disabled. Ryan notes that the snowball effects of benefit changes have pushed an estimated 650,000 disabled people into destitution, as defined by the Joseph Rowntree Foundation, with even traditional services such as meals on wheels scrapped by most local councils, and desperate people being refused wheelchairs and other essential equipment.

At the same time, Ryan continues, household poverty has meant the young children of disabled mothers are being taken into care, while thousands of older children are themselves left to care for disabled parents, in the absence of public provision. Disgracefully, as if to prevent the inexcusable from generating any social concern, the conservative media churned out pernicious narratives reviling the disabled as fakes and 'benefit cheats' throughout these damaging times. Benstead's comprehensive overview reveals the same devastating effects of Britain's recent 'welfare reforms' on those suffering from chronic illness or disability. Given this situation, it is no surprise to learn from the government's own statistics that an appalling 60 per cent of all deaths recorded from COVID-19 in England in 2020 involved disabled people, with tens of thousands killed by the inequitable treatment they faced.[16]

The same patterns were evident in the United States, three decades after the rights granted in the Americans with Disabilities Act of 1990. Rebecca Vallas, co-director of the Disability Economic Justice Collaborative, contends that disabled people are today twice as likely to live in poverty, with almost half struggling to pay their rent or have enough to eat. Disabled people of colour face even greater economic hardship, while nearly half of all incarcerated women have a disability.[17] The panorama could hardly be grimmer.

Disability Activism Today

So, where is the disability movement now? In the UK Jenny Morris continues to blog about 'ableism', and the appalling lack of care for the disabled. But a few years ago she mentioned missing the collective resistance of earlier years, confessing sadly: 'I used to spend my time using research and evidence to influence disability policy. I stopped doing that the week before the 2010 general election ... Now I spend my time gardening.'[18] However, new voices in this arena in the UK are determined to restore the activism, linking their disability research with rebuilding movement militancy. One is Luke Beesley, who worries that some recent books on disability, though rightly stressing the brutal assault on and neglect of the disabled, are no longer speaking from a site of struggle. Still, after a low point of crisis in the 2010s, Beesley in 2019 describes a renewal of resistance from disability activists, especially over the last few years.[19]

Today it's clear that disability activism has certainly not disappeared. This is evident in the work of campaigners from Disabled People against Cuts (DPAC), formed in 2010, with prominent participation from the remarkable artist and activist Dolly Sen. She and others surrounded the Department for Work and Pensions (DWP) in 2019, carrying large, red broken hearts, each inscribed with the name of someone who had died due to DWP cuts. Even more dramatically, the following year Sen donned a doctor's coat and 'sectioned off' the DWP with tape, declaring it 'a danger to itself and others'.

At the same time, China Mills, head of the Healing Justice group, was also stressing the links between people's deaths and welfare reform, while pointing out that any or all of their experiences of chronic pain, exhaustion, anxiety, police brutality, and lack of accessible transport mean that many who are disabled simply cannot make it to street protests. However, she suggests that resistance can also involve quieter modes, 'internalized, embodied and invisible', as well as 'forms of bearing witness and theory-making'. Surveying the body count from welfare reforms is heart-breaking, yet, as Mills reminds us, there are rich histories of resistance: 'This is a story of disabled people joining forces with bereaved families, bearing witness to welfare reform's deadly impact, pushing at the boundaries of what we think resistance looks like, and collectively envisioning justice.'[20]

In the States there have also been signs of resurgent disability activism. Combining queer and disabled activism, Robert McRuer and Anna Mollow in *Sex and Disability* assert the need not just to reject the cultural devaluation of disability, but also to recognize disability as a vital force that constantly reshapes our culture, despite ableist norms that would relegate it to a supporting role.[21]

In 2022, the Asian American Alice Wong, diagnosed with muscular dystrophy from birth, was active on many platforms celebrating the strength she gained from her disability activism. In her book *Year of the Tiger: An Activist's Life*, she writes: 'I want people to expect me to be in the same spaces as them … People still find it exceptional or surprising that disabled people have children, or careers, or amazing talents, or wild adventures. This is both a cultural and a political problem. And this is why visibility and representation are so important to me.'

Wong initiated the Disability Visibility Project, collecting stories about disabled lives, determined to focus on the wisdom of disabled people themselves, their struggles, and their often remarkable achievements, as well as their determination to connect and find ways to transcend isolation. Many stories appear in her edited collection *Disability Visibility: First-Person Stories from the 21st Century*. Here we see the role of race and ethnicity in further marginalizing disabled people within the mainstream, including the erasure of Indigenous people.[22]

Able-bodied or disabled, we need to pay far more heed to issues around disability, beginning with the realization of its extent: an estimated 1.3 billion people worldwide experience significant disability. It's because bodily and mental limitations are so immensely varied that stories of living with 'disability', or surmounting its challenging consequences, take so many forms. Every disability activist has their own, often riveting, mostly distressing, story of survival.

In her remarkable memoir *Golem Girl*, for instance, Riva Lehrer describes the mental and physical torments of growing up in Cincinnati with spina bifida in the 1960s, when disabled children met with daily abuse. Recalling the supposedly emancipated 1960s, it is startling to read Lehrer's account of how she was constantly persuaded that she would simply be written off in adulthood, like all the other disabled children she was schooled with: never expect to be able to work, or to have sexual relationships, or to have children.

Lehrer movingly depicts her intense dependence on her mother, and how at times she was desperate to escape that dependence. In her teenage years Lehrer found herself permanently in conflict with this overprotective mother, in a way that was destructive for both. She wanted, she explains, to put up 'walls in my head, boundaries that let me keep my mother out'. However, her life changed completely once she reached college and learned to embrace her disability and hitherto mortifying body. Before long she is describing herself as a 'queer, crippled Jew' who now sees rich opportunities for creativity and resistance, especially through her artwork.

Pain and problems remained, along with constant hospital visits (which in the States must be paid for). And yet Lehrer is eloquent on the magic and mysteries of disabled bodies 'that are thought to drool, slime, bleed and infect, if not in truth, then in the public imagination ... But perhaps we might think of leakage as a reaching-out, a desire to join the tribe of humanity.'[23]

Here in the UK, Frances Ryan, comparing the view she absorbs from her doctor as a wheelchair user and her own feelings about it, says much the same thing: 'This body, in all its joy and tears and moving edges, is loved completely – not despite its disability, but because of it.'[24]

Vulnerability and Care

It's very clear just how inspiring narratives of disability have proved for many, in their move away from discussions of vulnerability to emphasize instead creativity and collective action. The social model for disability both empowered activists and shifted perceptions of disability, sustaining the demand for change.

Yet it created problems for some well-known disability spokespeople, most evidently in the writing and media appearances of Tom Shakespeare in the UK. When his influential text *Disability Rights and Wrongs* appeared in 2006, many activists saw it as a betrayal because of its partial acceptance of a medical model of disability. Shakespeare sought to discuss the levels of distress and heightened vulnerability surrounding disability that cannot simply be reduced to a lack of social support. In a later essay, 'We Are All Frail', Shakespeare again disputed the idea that those with bodily or other impairments must reject the label 'vulnerable' lest it reinforce negative stereotypes. Such rejection weakened their criticisms of the failure of public funding to provide the facilities necessary for everybody's empowerment.

Somewhat at odds with disability rights activists in both Britain and America, Shakespeare insists that disability is not 'mere difference' but can – albeit not in every case – involve painful and challenging disadvantages. The medical and the social certainly intersect in creating the perils of disability. Witness the fact that disabled people are known to be two to three times as likely to suffer domestic abuse, in both Britain and the States, their dependence exploited in intimate relationships.[25] Moreover, many studies now show that it is the historical failure to acknowledge, let alone adequately accommodate, the sexuality of disabled people that has itself exacerbated their heightened vulnerability to sexual harm.[26]

Nevertheless, despite all these potential hazards, Shakespeare does agree that there is no sharp dichotomy but rather a continuum between the abled and disabled, for 'to be human is to experience bodily deficits'. To this I would add: and to suffer frequent psychic pain. Shakespeare concludes that as everyone is at risk, the solution is to 'make a world that can include everyone, regardless of their differences, as vulnerable to impairment and illness'.[27]

Once we accept that we are all vulnerable to frailty and

impairment, albeit to different degrees at different times, then it should be clear that we are all in need of support and care: all of us some of the time, and some of us all of the time.

In her enthralling and angry book *The Undying*, American poet and writer Anne Boyer tells how she lived through the most prolonged and excruciatingly painful treatment for a highly aggressive, triple-negative breast cancer she developed aged forty-one. The only way to manage at all, she found, was in somehow sharing her pain, not exalting or conquering it, but rather accepting it as real and something shared with others. She recalled other patients joining her during treatment, to whom she made clear how much the treatment she was undergoing really hurt. It was a strange but necessary solidarity: 'This is why I tried to write down pain's leaky democracies, the shared vistas of the terribly felt.'

Agency is not the issue in Boyer's memoir, as she rejects the dominant cancer narratives of 'fighting' and 'resilience'. It is a story of pain, which most people, she says, simply do not want to see or hear about: 'We are expected to keep our unhappiness to ourselves but donate our courage to everyone.' Boyer is also enraged by the gulf between those who can and those who cannot pay for the treatment they need, and the lack of any provision for care after treatment. This is why the death rates for single women is double that for married women from her form of breast cancer, and far higher again for those who are poor or Black. Some people are rarely considered worthy to be kept alive, she reflects: 'These women's deaths are racist and unnecessary, and our grief over them should tear open the earth.'[28]

As the New York feminist philosopher and disability theorist Eva Kittay notes in her important book *Love's Labor*, when dealing with 'extreme dependency' there can be no serious 'pretence of independence'. She knows this all too well from being the chief carer for her severely cognitively and physically disabled daughter. Nonetheless, Kittay stresses that we are all interdependent, which means we must search together 'for a knife sharp enough to cut through the fiction of our independence'.[29]

All things considered, I lean towards Shakespeare's more eclectic approach to disability and chronic illness, and endorse his mantra: 'True inclusion is to value people equally, regardless of their abilities. Happiness comes from acceptance of frailties.'[30] And if not happiness, then at least a sense of our shared humanity, and greater knowledge of the ineluctable ties between dependency, equality, and care. Sometimes, as Boyer illustrates, it may be the pain and suffering that we need to feel is shared.

Yet, while we are all vulnerable, it remains crucial to pay close heed to the contexts of care, support, or neglect, that moderate our degrees of vulnerability, as again Boyer illustrates through her own ordeal with cancer. We can reclaim the idea of shared vulnerability, and fight to remove its stigma, but at any one time some of us will be far more vulnerable than others. Of course, we are encouraged to believe that once past childhood it is only the disabled, the chronically ill, or the genuinely old who are vulnerable and in need of significant care. But, as we now know, we may find ourselves in moments of acute crisis and having to depend on others for care at any age, while our dependence on differing forms of care is evident throughout our lives.

Nevertheless, the ways in which we depend upon others can be easier to disavow at certain times, especially when young, able-bodied, and healthy. Hence, it is the particular association of dependency with more visible fragilities that makes the fear of ageing and mortality become more pressing as we progress through adulthood.

The Scandal of Ageing

'Age cannot wither her, nor custom stale / Her infinite variety', and it is true, though we probably never possessed the fabled beauty of Cleopatra, that people tend to grow more, not less, different as they age. Nevertheless, most of us prefer not to think about ageing, just as we avoid contemplating death. We know that with old age our status in the world drops, and even our visibility – especially if we are women. And we definitely lose authority. Mischievously, this is why some of the best women crime writers have favoured elderly female sleuths, from Agatha Christie's Miss Marple to the later, explicitly feminist protagonists of Amanda Cross, or Sara Paretsky's V. I. Warshowski, still active at sixty.

The cloak of social invisibility enfolding ageing women acts as a camouflage enabling these sleuths to upend expectations and to use their lifelong experience of the ways of the world to snoop around unnoticed, given cultural preconceptions of and disdain for older women, with their infertility and wrinkles. But, as that great optimist, the much-missed New York Jewish writer Grace Paley, asked, when commenting on ageing at sixty-seven: 'Invisible to whom? And so what? All the best minorities have suffered that and are rising nowadays in the joy of righteous wrath.'[31]

So what? Well, it's not always easy to be old and joyful, however righteous our anger at being disregarded in later life. 'Once we have reached a certain age it's hard to be reconciled to the fact that people are always going to be impatient with us', the Nobel Prize–winning Polish novelist Olga Tokarczuk writes in her acclaimed thriller *Drive Your Plow over the Bones of the Dead*.[32] Some may see this as an exaggeration, yet there is no doubt that assumptions of physical and mental weakness, along with increasing 'ugliness', underpin the legendary derision projected onto us once we become old ladies.

'Witches', 'crones', 'harridans', 'hags', 'old bags', 'old bats': the poisonous synonyms trailing ageing females are endless, whether positioning us as dangerous, repulsive, or pitiable. Indeed, old age itself tends to be gendered as female, because of its association with supposedly 'feminine' frailty. This is what haunts men in literature, as they fear they might be seen to be 'losing it' when the presentation of any wished impregnability becomes harder to perform. Hence the dread that old age turns men into women, or at least that growing older 'neuters' them: 'That is what old, even middle age, effectively does to males', lamented the American law professor Bill Miller in his book *Losing It*.[33]

There are, of course, disorienting aspects to ageing that do not reduce simply to ageism, physical weakness, and the lack of adequate social support – though they are never wholly detached from them. It is alarming how time seems to speed up as we age. In childhood a day can seem to last forever; later, years collapse into decades in a trice. Our bodies keep changing as we age, but our minds are rather different, in many ways largely unchanged, despite growing forgetfulness, at least before any serious cognitive decline.

Memory gives us access to experiences we have shared throughout our lives, allowing us to revisit our younger selves, and (at least when free from trauma, neglect, or extreme cognitive failure) enabling us to retain some abiding sense of self. Loss of memory, in the striking formulation of the neurologist Scott Small, is a chisel that chips away at the marble of our lives, with the qualifier that forms of forgetting are also necessary to preserve our selectively hewed image of ourselves.[34] Crucially, though, we need to feel affirmed by those around us, at least every now and then, if we are to retain any sense of our personal continuity through time. It is especially when others are interested in our past lives, when they take the trouble to remind us of 'ourselves', that we can most easily embrace again the sense of who we like to feel we have always been. This is the joy and significance of enduring friendships, as we relive, embellish, forget, and partially invent the past – together.

But if we find ourselves in uncaring contexts, treated with little dignity or respect, it is much harder, perhaps impossible, to meander back mentally, even in solitude. Old age makes us especially vulnerable to forms of rejection that can existentially undermine any sense of who we are, or our place in the world. This is the peril of loneliness and neglect in old age, where the absence of emotional, responsive care and empathy can prove quite as damaging as the denial of physical care.

It is particularly shocking today, when Age UK reports that half a million older people go at least five or six days a week without seeing or speaking to anyone at all, and two-fifths of all older people say that the television is their main company.[35] There is also overwhelming evidence that racial and ethnic minority groups, especially when migrant, are likely to enter old age in poorer health and at greater risk of vulnerability, due to lifelong discrimination.[36]

Similarly, in the United States vast numbers of elderly people say they are lonely, with even higher rates of reported loneliness among poorer people living in subsidized housing, accompanying high levels of depression. Again, race and ethnicity play a prominent role, with all research indicating that the combination of economic insecurity and limited social options can produce extreme isolation and even disability among African Americans.[37]

However, whatever their distinct belonging, it is always older women who are the most likely to end up living alone. Recent research in the UK shows that 60 per cent of women over seventy-five live alone, compared to 49 per cent of the whole population, and that those who do live alone are more likely to feel lonely, with half a million older women today saying they are severely lonely.[38]

Wherever possible, I have for some time been trying to use my own experiences of old age to confront ageism, while also looking for better ways in which we can support each other as we age. This includes fighting on all available fronts for policies that address improved care for the elderly. Moreover, ageing remains a critical feminist issue. For not only are older women far more likely to end their lives living alone, but it is also women overall who still have the most complex relations to matters of care. As supposedly the homemakers, women have a particular horror of becoming needy or dependent, reflecting the distress of thinking themselves a potential burden to those who for so long depended on them.

Nevertheless, the fear of increasing dependency is common to all of us, allied to the fear of a widening gap between who we feel we are, or would very much like to remain, and how our culture perceives us in old age. It explains why so many old people vehemently proclaim that they 'don't feel old', insisting that they can take care of themselves, thereby reinforcing the disavowal of old age and its distinct needs.

Enhancing old people's personal fears of fragility and loss is a social climate in which the deteriorating position of young people has intensified social resentment against the old. We find not cultural celebration but public alarm over people's growing longevity. Nowadays it is expressed in talk of a 'tsunami' of elderly people, claiming triple-locked pensions, requiring endless care and support from the state at the expense of younger generations. Indeed, we have seen much official and media orchestration of tendencies to blame the elderly for the very real plight of the young.

Always scenting which way the wind blows, the revered Canadian writer Margaret Atwood has magnified the possible trajectory of this resentment in some of her recent fiction. One of her apocalyptic short stories, 'Torching the Dusties', is set in an old people's nursing home whose residents are under siege from a murderous throng of violent young people, said to be part of an international youth crusade, under the banner 'Our Turn'. In an ageism that has turned deadly, young people have been setting nursing homes alight, determined to finish off the 'parasitic dead wood' that inhabits them, while wearing 'baby masks' and chanting 'Time to Go. Fast not Slow. Burn Baby Burn. It's Our Turn.'

Atwood highlights the media's role in helping to stoke young people's anger with their rhetoric of crisis and calamity surrounding the care needs of the elderly, as well as in pitting the young against the old in their talk shows. As Atwood's clever, semi-blind but feisty protagonist realizes, it is not the first time in history that the rage of the young has been fanned by 'scapegoating some of the most vulnerable in society'.[39]

Atwood's dystopian fiction echoes the true-life observation of many others, such as that redoubtable scholar of ageing Margaret M. Gullette, writing on the cultural impediments to ageing well. In a new book, bluntly titled *American Eldercide*, she argues that at the height of the COVID crisis the elderly were simply declared expendable. The inadequate care, or brutal neglect, of old people in nursing and veterans' facilities in the US resulted in a huge death toll in 2020.[40]

We saw a similar neglect in the UK, where the NHS was initially forced to release older patients back into their care homes without first testing them for COVID-19. The result was a dramatic rise in COVID mortalities in care homes, including of carers. Death rates in British care homes were soon a shameful thirteen times higher than, for instance, those in German care homes. Just as telling was the early nonchalance greeting the deaths of these fragile elderly in the UK, who were not even counted in the government's initial reports of daily COVID deaths. These were largely preventable deaths, publicly ungrieved at first: an overdetermined consequence of the scandalous state of elderly social care for decades, given the savage cuts to local government and the enforced privatization of care homes.

Far from lamenting this disregard, a reactionary few used their platforms in the British press – including Jeremy Warner, then assistant editor of the *Daily Telegraph* – to suggest the possible economic gain of COVID-19 in 'disproportionately culling elderly dependents'. The equally retrograde commentator Toby Young agreed that the potential death of thousands of old people could be seen as 'acceptable collateral damage'. Fortunately, such blatant ageism drew strong condemnation, and before long there was a surge of interest in the impact of the pandemic on the elderly. This was orchestrated by charities, such as Age Concern, and other spokespeople for the aged, whose reports highlighted the way many older people were falling prey to an often devastating anxiety, as the group most at risk from COVID-19.

Nevertheless, though we do hear more about the needs of the elderly today, Age UK reports that an estimated 1.5 million older people are currently living with unmet care needs. Over ten years ago, the *British Medical Journal* stated that there were up to 40,000 preventable deaths of older people annually, and that number has only increased since, with conspicuously rising mortality rates among certain groups of the elderly, particularly working-class women.[41] The reason is clear. Long before the pandemic, care services for the elderly had already been slashed and privatized, placing them out of reach for many. From 2011 private equity firms, many of them based in the United States, acquired several of the largest care chains, making huge profits out of financializing and overleveraging the homes. Meanwhile the growing numbers of underpaid workers in the care sector were forced into the corporate gig economy, leaving them overstretched, vulnerable, and less able to care.

As others have said, a good measure of any society is the way it looks after its vulnerable old people. On that score, ours remains morally bankrupt. We know that genuine care requires patience, empathy, and, above all, time, especially when dealing with the fragile elderly. Unfortunately, this is just what our current forms of privatized care preclude.

Again, in his work on caring for the vulnerable elderly, Tim

Dartington emphasizes the hazards of the presence of markets in our care delivery, which seems designed to discourage or inhibit compassionate interactions between the givers and receivers of care. This is most evident in the 'care' provided for the most helpless of all, especially people with dementia, resulting in much avoidable misery: 'Older people unable to feed themselves, facing malnutrition and dehydration, [are] overprescribed with antipsychotic drugs ... these are not deliberate policies to achieve an accelerated level of mortality, but the outcome of policies that are fatally disrespectful of dependency.'[42]

Whether in need of care or trying to care for elderly people we love, the toll on many people has been devastating. In 2017, the celebrated British sociologist Bev Skeggs, now one of our leading care advocates, wrote a heart-breaking essay on the lack of care experienced by each of her parents in their final years. That damning indictment, entitled 'A Crisis in Humanity', described the failure of her continuous efforts to secure adequate care for each of her parents, due to the dual institutional collapse of the NHS and of the caring systems where they lived, in the north of England, while she worked in London. Even when her elderly mother was hospitalized, Skeggs found that staff had no time to care, not even to feed her then blind mother, in her final illness: 'Neglect by design is the name of the game', she concluded.[43]

Yet, there is today no shortage of voices showing that with adequate resources it is perfectly possible for almost everyone to live decently and be cared for to the end. Ageing people themselves are already providing high levels of essential caring work. Were we to place care at the centre of social policy and community funding, devising schemes to reduce health inequalities overall, more people could live well into their old age and receive the care they need throughout their lives.

The epidemiologist Michael Marmot and his fellow workers have for decades been advocating ways of achieving this. As he says, it requires action across all the social determinants of health, including education, occupation, income, housing, and community resources.[44] Above all, it requires putting money into our appallingly underfunded and neglected care services.

Already, competing with pessimistic assessments of the neglect and disparagement of old people, a contrastingly cheerful current, most prominent in the States, can be found confidently celebrating the many ways it is possible to live well and flourish in old age. To take just one example, in 2020 the media scholar Susan Douglas published *In Our Prime: How Older Women Are Reinventing the Road Ahead*, which suggests that there is no reason why everyone should not be thriving in old age. She finds that today many older women manage to reject sexist ageism, and lead energetic, active, and socially fulfilling lives.[45] Yet, sadly, they are more numerous in some groups than in others.

Ageing Scandalously

A decade has passed since I started writing about the perils and pleasures of ageing at the end of my sixties. I drew, as ever, upon the enduring feminist faith that our own anxieties and challenges will be easier to surmount when shared. For '70s feminists, former worries about being heard and struggling to improve women's lives overall had mutated to include new fears around increasing frailties and approaching mortality. Now, in my late seventies, things have only got worse for so many.

I still believe that, with luck, we can retain a distinct sense of ourselves and keep our past identifications and current belongings more or less intact, so long as we feel connected to wider caring communities. It means, above all, that we still need to find ways of both giving and receiving care, understanding the complex interactions between the two and doing our best to support those who care for and about us.

However, I know how privileged I am for this to be true, when deepening inequalities on every front have left so many unable to access the essential care they need or to feel part of any caring community. Moreover, although I was able to keep working until I chose to retire, in my late seventies, data from across Europe suggests that ageism is the most commonly reported reason for work-related discrimination experienced by older workers, beginning in middle age, especially for women.[46]

Nonetheless, the small but intrepid band of ageist resisters, determined to tackle the cultural aversion towards the very topic of ageing, has unquestionably been growing over the last decade or so. They are mostly old women, prime targets of gerontophobia. From America comes the humour and insight of some of the writers who have moved me most, chiefly Grace Paley and Ursula Le Guin. Le Guin dares to write about beauty and ageing, noting that while beauty is always a part of youth, there are older people she finds beautiful as well: 'For old people, beauty doesn't come free with the hormones, the way it does for the young ... It has to do with who the person is. More and more clearly it has to do with what shines through those gnarly faces and bodies.'[47] It is not the loss of beauty, but the loss of identity that can become most frightening for old people.

In the UK, the British scholar and writer Jane Miller was seventy-eight when she began her book *Crazy Age: Thoughts on Being Old* with the confident assertion: 'I am old and I feel and look old.' She quickly adds: 'I like being old at least as much as I liked being middle-aged and a good deal more than I liked being young.' Two years later she would ask directly, 'What do the old want?' and reply, 'I suppose most people want some company and some independence.'[48] Nevertheless, the denigration of old age remains ubiquitous, which is why I opened my own book *Out of Time* rather less confidently: 'How old am I? Don't ask, don't tell. The question frightens me', moving on to suggest that 'it is alarming facing up to the fearful disparagement of old age'.

And yet writing that book helped me to confront some of the elaborate cultural denial surrounding the vicissitudes of old age, my own and others', even as – more cheerfully – I surveyed the possibilities for living fully and imaginatively in old age. Most happily, it brought me one or two new younger friends, also interested in the topic, whom I cherish to this day. Yet, with official talk of 'ageing well' still largely reduced to appearing not to have aged at all – or not becoming, as we all will, frailer and with specific needs in our old age – it is hard to capture the antinomies of our ageing experiences.

'I don't *feel* old' remains the habitual refrain from most people, whatever their age, which tells us more about the harmful stereotypes surrounding ageing than about anything else. As all the latest reports still find, negative associations with older people dominate all areas of society, including the media, advertising, and central and local government. Indeed, they are present across all age groups, including the elderly, although strongest of all in middle age.[49] Our first task, however, which today is more significant than ever, is to find ways to beat back the market mindset that post-retirement we become 'unproductive' and hence less valuable in the world.

This is all the more critical now that most of us will be living several decades beyond waged employment. Again, this means questioning the very notion of 'productivity' and insisting that caring itself is not only productive in its maintenance of life, but a way of relating that enriches all our personal interactions.

Nevertheless, I still find that addressing the myriad complexities of ageing is challenging. On the one hand, I want to celebrate all the ways in which it is definitely possible to lead busy and fulfilling lives, at any age. Indeed, approaching eighty, and despite retirement and the recent hazards and enclosures of COVID and lockdowns, I remain as politically engaged as ever, still sustained by friendships old and new, while even daring to hope (despite certain failures of short-term memory) that I may, at times, still have something useful to offer. Memories matter, even if recent ones often fade quickly.

On the other hand, I am more aware than ever of the chilling levels of neglect, cruelty, and abuse suffered by many in their old age, tied up with the obscene levels of inequality, especially over the last decade. The second observation threatens to overwhelm my first ambition. It is difficult to celebrate my own and others' positive experiences of old age, when it's clear how privileged our situations are. Additionally, there is great cultural pressure for us oldies to present cheerful, resilient stories of our ageing well, precisely to obscure the continuing neglect, even cruelty, suffered by so many others.

We must therefore tread carefully when meditating on possibilities for living well in old age. It can be all the more confounding amid the deluge of market promises that we can stay 'forever young'. All we need to do is buy pricey skincare lotions, swallow DNA-repair drugs, pursue hormone replacement therapy, or undergo plastic surgery – the list is endless – all supporting the massively profitable longevity industry.

No one was more critical of these invasive, class- and race-blind, rejuvenating regimes than Barbara Ehrenreich, still inspiring me at the start of this book, but whom I am now mourning at its completion. Approaching eighty, in her last book, *Natural Causes*, she ridiculed the widely promoted fiction that we can stay in full control of our minds and bodies with a little more self-love and self-care. In reality, we cannot control the decay of our bodies. What this ageing socialist feminist insisted upon, as she had throughout her extraordinary life, was that *mutual care*, not *self-care*, is what we need if we are to live a good life at any age: 'We could talk to each other, we could have more parties and celebrations, we could do more dancing. I know this sounds a little crazy, but I think that it's something that's very much missing in our lives.'[50]

How right she was. And more parties, more celebrations, are just what some older people, mostly women (myself included), have decided to generate. No longer invisible, we are determined to age scandalously, shedding that shroud of concealment. A few years ago in the States, Ashton Appleton published *This Chair Rocks: A Manifesto against Ageism*. It calls for us all to celebrate old age, and to join her in exposing ageist myths: 'The sooner growing older is stripped of reflexive dread, the better equipped we are to benefit from the countless ways in which it can enrich us.' Writing up her interviews with other oldies, she quotes the eighty-eight-year-old folk artist Marcia Muth, who tells her, 'Your life does change as you get older ... you get into what's important and what's not.'[51]

Such confident and assertive public resistance to ageism can also be found in the UK. Here, for instance, the poet and writer Leah Thorn founded Older Women Rock, a project involving poetry, retro clothes, performance, and film, all drawing upon conversations with other older women. Thorn and her companions stage theatrical events, each performer wearing gorgeous clothes emblazoned with bold anti-ageist quotes. They have created pop-up shops as spaces for tackling the many harmful ways ageing women, in particular, are impacted by the beauty industry, fast fashion, and more. Such defiance of predatory markets targeting older women then opens out to link it with the importance of resisting climate change.

Thorn is clear about her goals: first, to decry the near absence of older women in the media, except as frightening or comical stereotypes. She angrily denounces the small pensions many receive, leaving them in poverty due to their breaks in employment to raise children, or care for ageing parents. She also lambasts the fortune made by the beauty industry from 'older women's insecurity'. Finally, Thorn seeks to counter older women's tendency to conceal or be 'discreet' about physical changes such as greying hair, facial hair, or incontinence.[52]

Women are aged by culture faster than men, and we more visibly try to resist the ways in which we are written off a good decade earlier than men. Yet, it is men as they age, especially men over sixty-five, who are most at risk from suicide. In the United States, 85 per cent of all suicides among older adults are those of men over sixty-five.[53] The usual explanation for this is that older women on average have larger social networks and maintain more ties to people outside of their household than older men.[54]

Lately, however, there have been efforts to rectify the lack of research on older men, with films and books beginning to explore the experiences of men in old age. The most popular from Hollywood include *Gran Torino* (2008), *Nebraska* (2013), and *Cry Macho* (2021). The point about these movies is that their well-known stars are not, for once, being cast as romantic leads (as they usually have been, whatever their age), but as gloomy, alienated, or washed-up old guys. A type of progress, with its greater, if gritty, realism!

Throwing light on some of this gloom, one study from Australia examining the high risk of suicide in older men found their sample of octogenarians unhappy 'about [their] increasing social alienation, related to losing their historical position within families and the community, and their limited ability to initiate friendships and maintain meaningful connections'. Sadly, but significantly, some participants suggested that suicide was simply the most rational alternative to 'dependence' in their final years. In agreement with other studies, this one mentioned that women were better than men at coping with ageing, differences they saw as 'stark and unchangeable'.[55] Other studies have found that suicide is less common among sexual minorities in old age, suggesting that such men might have gained more 'crisis competence', having already faced more adversity, and being less privileged to begin with.[56]

Caring across the Generations

Whatever older people's identifications and commitment to embracing the hurdles we face as we age, we know that at some point we are all likely to need more distinct forms of support, a situation already familiar to the disabled and chronically ill. Many observers have been warning of the increasing dangers of age ghettoization. On this topic, Anne Karpf, the British sociologist who has written much on ageing and ageism, notes that when a large sample of Facebook groups created by twenty- to twenty-nine-year-olds was examined by researchers at Yale School of Public Health, three-quarters of them denigrated the elderly, while more than a third, extraordinarily, advocated banning old people from public activities like shopping.[57]

In the UK, young people harbour equally negative attitudes towards us oldies, while their high levels of digital activity cut them off further from contact with us. Judging from the reports about these problems, there seems just no space at all for care or solidarity, let alone friendship, across the generations. Throughout Europe there has also been much discussion of the need to reduce the generational digital divide, which despite mediating circumstances remains a chasm.[58]

This apparent failure to build better, or indeed any, social bridges between the generations is harmful to young and old alike. For ageing is a bridge all must cross, short of an early death. Hence, as others have noted before me, ageism is actually a prejudice against our dreaded future selves, which explains the prevalence of mid-life crises. One of the main ways to break down those fears of old age is obviously by finding better ways of promoting contact between young and old, especially when many old people, with adequate resources, are both flourishing and eager to engage with life in all ways possible.

I know I have been lucky in maintaining close contact with many younger friends, whether in my Care Collective or through other means, as well as, happily, via social media.

When you actively share political outlooks and come together in collective engagements, precious bonds can be maintained across the generations. It was not only at Greenham Common that young and old could unite. Today many enjoy such encounters in climate activism, fighting austerity, defending community resources, offering mutual aid at food banks, or in a multitude of other ways involving shared goals, both distant and near.

Thus I hover between hope and foreboding when looking ahead at possibilities for strengthening cross-generational ties. The foreboding stems primarily from the cruel contrasts in older people's well-being and access to care. Elana Buch, in her *Inequalities of Aging*, exposes the troubling dynamics of the American home care industry, in a system that glorifies independence while providing little or no public help to preserve it. The ugly secret at the heart of care provision in the US, she suggests, is that those who care for the most vulnerable are themselves rendered vulnerable in the process. Buch does the rounds with one care worker, Maria, watching her constantly putting herself out, engaged in multiple imaginative tasks to enable her elderly employer to preserve her old sense of self, but typically getting very little in return.

Buch sees care workers, who are usually Black and ethnic minority women, committed to 'maintaining their [wealthier] clients' physical health, sustaining their subjectivities, and enabling them to be seen as independent'. But such labour comes at the expense of carers' own well-being, when home care jobs provide little status and no health insurance, sick pay, or retirement benefits. Thus, Buch concludes: 'In a nation founded on a belief in political and personal independence, we struggle to accommodate the profound interdependencies that make life possible. It is a system that consumes those who sustain it.'[59]

In the UK we have been heading the same way for some time. We remain in dire need of increased social care funding to improve both access to and quality of care, whether for home care, or that provided in care homes. It is why the British Medical Association has repeatedly urged the government to widen access to care services by making them free at the point of need, as well as to invest in the social care workforce and properly value its workers. But despite repeated commitments from government, we have seen no real progress at all. Hence there remain well over 100,000 vacancies in social care in England alone, which is currently likely only to increase, according to research by the think-tank the King's Fund.[60]

Although some of us will be far more at risk than others, it is clear that hostile attitudes towards old age remain endemic everywhere, all tending to depict old age simply as a process of decline. Yet, as we've seen, there are also counternarratives, sometimes issuing from those same habitually ageist places. In the UK they are rehearsed by various well-established campaigns and institutions, such as Age Concern, or the Centre for Ageing Better. Moreover, especially during the COVID pandemic, we saw more people challenge the principle that unless you are maximally productive, you are of little interest to anyone.

As we've seen before, when the pandemic first hit, there was a mushrooming of mutual aid groupings around the country, helping some, though sadly far from all, elderly people who lived on their own to feel less isolated and neglected. At the same time, old people themselves extensively participated in supporting food banks and helping their neighbours. Personally, like many vulnerable older people, the pandemic did indeed force me to remain largely housebound. And I am surely not alone in the way this experience taught me to cherish my ties and commitments to others even more. Today, I am probably in as much daily contact as I have ever been with friends, neighbours, and political comrades, if still often virtually.

COVID-19 clarified to an unprecedented degree that one way or another, and at whatever age, we all rely on care from others. I am left hoping that this might encourage more of us to fight to ensure that we all have more time, and more resources, to expand our possibilities for both giving and receiving care. Broadening this out, as the US care theorist Joan Tronto insists we do, it is now crucial for us all to realize that for human life to continue to flourish on this earth, we must rethink the centrality of care in 'the new age of limits', attending to all those social movements which are engaged, at whatever level, in maintaining and repairing the world.[61]

Most of us are only just beginning to register the limits to the continued flourishing of life on our planet. The urgency of the need to address our relation to the world around us now moves me on to address the most expansive of caring practices, caring for the world itself.

5

Repairing the Planet

There are many ways of caring, which always need to be fluid and adaptable. However, caring for nature and the world itself has now become the most challenging of all, requiring new sensitivities and imagination, along with innovative policymaking, on a global scale.

In Western thinking, 'nature' exists to serve us; it is ours to exploit. With its basic elements of earth, water, fire, and air, nature is regarded as valuable above all when providing resources for human consumption, use, or recreation.

But nature, itself threatened, is becoming more threatening. Ecological shifts are resulting in melting ice sheets, rising sea levels, flooding, hurricanes, wildfires, droughts, and widespread extinction of species. Climate change is seen as the trigger, caused by our failure to care about depleting the earth's resources. It is now affecting everything – from national economies to global politics, migration, and our long-term future on this planet.

Yet Western countries have been reluctant to heed decades of scientific warnings about the human production of global warming and environmental deterioration. It is only very recently that most nation-states have reluctantly conceded the need to tackle fossil fuel carbon emissions, and so far only in largely constrained and self-serving ways.

The first Conference of the Parties (COP), established by the UN to tackle the climate emergency, took place in Berlin in 1995. At that time fossil fuels made up about 80 per cent of energy production worldwide, responsible for the release of carbon dioxide, the greenhouse gas most implicated in global warming. After almost three decades of annual conferences, fossil fuels make up exactly the same 80 per cent of global energy production, with temperatures still rising. Since climate activists and scientists have been warning of the power and peril of climate change for years, most of us, and above all our governments and transnational corporations, remain in a form of deliberate denial.

As I write, the latest UN Intergovernmental Panel on Climate Change (IPCC) report on the climate crisis predicts that heat-waves and water shortages are set to increase, and governments are simply not doing enough to prepare for, let alone combat, climate change. Indeed, they are doing the opposite, with most of them still contributing to the calamities ahead, as if pursuing a determined refusal to care.

The esteemed Indian writer Amitav Ghosh wrote of his surprise twenty years ago, when, during research for a novel he was planning to set in the Bay of Bengal, he observed first-hand the devastation of climate change: 'People spoke of their homes disappearing, of sea levels rising and saltwater erosion, but no-one knew what was happening ... And as the years went on the signs became clearer and clearer.' Moreover, Ghosh argues, it was the British pillaging of lands and killing of Indigenous people that laid the foundation for this climate emergency.[1]

The British scholar and journalist Anne Karpf notes in her book *How Women Can Save the Planet* that, as with so many human catastrophes, those already suffering most from the climate crisis are the people least responsible for it. The world's richer nations are responsible for 86 per cent of global CO_2 emissions, caused primarily by burning fossil fuels, mainly coal, oil, and gas. The average Briton emits more carbon in two weeks than a citizen of Uganda, Malawi, or Somalia does in a year.[2] It helps explain why some of the very first and still-ongoing environmental movements emerged in poorer parts of the globe, most prominently with the Gandhi-inspired, tree-hugging Chipko movement, or Chipko Andolan, in India in the early 1970s. This alliance aimed to preserve forests in the Himalayan region of Uttarakhand and has become a rallying point for non-violent environmental movements to this day.

Clearly, then, when it comes to understanding the climate crisis, we are all connected. But many still refuse to recognize those ties, whether historically or in the present. The repudiation is all the stronger when people are seeking to disown the harm they have caused and often continue to cause. It means we need to look carefully at our past and present engagements with the natural world, whether on our doorsteps or far away. Especially in modern times, the majority have tended to have an unconcerned or somewhat ambivalent relation to nature, with scant curiosity about our impact upon or place within it, at least until lately.

When not treated purely instrumentally, nature is often prized as inherently nurturing, offering us moments of solace and beauty. As poets have often celebrated, nature is where we can be soothed and healed. For some, however, the natural world offers more of a challenge, as something to be conquered and controlled. For others, unmitigated nature is usually scary, a place arousing dread and foreboding, especially when clouds darken, rivers surge, or wild animals are on the prowl.

We know that our forager ancestors survived as hunter-gatherers, recognizing themselves as part of natural cycles of birth, growth, and death, while infusing nature itself with spiritual values to help forestall natural catastrophes. Ties linking humans to other creatures were evident, for instance, in prehistoric cave paintings such as those discovered in Chauvet in the south-east of France. These portrayed beings that are half animal, half human.

Nurturing Nature

In modern times, those poets and artists known as the Romantics stood in awe of nature, worrying about the effects of industrialization and urban expansion. Everyone is familiar with William Wordsworth's joyful encounter with 'ten thousand' daffodils, lifting the human spirit, a poem he wrote in 1804. John Keats, lying on his sickbed a decade later, knew that simply gazing outwards at nature could restore his mood, even a transient sparrow enriching his existence.[3]

Declarations of the significance and power of nature were equally common in the US at that time, as writers pondered the relationship between nature and civilization. In his classic essay 'Nature', the philosopher Ralph Waldo Emerson wrote of the transcendental pleasures of feeling at one with the natural world, while also warning readers of the need to curtail the ongoing destruction of the 'wilderness'. Later, those same sentiments were echoed in the writing of his disciple, Henry David Thoreau, seeking solitude in the forest in his seminal ecological treatise, *Walden, or Life in the Woods*, which has inspired generations of environmentalists to this day.[4]

Most passionately of all, however, the American Walt Whitman believed it to be his mission as a poet to bring 'man' closer to nature. His extraordinary epic poem *Leaves of Grass* first appeared in 1855, and he kept returning to it throughout his life. It began with an exhortation to despise riches and instead 'love the earth and sun and the animals'. Whitman deplored people's distance from the nature he worshipped, and in later editions expressed the hope that, thanks to the work of poets, one day 'Nature and Man shall be disjoin'd and diffused no more'.[5]

Preserving that reverential tradition, today we have a cornucopia of literature on the nurturing capacities of nature. In the UK, the academic and naturalist Robert MacFarlane expresses the visual, emotional, and visceral satisfactions of nature in all his writing, including *Landmarks*, where he sets out explicitly to expand our lexicon of the natural world, and deepen our 'literacy of the land'. Not unlike Whitman, MacFarlane sought to 're-wild our contemporary language for landscape', which he hoped might also help to defend the environment. Similar ideas animate Richard Muir's *Landscape Encyclopaedia* and ripple through the beautiful texts and mellow pencil drawings of the late Roger Deakins. In his *Wildwood: A Journey through Trees*, Deakins celebrates the place of woods in our lives and culture. All these nature-lovers aspire to alert us to the wonders of everything that is now either threatened, or fast disappearing in the natural world.[6]

Unsurprisingly, from the time of Henry Thoreau ('We can never have enough of nature') in the mid-nineteenth century through to the present, the best-known lyricists of nature are men. Yet, if with a little less cultural fanfare, women have also been recording their delight in landscape and the natural world. This prompted the British writer and nature-lover Katharine Norbury to put together a collection of women's thoughts on nature. Searching for what might be women's distinct perspectives on the subject she sifted through novels, diaries, poetry, even gardening notes and household planning, for her anthology *Women on Nature*.

Her compilation includes writing from over 100 women, dating back to the fourteenth century, and including voices from Africa, India, the Caribbean, Japan, even a poem from the famous African American slave Phyllis Wheatley, 'A Hymn to the Evening', written in 1773: 'From the zephyr's wing, / Exhales the incense of the blooming spring. / Soft purl the streams, the birds renew their notes, And through the air their mingled music floats.'

But Norbury is well aware that both 'women' and 'nature' are slippery concepts, their meanings shifting across time and place. On the one hand, women have been seen, in different ways, as somehow 'closer to nature'. On the other, Norbury suggests, the very word 'nature' is implicitly anthropocentric, something defined by and distinct from 'man' or 'humanity', rather than humans being a part of it. Her goal in assembling the anthology was also to persuade everyone to act to conserve and renew the world around us, 'not merely to observe and catalogue its fall'.[7]

Similarly, the Scottish poet Kathleen Jamie urges us to look with fresh eyes at the 'natural', observing its historical fragility, while also noting that the human impact upon the world around us connects with the alarming drop in the population of certain species. Thus, in *Sightlines* Jamie concludes her astute, intensely lyrical observations, whether of the wildest of landscapes or the seemingly fixed presence of the earth or sea around us, with the thought 'A wing's beat and it's gone'.[8]

Speaking personally, I realize somewhat sadly that I have never been closely engaged with nature. Nonetheless, one of the real comforts of my life is seeing the giant eucalyptus tree at the back of my garden, which I planted as a sapling, now grown from 3 feet to well over 100 feet. That tree, together with everything else that I have managed to plant and grow, from tulips to tamarisk tree, certainly helps to keep me cheerful, along with happy memories of the amazing beaches, bushland, and blue mountains so often visited when living in my first homeland, Australia.

So perhaps I am a nature-lover after all, if a highly domesticated one. Moreover, as we age, I notice more and more people, indeed every single one of my older friends, turning in one way or another to the solace of nature, often through an interest in gardening, however small and constrained the space. Sometimes a window box has to suffice. In Jamaica Kincaid's cheery collection *In the Garden: Essays on Nature and Growing*, the writer Penelope Lively, at the time approaching ninety, promises:

Once a gardener, you find yourself offered a whole new dimension of experience, and an insight into the world of things that grow. You not only want to have a go at it yourself, whether you have a window box, a few square yards of basement space, or one of the substantial gardens up and down the land, but you also now have a permanent interest and curiosity – you want to see more, know more.[9]

So convinced have many become of the healing properties of nature that some health professionals have begun prescribing 'nature cures' for selected patients, especially those suffering from depression. A few years ago, GPs at five different practices in Edinburgh began encouraging nature treatments for improving mental health and reducing anxiety, in association with the Royal Society for the Protection of Birds.[10] Similar moves came from doctors in Canada, who began to prescribe free passes to national parks for patients who might benefit from more time spent in nature. One advocate enthused: 'Nature is good for a wide variety of conditions … there's almost no health condition that nature does not make better.' Similar practices emerged from clinics in the States, with some doctors arguing that more time spent in nature can make for a healthier planet with healthier people in it.[11]

However, even as we hear from all sides this soothing talk of nature's gifts to human welfare, bleaker voices warn about the relentless human assault on this natural endowment.

Ravaging Nature

Those visionary forebears who were busy eulogizing the natural world, feeling themselves part of it, were also painfully aware of the threats it faced from rapid industrialization. Like others of their day, they were alarmed by precipitous urbanization and the mechanized factory system, with workers packed into cramped housing, generating widespread disease and rising mortality, including of children. The immediate devastation accompanying these new manufacturing processes gave rise to varied forms of resistance across Europe and the United States.

It is why the early nineteenth century saw the emergence of a type of utopian socialism, hoping to build a 'New Moral World' that could improve both domestic and working life, expanding educational and cultural resources for everyone, while caring for the earth's resources.

French radicals such as Charles Fourier and Henri de Saint-Simon, as well as the Welshman Robert Owen, argued for cooperation and fairness between classes in establishing more nurturing, self-supporting communities.[12] As we have seen, for several decades Owen was able to maintain his model factory with its own welfare and education programmes, including housing, healthcare, and free schooling for all its workers, many of whom soon formed part of a progressive, compassionate, Owenite movement, encompassing early feminist ideas.[13]

These humanitarian forms of utopian socialism evinced a more respectful, less predatory view of nature. However, the revolutionary Marxist movement which replaced them from the mid-nineteenth century presents a rather different vision. With its commitment to technological progress, productivity, and improving the conditions of workers, Marxism has been seen as having no more concern for the environment than the capitalist system it opposed. While radical thinkers often agree that Marxism remains the most powerful critique of capitalism and its continuing, if shifting, impact on our politics and culture, they would question its green credentials. Yet recently several scholars, including John Bellamy Foster and Paul Burkett, have shown that both Marx and Engels were critical of capitalism's adverse environmental impact.[14]

In the first volume of *Capital*, in 1867, Marx suggested that capitalist production 'disturbs the metabolic interaction between man and the earth ... Capitalist production, therefore, develops technology ... only by sapping the original sources

of all wealth – the soil and the worker.'[15] Similarly, in his most
influential book, *The Origin of the Family, Private Property
and the State*, Engels warned that there should be no celebration of 'human victories over nature', noting the unpredictable
consequences of our interventions:

> For each victory nature takes its revenge on us. Each victory, it is
> true, in the first place brings about the results we expected, but
> in the second and third places it has quite different, unforeseen
> effects which only too often cancel out the first ... Thus, at every
> step we are reminded that we by no means rule over nature.[16]

Nevertheless, by far the strongest criticisms of the early depre-
dations of industrial capitalism in devastating the environment
appeared in the closing years of the nineteenth century. Few
were more keenly aware of the threats to the landscape through
mass production and the concentration of hundreds of thousands of downtrodden people in cramped living conditions
than the decorative artist and revolutionary socialist William
Morris, as he watched with disquiet village life disappearing
into the ugly sprawl of expanding cities. From the nineteenth
century until well into the twentieth, workers were still doing
twelve-hour shifts, with women and even children toiling long
hours in factories or coal mines. Repelled by the capitalist fixa-
tion on profit, Morris called for a radical rethink. In a lecture he
delivered to the Hammersmith branch of the Socialist Democratic Federation in 1884, entitled 'How We Live and How We
Might Live', Morris thundered that 'the time will come when
people will find it difficult to believe that a rich community
such as ours ... could have submitted to live ... such a mean,
shabby, dirty life as we do'.[17]

Most famously, Morris fleshed out an alternative vision of
the future in his utopian novel *News from Nowhere*, in which
he imagines a landscape no longer blighted by industrial
capitalism, but the abode of respected craftsmen once more
producing the goods people need, now working in harmony

with the natural world. In arguing for simplicity of lifestyle, community self-reliance, production only for need, and reduction of waste, Morris's vision chimes with more recent notions of green or sustainable societies.[18]

At much the same time, the writer, poet, and philosopher Edward Carpenter was also extolling the virtues of a return to the land and the simple life. He set up an alternative estate at Millthorpe in 1883, establishing a small market garden and producing leather sandals. In his poetic book *Towards Democracy*, nature is presented as the grand alternative to industrial capitalism, and Carpenter argues for a freer, more just society that might finally put an end to 'the long vain fight of man against Nature'.[19] Another Victorian critic and philosopher, John Ruskin, described nature as the ruling passion of his life, wanting to see a fusion between art, science, and nature that could enhance the care of nature. As if anticipating today's climate emergency, in two lectures he delivered in 1884, later printed in *The Storm-Cloud of the Nineteenth Century*, Ruskin mentions the ominous effects of industrialization on weather patterns.[20]

Despite these visionaries hoping that the time will come when humans everywhere choose to live their lives as part of and in harmony with nature, that time has yet to arrive. And many now fear that we have left everything far too late for its realization.

Nevertheless, there was constant pressure to try to curb the damage wrought by rapid industrialization and resultant air pollution on humans throughout the early to mid-twentieth century, with some modest results. In the UK a breakthrough was thought to have arrived after the injurious effects of heavy smog led to the Clean Air Act of 1956. This introduced smokeless zones to cap the fumes and other dangerous particles released into the atmosphere. With greater controls on urban planning, plus the decline in heavy industry, followed by another Clean Air Act in 1968, there finally did appear to be less pollution, and certainly a decrease in thick smog in Britain's cities.

Similar 'clean air' acts were passed in the US Congress, beginning in 1963. Programmes to reduce air pollution also emerged in different European countries, especially within the European Union from 1970.[21] Tragically, however, none of these efforts have done more than eliminate the smog of a century ago: the damage of air pollution continues everywhere. Shockingly, doctors in Britain recently suggested that 40,000 deaths each year are linked to air pollution.[22]

Moreover, while the focus of environmental concern has been on how humans have been harming themselves with the reckless burning of fossil fuels and ensuing greenhouse gas emissions, the fundamental problem is rather different, and altogether greater. We have been damaging not just ourselves, but our planet itself. We are only now beginning to understand the complex forms of our dependence on the natural world. Worse, we learn that earlier action could have averted what we are told is the imminence of total environmental catastrophe.

Timely measures could have forestalled the radical dangers we now face, and every year of inaction has made matters worse. Our situation might have been different *if* extractors of fossil fuels had sought alternatives; *if* manufacturers had wanted to make sustainable goods; *if* governments had regulated fossil fuels and subsidized green alternatives; *if* consumers had been made more aware of choices and of the environmental crisis.

Asking who is most to blame for climate change is a complex question, but one thing is undeniable: the greatest problem is the failure to regulate the fuel-producing capitalist corporations. Even now we allow them to control us and to set the public agenda.[23] At COP27 in 2022 there were more than 600 fossil fuel lobbyists, more than at any of the previous twenty-six conferences, which have, to date, managed to achieve no emission reductions whatsoever.

So, let's be clear. We know that a mere 100 fossil fuel producers are responsible for 70 per cent of greenhouse gas emissions, with the top twenty producing a third of those emissions. Secondly, we know that these producers *did* understand the dangers of their product and yet failed to curtail or alter its use. Instead, for decades they poured money into denying to the public the hazards of fossil fuels and other dangerous substances. In their book *Merchants of Doubt*, two historians, Naomi Oreskes and Erik Conway, exposed the funding of a small group of right-wing US think-tanks with links to the fossil fuel industry. In order to forestall any kind of preventative legislation, fuel corporations supported a handful of scientists who distorted the public debate by contesting the accumulating scientific knowledge on climate change and other environmental issues.[24]

Similarly, in *Exxon: The Road Not Taken*, a group of specialized journalists from Inside Climate News revealed that the giant oil corporation Exxon had itself pioneered critical research over fifty years ago that foresaw the environmental damage their business would do. However, as was confirmed again recently, after briefly embracing the prospect of turning to renewable forms of energy, by the 1990s Exxon switched to investing in the promotion of climate-crisis denial.[25]

Another perverse manoeuvre of the most polluting fuel corporations is to blame the consumer, insisting that they are only bowing to what people desire. In fact, if we look at consumption patterns, the first thing to notice about fuel consumption is how uneven it is. The latest analysis by the UK think-tank Autonomy shows that in the twenty-year period from 1998 to 2018, the top 1 per cent of earners in the UK, the 'polluting elite', used as much carbon as the bottom 10 per cent. In the light of comparable figures from around the globe, it's clear that the poorest are responsible for only a tiny fraction of greenhouse gases. As Will Stronge, director of research at Autonomy, comments: 'The enormous release of carbon emissions by the very richest in society over the past few decades is astonishing. Our analysis suggests that the most effective way for the government to tackle climate change would be to properly tax the rich, through a well-targeted carbon tax scheme.' A carbon tax on the top 1 per cent would have earned the UK £126 billion over the aforementioned twenty years, which could have been invested in anti-pollution measures. What a lost opportunity![26]

Disingenuously, energy companies always insist that shifting to renewables would hit the poorest hardest, since alternative forms of energy would cost more. It is apparently unthinkable that there could be a fairer tax system, yielding different types of subsidies for tackling energy inequities. Since the gross inequity in responsibility for climate emissions within countries is equally manifest between countries, the obvious conclusion for anything resembling climate justice is that richer countries must decarbonize faster, as well as help low-income countries transition to cleaner energy technology.[27]

We can never reduce climate damage without overturning the countless forms of evasion and denial that remain as strong as ever. The leading climate scientist Peter Stott describes his personal struggle to disseminate the facts in the face of forty years of climate denial. His book *Hot Air: The Inside Story of the Battle against Climate Change Denial* exposes the concerted efforts of an unofficial alliance of commercial lobbies, politicians, well-funded maverick scientists, and professional contrarians to smear and undermine serious climate research. Dangerous as this lobby remains, Stott notes that their dishonest provocation would remain itself largely hot air if it didn't serve the interests of irresponsible politicians averse to taking any radical climate action for their own short-term electoral reasons. Moreover, denialism pays well, being so generously rewarded by fossil fuel companies.[28]

Similarly, the indefatigable George Monbiot has spent almost four decades condemning the utter carelessness of most governments in protecting and subsidizing the world's most destructive industries. At some personal cost, he has worked heroically to publicize the extent of environmental damage worldwide. His research reveals that UK government money has uninterruptedly subsidized our three most damaging industries: fossil fuels, meat farming, and fisheries. Indeed, shockingly, he finds that the more destructive the business, the more likely it is to enjoy state protection: 'The "tough", "masculine" industries driving Earth systems towards collapse are pampered and protected by governments, while less destructive sectors must fend for themselves.'

In what he calls 'the pollution paradox', Monbiot explains how the political protection of destructive industries gets woven into government procedure, because the most pernicious commercial enterprises pay the most to buy their protection. In recent years Tory leadership campaigns have been handsomely funded by various fossil fuel producers, such as BP. In return, in 2021 oil and gas prospecting and production received £53 billion in subsidies.

Every year, Monbiot adds, governments around the world spend a massive $500 billion on livestock farming, which mostly disregards environmental protection, while around $60 billion is spent on industrial fishing, even as marine ecosystems are collapsing. The point is, either we protect the living world, or we protect the companies destroying it. At present we protect only the latter.[29] This is why, as Secretary General of the United Nations António Guterres recently put it, 'The world's biggest polluters are guilty of arson of our only home.'[30] And our governments encourage it.

Feminist Environmentalism

Such ruinous facilitating of environmental damage has not happened for lack of protest. For decades, environmental activists have tried to persuade us all to reframe our relation to each other and to the planet itself, knowing the urgent need for us to care for and protect the natural world. Over sixty years ago the American marine biologist and nature-lover Rachel Carson laid the cornerstone for Western environmental politics when she began researching the death of birds and other creatures in the late 1950s. Her book *Silent Spring*, published in 1962, was an immediate best-seller, with its impassioned attack on the unregulated use of DDT and other chemical pesticides. Carson argued that these pesticides were irrevocably harmful, decimating many species and contaminating the world's food and water supply.[31] Trying to open the public's eyes, she would say when discussing her book: 'Man's attitude toward nature is today critically important simply because we have now acquired a fateful power to alter and destroy nature. But man is a part of nature, and his war against nature is inevitably a war against himself.'[32]

Silent Spring did result in a nationwide ban on DDT for agricultural uses, though not before the agricultural industry had spent over a quarter of a million dollars vilifying Carson's research and Carson herself.

Carson's early death from cancer in 1964 predated the birth of second-wave feminism by just a few years. Right from its inception in the closing years of the 1960s, that movement was critically engaged with our relation to the natural world, albeit in varying and sometimes controversial ways. The radical feminist and American philosopher Susan Griffin, for example, wrote her lyrical text *Woman and Nature: The Roaring inside Her* in 1978, to denounce the disparaging identification of women with nature so common in patriarchal Western philosophy, religion, language, and culture generally.

Men have declared their dominance over women and nature alike, she argued, setting themselves above both. Women and nature were both exploited and silenced, seen as 'passive and inert', with women thought to be less evolved than men.[33] That book sold over 100,000 copies, and is usually cited as the first feminist text drawing connections between sexism, racism, and ecological destruction.[34]

Most second-wave feminists agreed that it is androcentric thinking, aligning women with nature, which in different ways assists men in exploiting them both, while obscuring the interconnections between humans and the rest of the world. The late French radical feminist Françoise d'Eaubonne had coined the term 'ecofeminism' in her fiery text *Feminism or Death* (1974), in which she accused the patriarchy of destroying women and nature alike.[35] On this view, only feminism, combined with environmentalism, could enable the planet to flourish.

Ecofeminism proposed an alternative worldview that saw the earth as sacred, knowing that all of us depend upon it. However, many feminists, including myself in my first book, *Is the Future Female?* (1987), had reservations. For ecofeminism mimicked aspects of androcentric essentialism by associating women with the 'feminine', or the 'maternal', thus indeed suggesting that women overall remained closer to nature than men, at least culturally, and therefore it was women who had to lead the struggle to save the planet. We see this view again in the influential feminist spirituality expressed by the US activist and author Starhawk. Her goal was the creation of nurturing human communities responsive to the cycles of nature, as imagined in her book *The Spiral Dance* (1979).

Along similar lines, the renowned Indian scholar and activist Vandana Shiva has been writing and speaking for decades about the ways in which women's daily engagement in reproductive and domestic work, involving diverse skills that resist specialization, equips them to perform multiple caring tasks and gives them a special connection to the environment. This is even truer in subsistence economies, where women are always aware of their reliance on nature. Through her many books, including *Staying Alive: Women, Ecology and Development*, first published in 1988, Shiva became a figurehead for local resistance movements in India, fighting against the aggressive incursions of multinationals bent on destroying agricultural resources and other public space.[36]

Yet, if ecofeminism was seen by many as 'the fluffy end of feminism', it nevertheless played an important role in the growth of the environmental movement, nowadays so crucial in climate activism. It begins with the acknowledgement that we indeed form part of the natural world, the most destructive part. Therefore we must totally transform our relationships to one another and to the natural world – indeed, to the planet itself. The compelling writing of the late Australian philosopher and green activist Val Plumwood, published from the early 1970s, played a key role in developing the kind of eco-philosophy that now forms part of an influential critical ecofeminism.

Plumwood's best-known work, *Feminism and the Mastery of Nature* (1993), begins by disowning the dominant form of Western rationality that denied humans' dependence on the non-human, and saw 'Nature' as the realm of those defined as 'inferior'. Gender, race, and class oppression all connect with this denial of the links between humans and other animals within the natural order – which when humans are involved, she suggests, is perhaps better described as natural chaos.[37]

After presenting awareness of our connection to nature as pivotal for feminism, Plumwood moves on to show that a more egalitarian relation with nature necessarily includes the virtues of friendship and openness to the needs of others, in the broadest possible sense. Indeed, in agreement with what I have suggested throughout this book, Plumwood argues that such democratic openness follows from the recognition of our shared human dependency, responsibilities, and interconnections, which will vary along with the distinct nature of the regions we inhabit.

Indigenous People and Climate Change Resistance

Plumwood's writing overlaps with the analysis expressed in much Indigenous writing and activism. For instance, the scholar and militant Kim TallBear, born on a South Dakota reservation, writes of the physical elimination of Indigenous people in the US, along with the violent dispossession of their lands and culture. Echoing extensive Indigenous activism from around the world, not least in my birthplace in Australia, she discusses the sapping effects of settler colonialism wherever it occurs:

> The issue is not only that material dispossession of land and 'resources' builds the settler state but also that 'dispossession' undercuts co-constitutive relations between beings. Property literally undercuts Indigenous kinship and attempts to replace it. It objectifies the land and water and other-than-human beings as potentially owned resources.[38]

Back in 1992, the Guatemalan Indigenous campaigner Rigoberta Menchú was awarded the Nobel Peace Prize for her work on the rights of Indigenous peoples and the need for reconciliation between ethnic groups. However, there has been limited progress towards this goal. Instead, the dispossession of Indigenous people has continued around the globe. It is therefore hardly surprising that Indigenous people have spearheaded so many ecological campaigns to defend their lands and resources. Most climate activists are well aware that deferring to Indigenous knowledge and involving local communities is one of the best ways to protect forests and other natural resources, in hopes of keeping climate change in check.

In southern Africa, this includes wildlife protection in transfrontier conservation areas, such as the Selous–Niassa corridor along the Tanzania and Mozambique borders. There have also been continuous struggles to protect the rich forests and nature reserves along the Amazon River, above all in the Cordillera del Condor that borders Ecuador and Peru. This has been fought over by those two countries for decades, and especially since copper-rich ore was found there in 2000. Despite protests from the Indigenous Shuar and Saraguro Kichwa communities, the Ecuadorian government handed out concessions to multiple international mining companies, leading to the contamination of rivers and the forcible eviction of local families by the mining companies.

The Amazon Basin, which contains the world's largest rainforests, is home to Indigenous people from nine different countries, ethnic groups who have struggled for generations to make their voice heard on the global stage. In 1984 the Confederation of Indigenous Organizations of the Amazon Basin (COICA) was founded in Peru, under the coordination of José Gregorio Díaz Mirabal. Díaz not only describes COICA as fighting to halt deforestation and preserve land, but also links their struggles to global climate change, the battle to preserve human life overall. Practically, COICA has been calling on COP forums to guarantee that 80 per cent of the Amazon will remain protected by 2025.

It is now widely recognized that the natural world is richer and more diverse where Indigenous people live, since their lifestyle keeps them directly in touch with the land. However, struggling to protect that land, especially against invasive mining or farming companies, has led to enormous suffering and loss of life for Indigenous people. Another deadly conflict involves the Karen, a major ethnic group in Myanmar, who have been fighting for autonomy for about seventy years. Massacres and persecution have forced tens of thousands of Karen from their homes. Myanmar's eastern frontier with Thailand is an important strip of biodiversity that combines the ancestral lands of about 350 Indigenous communities who collectively manage the area. However, here as elsewhere we find arrests and murders amid the displacement of tens of thousands of Indigenous people, despite previously agreed entitlements to protect their landholdings.[39]

Some of their leaders who manage to survive have been able to find a voice working with the UN on the Rights of Indigenous Peoples. One of these is the Filipina activist Victoria Tauli-Corpuz, who helped organize Indigenous struggles against the destructive Chico River Hydroelectric Dam project under Ferdinand Marcos in the 1980s. She has reported regularly on the appalling number of forest dwellers and defenders who were declared 'terrorists' and killed, simply for trying to protect their lands.[40] Another report, from 2020, revealed that over 300 environmental activists were killed in that year alone, again mostly Indigenous people campaigning to protect their land rights against logging, mining, large-scale agribusiness, hydroelectric dams, and other intrusions, with half of those murders occurring in Colombia. Tragically, Global Witness estimates that well over 1,000 environmental defenders have been murdered since the Paris Climate Accords were signed in 2015, and that number continues to rise.[41]

Very much in harmony with Indigenous struggles, the Black Lives Matter movement (BLM) has pointed out that the climate crisis is a racist crisis, linked historically to slavery and imperial aggression, along with industrialization, which now requires a reparative redistribution of global resources. As the Black British film director and climate activist Ashish Ghadiali points out: 'Successive climate summits have disregarded the needs of the world's most vulnerable communities and delivered control of the international climate conversation into the hands of global corporations, including BlackRock and Shell.'[42] These are precisely the corporate groups that have obstructed decarbonization for years, and acted purely in their own interest, even when ostensibly declaring their conversion to a new green capitalist transition, or Net Zero by 2050.

The hollowness of this conversion is evident in the total lack of corporate concern for global inequality and related water and food shortages. In contrast, any genuine engagement with climate issues has to begin by addressing the immediate impact of planetary heating, which requires nothing less than a global transformation of the relationship of all people towards each other and the natural world we share. As we've seen, this runs thoroughly counter to the present state-protected, deregulated, capitalist relations of production and exchange, which will always be driven by hunger for growth and profits. Market growth is the problem, not the solution.

Climate Justice

We keep hearing that the window of opportunity to act on the climate emergency is closing rapidly. As I write, it's reported that temperatures in parts of Antarctica are an extraordinary 40°C (or 104°F) degrees higher than the seasonal average; they have also reached 30°C increases at the North Pole. Lisa Schipper, from the Environmental Change Institute at Oxford University, exclaimed despairingly in March 2022: 'If these extreme temperatures don't wake people up about this urgency, at the same time as war threatens to encourage more fossil fuel extraction and use, I don't know what will.'[43] Nor do I.

We know that before any real progress can be made, nation-states, especially richer states, must drastically change gear and pour money into alternative, non-combustible energy solutions. This was the whole point of the UN's IPCC, reminding states that year-on-year the failure to cut fossil fuel emissions was making the world terrifyingly unsafe. That first Kyoto Protocol of 1997 included the acknowledgement that highly developed, historically more polluting countries should take most of the responsibility for curbing emissions, under the principle of 'common but differentiated responsibility and respective capabilities'.[44]

Yet, despite all the subsequent meetings, including the historic 2015 Paris Agreement in which the participants committed to keeping the rise in global temperatures below 2°C, and to strive to limit it to 1.5°, *not one* of these pledges has been met. Not only has fossil fuel consumption hardly fallen in most richer countries, but in the United States, Canada, and Australia it has *increased*. In the UK, employment in the low-carbon and renewable-energy economy has actually shrunk, especially in factories producing energy-efficient products, onshore wind, and solar energy.[45] Given that Western nations continue to enable and reward over-consumption, how do we strengthen resistance to global warming?

Facing the nonchalance and denial of most governments, refusing even to begin to engage seriously with the scale of the emergency, some climate militants have called for a shift to a full-fledged revolutionary agenda. Most conspicuously, the Swedish historian and radical activist Andreas Malm, backed by others in the Swedish Zetkin Collective, has already produced three texts promoting the building of rebel cadres to overcome the escalating catastrophe mismanaged by our vacillating states.

Malm scorns the non-violence of existing climate activism, along with the climate fatalism of those who fail to act at all. His most provocative text, *How to Blow Up a Pipeline*, proposes revolutionary sabotage. On this view, nothing short of extreme climate militancy can prevail, requiring a movement of millions organized around one goal: 'Damage and destroy new CO_2-emitting devices. Put them out of commission, pick them apart, demolish them, burn them, blow them up. Let the capitalists who keep on investing in the fire know that their properties will be trashed.'[46]

Elsewhere, in *Corona, Climate, Chronic Emergency*, Malm argues that the climate crisis was also responsible for the COVID-19 pandemic. It had been predicted and was preventable! Yet persistent warnings were, as usual, simply ignored, and wild animals continued encroaching into human eating chains. Moreover, without drastic change, Malm notes that more pandemics are certainly on the way. Deforestation in south-east Asia is expected to force 99 per cent of the region's bats to migrate by 2050, with 3,000 strains of coronavirus circulating among these bat species. Malm lists various moves that could defuse these disaster scenarios: the nationalization of oil and gas companies and their conversion 'into organizations for carbon dioxide removal' (through air capture technology); a ban on wildlife meat consumption and the phasing out of all meat; an end to most air travel. 'We must say that some forms of consumption are non-essential and outright destructive, and exacerbate the risk of future pandemics, and these forms will have to be regulated.'[47]

Of course, Malm knows how hard it will be to get nation-states or global corporations to end their investment in fossil fuels – not least since Russia's war in Ukraine set off a scramble for immediate new gas and oil supplies to prevent a looming energy crisis. Indeed, even before Russia's invasion in 2022, Western governments were directing tens of billions of recovery funds to industries involved in fossil fuel production.

Meanwhile, these same exploitative corporations were busy 'greenwashing' their products to hide the reality that their mode of operation is always to put profits before people, or any concern for the environment. Indeed, almost all major brands today, and some governments, make brazen claims of being environmentally friendly trying to conceal the significantly polluting or ecologically damaging reality. Ryanair's claim that their planes produce 'low emissions' was simply among the more absurd. Another egregious example is that of Innocent drinks, which advertises on TV with cartoons of cute animals singing about recycling and fixing the planet. In fact, the company is owned by Coca-Cola, recognized as one of the worst polluters in the world.

To point out that state investment following COVID was a lost opportunity for environmental justice is a colossal under-statement.[48] Ominously, too, the current rise of the far right is distinguished by defence of fossil fuels and denial of the climate crisis. This was patent in Trump's withdrawal from the Paris Agreement in 2019 and Bolsonaro's aggressive deforestation in Brazil, as well as in the programme of Alternative for Germany or of the far-right Swedish Democrats.

Yet, frightening as these challenges remain, as more people witness the effects of climate breakdown, near and far, there exist some forms of leverage for defending the environment apart from, or perhaps alongside, Malm's revolutionary road. Not only are non-violent climate activists of every stripe tirelessly demonstrating for radical change, but so, too, are many mainstream organizations globally, beginning with the UN, all preaching radical transition. The left, green, or social-democratic factions in most progressive political parties are now unanimous that urgent action is needed, all too aware, as we saw above, that earlier action could have softened this predicament.

Moreover, a few countries, including New Zealand under Jacinda Ardern and Finland under their recent prime minister Sanna Marin, had already led the way in integrating educational materials on climate change and environmental protection into the school curriculum. Jeremy Corbyn, when leader of the Labour Party, placed green politics at the centre of his 2019 manifesto. That manifesto promised a national investment bank and 1 million jobs in green energy, reskilling the population to help reach a zero-carbon economy. That same year, Alexandria Ocasio-Cortez, from the small but conspicuous left wing of the US Democratic Party, submitted a Green New Deal to the House of Representatives. It called for the achievement of 'net-zero greenhouse gases within the decade and a full transition away from fossil fuels', and pledged to refit every building in the country to meet new energy-efficient standards.

The people who have campaigned for the longest, publicizing and even rendering fashionable the idea of some form of Green New Deal, place climate justice at the heart of environmental politics, in tandem with an end to capitalism as we know it. They include the British feminist economist Ann Pettifor, or the renowned Canadian author and activist Naomi Klein, with her influential *Leap Manifesto*. They know, of course, the herculean task of detaching nation-states from the corporate interests that have been funding and influencing them, often despairing over the difficulties of pushing states to change course and legislate against the extractive industries.

We also know this needs to happen first and foremost in the richer countries, while they donate the money needed for clean energy in poorer nations, along with projects for rewilding and the prevention of deforestation. However, Pettifor and Klein agree with climate activists everywhere that defeatism is not an option, despite the daunting sums required to begin to repair past environmental damage.[49]

This is why hopes for change continue to circulate within the mass resistance of hundreds of thousands globally, from schoolchildren to nonagenarians – from Greta Thunberg to Phil Kingston, in his late eighties, or the Indigenous Brazilian leader Raoni Metuktire, in her nineties. Alongside the many reasons for gloom, resistance continues, with climate leaders believing they have not only an obligation to resist, but a duty to keep hope alive, caring for each other and the world itself in the process.

'Every protest shifts the world's balance', or at least contributes to doing so, the American eco-activist and storyteller Rebecca Solnit assures us.[50] Monbiot concurs as he searches for ways 'out of the wreckage', suggesting that altruism and concern for the feelings of others are part of our evolved humanity, however much orchestrated individualism tries to undermine them. Our goal needs to involve passionate calls for greater democracy in every area of life, from the local to the global to enable each of us to feel a shared belonging as, step by step, we wrest spaces back from the market into genuine public ownership. This would bestow on everyone a sense of private sufficiency in the midst of broader public luxury, as opposed to what we have now – limited private luxury in the midst of widespread public squalor.[51]

A similar argument in praise of 'communal luxury' is developed by Jason Hickel in his popular book *Less Is More: How Degrowth Will Save the World*, contending that 'degrowth' policies can regenerate our damaged planet and avert catastrophe. This vision is one in which food and other forms of essential production, including supplies of renewable energy, would be more localized, with real democratic control over them and greater use of public infrastructures generally, such as transport.[52]

Finally, despite the hot air from governments only pretending to invest in alternative energy, the possibility that wind and solar energy *could* keep the global electric grid running is not just a pipe dream, at least according to Mark Jacobson and his fellow researchers at California's Stanford University.[53] Indeed, some nations – including Iceland, Costa Rica, Namibia, and Norway – are already producing more than 90 per cent of their electricity from clean sources.[54]

Negating Despair by Building Climate Agency

Many of us are familiar with Rosa Luxemburg's powerful slogan 'Socialism or Barbarism', formulated over a century ago during the First World War. Today, 'Ecosocialism or Barbarism' seems too weak to encompass the perils of planetary collapse prophesied by so many climate scientists – 'Conversion or Catastrophe', perhaps.

Catastrophic thinking has traditionally been treated by clinicians as pathological. But at a time when the International Psychoanalytical Association recognizes climate change as 'the biggest global health threat of the twenty-first century', psychologists and clinicians alike are recommending it: 'The cataclysmic realities of climate change call upon all of us to cultivate catastrophic thinking.'[55] Accordingly, the American psychoanalyst Susan Kassouf, having listened to her patients' frequent alarm over climate change, says she has learned from such catastrophic thinking that a certain sense of powerlessness, dependence, and despair does not necessarily entail a loss of agency or the shutting down of social and political action.

On the contrary, she reflects that 'vulnerability does not mean weakness ... our bodies are porous and fragile'. We should hardly need reminding. Kassouf quotes one of her patients saying, 'I got where I am because I led with my vulnerability.' Acknowledging trauma, indeed thinking through trauma, however troubling, she now believes, helps us all to recognize what should be our shared anguish in relation to climate change. Perhaps in cultivating more 'catastrophic thinking in our lives and practice', she concludes, 'we can become more conscious of a renewed thankfulness to be alive at all.'[56]

Thinking along similar lines, the Welsh psychologist Stuart Capstick contests the view that acknowledging the climate crisis means living dismal and restricted lives of self-denial.[57] It's true that melancholic resignation might seem inevitable, when on the one hand we hear government lies and evasion, and on the other, news bulletins berate us that 'it's now or never' for avoiding the end of the world.[58] Yet it is interesting to read that the sweeping global research conducted by Capstick and his colleagues on environmental attitudes found a persistent correlation between concern for the environment and personal well-being.[59]

Data was collected from nearly 7,000 people across seven countries, and in each case a measure of involvement in conservation work, reducing waste, or buying green products accompanied greater personal satisfaction scores, in both high- and low-income brackets. Of course, the researchers are aware that this correlation can mean that a personal sense of well-being may be what drives ecologically caring behaviour, as much as the reverse. However, it does support the idea that managing, in whatever way possible, to feel some small sense of agency in relation to environmental issues is one way of preventing crippling anxieties from overwhelming us.

Nevertheless, this is no substitute for forcing states to stop investing in polluting corporations and damaging industries. But we need to work on many fronts to help us get there. For instance, at local levels in the UK, municipal councils have been pursuing a diversity of anti-pollution policies: Bristol Energy Cooperative is a community-owned initiative to build a low-carbon energy infrastructure for that city, tied in with the council's City Leap project.[60] Within the EU there are also already diverse packages aiming towards a sustainable green transition. In the US it is Vermont, whose senior senator is Bernie Sanders, that has the most renewable-energy resources of any state. The city of Burlington, Vermont, already generates almost 100 per cent of its in-state electricity through wind and solar power.[61]

Yet, in our already overheated planet, only attempts at climate *justice* can take us to the heart of the problem. There will need to be global support from richer nations for global reforesting, as well as provision for small-scale farming and a wholesale decrease in intensive agribusiness, with an end to the factory farming of animals. Thinking globally means richer nations assisting public ownership of clean energy projects in poorer ones, along with resources for the expansion of quality public transport, water, and housing infrastructures, accompanying universal public healthcare provision.[62]

However, smaller actions of many kinds are also relevant for promoting more environmentally sustainable lifestyles, advancing alternative forms of collective consumption and shared pleasure. This is what the philosopher Kate Soper, among others, has been exploring for some time.[63] There are real pleasures to be had in moving away from carbon-heavy lifestyles to invent instead more collective models, while rebuilding notions of neighbourliness and putting our imaginations to radical use in fighting for or helping to deliver improved caring facilities for everyone. The push for a shorter paid working week is crucial here, and nowadays it seems to be gaining real traction.

Once again, these ideas tie in with feminists' consistent calls to place care at the heart of politics. As we outlined in our *Care Manifesto*, what we need is inventive forms of collective care at every scale of life – from our most intimate ties to our relationship with the planet itself. For care work is green work, wherever it is done, as opposed to carbon-intensive technological investments. Prioritizing care at any level, as we have seen, means reinvigorating welfare states and building communities strengthened by cooperative and public ownership, rather than relying upon profit-led global corporations. It is work that can improve all our lives, especially when in need, as well as providing meaningful and necessary work. Care work will be all the more rewarding once we invest in it and make sure it is adequately paid.

There are many more strategies to push for that promote the immediate, practical changes needed to enhance our daily lives and improve public infrastructures through switching to technologies that are minimally polluting and extractive. Encouraging this, of course, means moving right away from the competitive individualism of recent decades, knowing that there is no healthy, nor even viable, future unless we put our relationships to each other first and cherish the natural world we inhabit. Often the obvious has to be endlessly restated, and fought for many times over, though fortunately we have a small army of eco-warriors doing just that.

This army consists primarily of dedicated climate campaign groups such as Extinction Rebellion (XR), now active globally. Its thoughts are laid out in a rich and exuberant manifesto, *This Is Not a Drill*, surveying the impact of environmental damage on different populations everywhere, and pondering how best to resist. Sidestepping all the cultural roadblocks placed in the way, the manifesto aims to inform people about the many practical things they can do. With contributors ranging from an Indian farmer to a Californian firefighter, and including the visionary feminist economist Kate Raworth, the Indigenous activist Hindou Oumarou Ibrahim, the Green Party MP Caroline Lucas, and Clive Lewis from the Labour Party, the variety of pressure and activism methods described here reaches well beyond XR's fluid tactics.[64]

As the powerfully persuasive Rowan Williams concludes, cautiously, in the afterword to the XR manifesto: 'It might work. It is just possible that sustained pressure will bring about a modest change of heart among decision makers and "wealth creators" and some serious adjustments *might* be made.'

However, he, too, knows just how hard it remains to persuade our politicians and corporate entrepreneurs to switch course, away from the massive distortion and denial to which they cling. Too many have successfully suppressed any sense of what it means to live in alignment with the rest of the world, able only to think in terms of technological triumph. Yet, in surprisingly radical language, Williams finally decides that, paradoxically, only a revolution can now bring us back from the 'insanely dangerous places' we now inhabit. 'Anger, love and joy may sound like odd bedfellows,' he says, 'but these are the seeds of a future that will offer life – not success, but life.' For those of us alive at this moment in history, he concludes, it is our job to join that revolution.[65]

From the US, the influential feminist scholar Donna Haraway clearly agrees: 'Our task is to make trouble, to stir up potent response to devastating events, as well as to settle troubled waters and rebuild quiet places.'[66] We certainly have ever more devastating events to respond to right now. Yet, I suspect we can only continue to do this if we also rebuild those quiet places, reaching out as often as we can to mitigate the resentment between people and to create connections across differences, and across borders.

It is true that the climate emergency cannot be addressed simply at local or national levels, though it certainly must begin there. It means rebuilding our locally based services and devising community wealth projects, while always appreciating the ways in which we are all interconnected well beyond these levels. Thinking globally surely confirms that any long-term future for the human species means finding alternatives to the continuing capitalist present, which has been so destructive of the lifeworld on which we all depend.

6

Caring Futures

Life at present is plagued by drama and emergencies. My own generation, born in the mid-twentieth century, has been called the golden generation – often upwardly mobile and likely to lead better lives than any generation before or, crucially, since. As the twenty-first century progressed, tough times began to hit a multitude of people of all ages. Essential resources are now harder to access, whether for housing, healthcare, or sometimes food – even some of the employed are forced to use food banks. Yet, practices of resistance and hope have not disappeared, and nowadays they often involve the need not just to prioritize care but to revolutionize it.

In small ways this is happening all around us. On my doorstep, I see friends and neighbours helping out at local food banks or preparing and serving meals at numerous community venues. These include the Second Chance Café in Stoke Newington, where nowadays I often go on a Friday for a delicious lunch – free for those on a shoestring, with voluntary donations from others. The goal is not just to meet basic needs, but to help create and nurture an alternative sense of community, in a world where self-interest and profit supposedly rule supreme. Similar alternative ventures are now popping up in many community settings, even as traditional resources, including once flourishing commercial life, are increasingly imperilled.

Essential workers, whether in health, transport, or education, have been taking to the streets in recent years demanding better wages and conditions, knowing how far their living standards and working conditions have deteriorated, while profoundly troubled by the impact this has on the care and provision they can provide. Unusually, their militancy has met with much public support, despite the difficulties they create for people. Further afield, activist volunteers are attempting to offer care and assistance around the globe for those in most need.

It seems clear that more people than ever are coming to see that we can only ensure human survival once we start to place care and concern for each other at the heart of our politics, and the centre of our lives. If we are to avoid a calamitous future, we have to move away from a world based on private accumulation and replace it with a politics of care, solidarity, and equality, cultivating a caring consciousness in all our social interactions.

The missing element, however, is any move to prioritize care at government or corporate levels, other than speciously. As one of my British care collaborators, Bev Skeggs, comments: 'One thing that never stops astonishing me is how our society rewards the most careless, those who can and do care less about other people.'[1] That is why wherever we look we see evidence of chilling cruelty towards those in greatest need, often coming precisely from the people with greatest power to act otherwise. 'Cruelty towards other people is a cornerstone of government policy', says the British Pakistani writer Kamila Shamsie, lamenting the tragic effects of ten years of 'hostile environment' in the UK – a policy deliberately designed to make life impossible for undocumented migrants, even though many of those targeted and often deported were actually entitled to stay, resulting in horrendous suffering.[2]

Moving beyond Pessimism

In Britain we now know that a decade of heightened welfare cuts, combined with the harmful effects of Brexit and the global pandemic, have left over 14 million people in poverty, almost half of them disabled or living in a family with someone who is. In the United States, still the wealthiest country in the world, nearly 40 million people (11 per cent) live in poverty. Indeed, the eminent French economist Thomas Piketty concluded from his research there some years ago that steeply rising inequality is now simply the normal state of affairs, with zero growth in incomes for the bottom 50 per cent over the last thirty years, while the incomes of the top 1 per cent grew by 300 per cent. As he concluded in his book *Capital in the Twenty-First Century*, the top 1 per cent have 'behaved like bandits' at the expense of the 99 per cent. Such chronic, and now worsening, structural inequalities inevitably leave millions of working families in poverty, especially those who have always been marginalized in the United States: its Black and Brown citizens, as well as immigrants and refugees, with disproportionate numbers of women and girls.[3]

In such harsh times, it can be difficult to move on from simply listing the endless inequities and horrors of the moment to focus instead on glimmers of hope. We have only to heed the UN estimate of over 84 million displaced people globally to feel a certain helplessness.[4] But this is not the first time that people have felt beleaguered by despair, even when stoutly trying to offer an affirming flame. If W. H. Auden could manage to express such a longing on the eve of 'September 1, 1939', we must realize that the search for affirmation against despair is the only place to begin – although, like Auden, we will surely remain 'uncertain and afraid', even when refusing to succumb to illusion or denial.[5]

At the end of the twentieth century, the romantic figurehead of the Chiapas Indigenous uprising in Mexico, the Zapatista leader Subcomandante Marcos, wrote dramatically of the 'Fourth World War Against Humanity'. His summary of the global situation is concise and convincing: he limns the obscene concentration of global wealth by the very few and the extension of 'hopeless poverties'; the contraction of democratic controls and the intensification of state repression; the breakdown of communities; enforced emigration; the inevitable creation of surplus populations – the landless, the homeless, and the imprisoned, who are treated as social 'waste'. Yet his conclusion was equally clear – not to despair, but rather to build a 'new world' to defend the 'redundant' and the 'next-to-be-eliminated'.[6]

This is how the people who impress me most, near and far, are determined to proceed. I feel lucky that in my early political life our shared visions of new and better times were rarely clouded by intimations of despair. Though aware and supportive of anti-colonial struggles, Western activists back then were less attuned to extreme hardship in certain parts of the world – other than in exceptional times of conflict, as when almost two million Biafrans died of starvation during the Nigerian civil war at the close of the 1960s.

Decades later, as a person of Jewish descent, I became involved in the Palestinian struggle for peace and justice. And that was when I did experience not just frustration but often profound despair before the perpetual impasse in Palestinian attempts to stop Israeli land grabs and military incursions into what little remains of their ancestral lands. Daily atrocities are multiplying even as I write.

To date, for many Palestinians yearning for free movement and an end to brutal occupation, the only options are either simply resisting or surviving despair, though any form of collective defiance helps. So many remain at all times sitting targets for bombs or bullets coming from the Israel Defense Forces (IDF), which are never far from their doorstep. Yet, against all possible odds, their struggle continues, as does that of the Jewish Israeli leftists who support them. This includes those producing +972 magazine, or who are active in Breaking the Silence, and all who work to support the six leading Palestinian human rights organizations, committed to peace and justice, which were so fraudulently declared 'terrorist organizations' by the Israeli state in 2021.

Back in the UK, when government policies depressing wages and welfare have jeopardized the economic survival of millions, combating despair is sometimes necessary on my own doorstep. It is more urgent than ever to acknowledge the absurdity of this situation, given how wealthy Britain remains as a nation, whatever its global decline. I have now spent over five decades being politically active here, with redistribution, equality, and cultural respect for difference and diversity as my constant goals. However, today I would begin by highlighting the role that care and compassion must play in our politics as we work for any worthwhile and sustainable future.

The radical notion of care, defined broadly to include all activities that enable human life to flourish, alongside the nurturing of non-human and planetary well-being, is quite distinct from benevolence or pity. 'Pity would be no more, / If we did not make somebody Poor.' In the meantime, respect and dignity for all life must be our goal, as it was for Blake, 'in this valley of misery and happiness mixed'.

Many of my political friends and acquaintances, who have also spent much of their lives working towards kinder, more egalitarian times, had begun hoping that the global pandemic might help amplify calls for change. Surely it was finally time to turn against the sponsoring of inflated individualism and unfettered market practices that had been wreaking such social havoc over the last four decades.

Might not this 'pan-demic', this threat to 'all-people', encourage some new thinking in relation to our shared vulnerability? It had spotlighted so strongly our global interdependence, and our lifelong needs for differing forms of care and support – which hitherto most people had usually preferred to ignore. Moreover, as we saw, at its height the pandemic *did* stimulate heroic efforts of sacrifice and nurturing from care workers globally, as well as generate a host of grassroots practices of mutual aid for those in want of care and companionship, some of which continue today.

However, among those in a position to change things, memories are short and actions habitually duplicitous. Globally, we clapped for our 'carers', especially those working in hospitals, during the height of the pandemic. Then, without batting an eyelid, our governments continued to ignore or devalue much of the essential labour that sustains us all. Care workers are still as underpaid as ever, while few if any public resources remain available to support those engaged in unpaid caring work at home. At the close of 2022, nurses in the UK reluctantly came out on strike for the first time ever, while other workers across our essential services – in transport, education, mail, energy, and the civil service – were forced to take strike action to prevent their already sinking wages from falling even further, heightening the rampant cost-of-living crisis.

Looking towards the future, obviously we all start from very different places: some in wretched physical displacement from former homes and livelihoods, others adequately affluent if often time-poor, a significant minority facing alarming deprivation, even homelessness. But many, perhaps most, of us are worried about the world we will be leaving behind for future generations. However, once we factor in environmental concerns, along with all the shifts needed to enable us to place care for others at the centre of our politics, it's not so difficult to see what needs to change.

The Cameroonian anti-colonial theorist Achille Mbembe, who has written extensively about the horrors of slavery, colonial depredation, and contemporary dispossession, proposes that today, 'the political in our time must start from the imperative to reconstruct the world in common'. Colonizers once travelled to different parts of the world to exploit them, reallocating resources from the lands they seized and from the people who had long resided there, while claiming possession of what had never belonged to them. Today, as Mbembe eloquently summarizes, the reverse needs to be done. Humans must admit that we 'coevolve with the biosphere, depend on it, are defined with and through it and owe each other a debt of responsibility and care'.[7]

Of course, everything still remains to be fought for if we are to begin to turn around the unrelenting capitalist search for profits, which, in the process, so often disrupts lives and livelihoods, sometimes rendering people discarded and destitute. It's why so many progressive activists have been involved in battles against incarceration, as well as in attempts to provide shelter and assistance for refugees and asylum seekers, supporting them in their journey to find safe havens in new homelands.

Caring Abolitionists

In the midst of continual setbacks there has been occasional good news, which highlights what can happen when a caring politics takes on the careless cruelty routinely tolerated. For instance, in the world's richest 'democracy', which preserves its spectacular inequality with the world's highest incarceration rates, US prison abolitionists and champions of radical criminal justice reform have won a few significant victories. They point the way towards what could be more caring futures.

In Los Angeles in 2022, programmes for reducing incarceration by providing alternative forms of care attracted serious attention. Three years earlier, in 2019, one of the many coalitions against mass incarceration in Los Angeles, involving more than fifty local community organizations, unions, and activist groups, succeeded in stopping a large prison expansion plan, gaining instead official endorsement for their programme of alternatives to prison through expansions of welfare. The following year, Los Angeles adopted a 'Care First, Jail Last' strategy, promising 'treatment and services to those in need, instead of arrest and jail'.

The police murder of George Floyd that same year (May 2020) was pivotal in turning Black Lives Matter, at least briefly, into one of the largest movements in US history, with their calls to 'defund the police'. It was also crucial in reinforcing the apparently less threatening Care First, Jail Last agenda. Always highlighting the role of racism and poverty behind detention rates, anti-prison organizers successfully pushed for 10 per cent of the county's available general funds to be invested in implementing their welfare agenda.

As the whole of the world soon learned, George Floyd was a Black man who had lost his job not long before the white police officer Derek Chauvin knelt on his neck for almost ten minutes, as he lay handcuffed, face down on the street. Before being crushed to death, Floyd was crying, 'I can't breathe', as three other officers looked on. Well over 1,000 more people have been killed by police since Floyd's death, but while police violence continues unabated, many states have been watching the success of anti-prison activists in Los Angeles, wondering what they can learn from their 'groundbreaking roadmap for decarceration and service expansion'.[8]

However, any success has been a very long time coming. It is over fifty years since America's most famous prison reformer, a global icon of Black resistance, Angela Davis, edited her very first book, *If They Come in the Morning: Voices of Resistance* (1971). In that compilation of essays, letters, poetry, and articles, twenty-seven Black militants, including Davis herself, describe their own struggles against incarceration and the systemic use of arrest and imprisonment to crush Black struggles in the US. As has often been reported, it was her understanding of the role of prison in suppressing Black struggles that led Aretha Franklin to offer to pay Davis's bail, whatever it cost: 'Jail is hell to be in. I'm going to see her free ... because she's a black woman and she wants freedom for black people.'

Today, Davis fights on, as energetically as ever, alongside thousands of other abolition activists, including her friend, the

Black scholar and activist, Ruth Wilson Gilmore. Gilmore has spent the last three decades compiling a carceral geography across the States. The point these activists and writers are all making is that prison abolition is a constant cause. For it is about working for societies where the conditions of neglect and carelessness that push people along the route to prison must themselves be abolished. As Gilmore says, the struggle 'isn't just absence ... abolition is a fleshly and material presence of social life lived differently'.[9]

As all abolitionists spell out, defunding prisons requires the wholesale restructuring of our economic order, overturning the capitalist avariciousness that immiserated so many. They elaborate what those changes will involve if we are to rid societies of most forms of theft and violence: an end to homelessness through public housing; investment in all forms of welfare, including healthcare, childcare, education; the growth of democratically run jobs and inclusive communities, all geared towards nurturing each other, along with the earth's resources.

Davis, Gilmore, and other abolitionists have been making these points for decades, and they are reflected today in the outlook of Black Lives Matter (BLM). BLM's 2016 manifesto, 'Vision for Black Lives', lists six demands, including divestment from prisons and investment instead in education and healthcare, along with 'economic justice for all and a reconstruction of the economy to ensure our communities have collective ownership, not merely access'.[10]

The UK's anti-carceral movement has not been as vigorous. However, it is growing, and making all the same points about the need for investment in welfare, along with democratically run workplaces and communities. Here, too, the movement is led by Black activists involved in BLM. As one of their spokespeople, Adam Elliott-Cooper, describes in *Black Resistance to British Policing*, Black people are continuously confronting police racism in this country. This can be seen in the routine, and sometimes lethal, police violence against young Black men, along with the far harsher prison sentences handed out to Black defendants in the courtroom. Indeed, in a recent survey of legal professionals, over half of them reported seeing judges acting in a racially biased way.[11] Like US abolitionists, Elliott-Cooper argues that the fundamental struggle is to 'erode society's reliance on the police and prison systems, and instead empower community-led and social solutions to the inequalities that lead to harm in the first place'. Additionally, he points out that much of the resistance to police racism and the calls for prison abolition have been led by Black women.[12]

Black British women's anti-prison activism is reflected in the work of the Cradle Community, which recently published its first important intervention, *Brick by Brick: How We Build a World without Prisons*. This reveals that the UK's prison population is the largest in Western Europe, with some of the very worst conditions when compared to EU countries. Indeed, chillingly, someone dies in prison every four days. Also highlighting the social deprivation behind incarceration, the Cradle Community notes that two-thirds of prisoners are unemployed when arrested, with 15 per cent homeless and many suffering from mental health problems.

Furthermore, prisons comprehensively fail to provide any safe space to undo the cycle of violence and neglect that so many prisoners have been caught up in prior to their arrest. Nor does prison nowadays enable inmates to acquire useful skills with which they might contribute to society following their release. The Cradle Community puts forward a set of immediate demands to keep people out of prison, such as the decriminalization of sex work and the repeal of drug and vagrancy laws, along with the abolition of Stop and Search. Overall, however, they, too, believe that dismantling the carceral state means transforming society by removing the underpinnings of inequality, beginning with the provision of healthcare, education, and housing justice free from racism, along with an end to the criminalization of migrants.[13]

In the meantime, as the British criminologist Joe Sim has been explaining for decades, our prisons remain places of systematic humiliation, neglect, and indifference, generating desperation and despair for almost everyone who ends up inside them. His research in, for example, *Punishment and Prisons* not only confirms the pitilessness of prison regimes, but also describes their comprehensive failure to generate any form of rehabilitation.[14]

Sims emphasizes that most law-breakers rarely land in prison, especially those involved in corporate or state criminality. Prisons, as we have seen, are overwhelmingly reserved for the dispossessed, and increasingly racialized. With rare exceptions, in Sim's experience, the only care and compassion he has witnessed inside prison has come from fellow prisoners. Documenting the colossal levels of self-harm in men's and especially women's prisons, Sim argues that there will be no end to this cruelty until we see well-funded alternatives to custody operated by trained and committed staff, while simultaneously tackling the unpunished criminality of the powerful.

Supporting Refugees

Radical moves towards prison abolition are an essential part of any caring future. However, perhaps an even more urgent task today is that of tackling the global humanitarian crisis of displaced people in search of asylum. Over the last decade, there have been massive movements of migrants seeking refuge from places of conflict or destitution in their homelands of Africa, Afghanistan, Syria, and other parts of the Middle East. Instead of rising to the challenge, most European states have mercilessly fortified their borders, resulting in tens of thousands of migrant deaths annually.

The bodies of refugees now carpet the Mediterranean, turning it into the world's largest burial ground. This follows the reluctance of British and European states to rescue migrant boats in trouble, in what is called the 'left-to-die' policy following the death of sixty-three migrants heading to Italy from Libya in 2011. Despite sending distress signals, and while under NATO's watching eyes, they were left to drift for fourteen days until their small boat sank and all but nine were drowned.[15]

The British government's current shameful attempts to deport unauthorized refugees to Rwanda has rightly been described as treating refugees like 'human waste', all the more so when Rwanda is known to be a country where detention and torture are the norm for internal critics. It is even more despicable when there are no safe and lawful routes available to most refugees hoping to reach Britain, as shown in a recent report from Amnesty International UK. We already accept far fewer refugees than most other European countries and keep them in detention for longer.[16] Nevertheless, despite such murderous indifference, flagrant on so many levels, we have also seen impressive mobilizations of solidarity, care, and support for migrants, although rarely from official agencies.

In her inspiring collection *The New Internationalists* (2020), my friend Sue Clayton presents the reflections of sixty people from among the thousands of activist volunteers countering the inhumanity towards those in need of asylum.[17] Clayton herself worked to assist many children she found stranded in the Calais Jungle, documented in her impressive film, *Calais Children: A Case to Answer*. Other volunteers provided emergency aid for refugees, conducted sea rescues, or helped to organize protests and advocacy in support of migrants. These activists register the catastrophic failures of international NGOs, unable to do more than stand by as refugees are herded into oppressive 'holding grounds', waiting interminably for asylum applications to be processed. Witnessing the suffering of migrants of all ages, including many children travelling alone, volunteer activists sometimes themselves experience mental health issues, suggesting a need for psychological support for them, as well as for those stuck in limbo often for years.

As Clayton argues, these volunteers provide us with new examples of civic responsibility and practices of care and solidarity. Activists worldwide have, in different ways and with varying success, been striving to establish spaces of refuge and welcome for those who need it, while publicly calling out the inhumanity of the authorities.

There are other dilemmas for volunteer activists, some of whom may wonder just how useful they can actually be, while others face concrete threats from governments simply because they have assisted refugees. As I write, a group of two dozen volunteers in Greece are facing trial on charges including espionage, after rescuing refugees arriving on the island of Lesbos. One of the defendants is the former Syrian refugee and champion swimmer Sarah Mardini, whose story of helping fellow refugees cross the sea from Turkey to Greece inspired the film *The Swimmers*.

The harrowing experiences of refugee activists are currently being recorded in Refugee History posts, including those by Tess Berry-Hart, the British author and playwright who helped establish the remarkable and still-ongoing grassroots charity Calais Action, in the summer of 2015.[18] Ever since, Calais Action has collected supplies for shipping containers offering succour to refugees in Calais, Dunkirk, Samos, and Athens. Such work is supported by the French volunteer group L'Auberge des Migrants, and many other grassroots organizations across Europe, especially visible in Greece, where so many refugees seeking entry to Western countries find themselves backed up. This includes the creation of the Athens Solidarity Centre (ASC), supported by the municipality, plus a swathe of other grassroots initiatives committed to assisting refugees, including those escaping from detention centres such as in Lesbos.

Working for a more caring future thus means listening to the unheard stories and reflections of refugees themselves, explaining why they have been forced to flee their birthplaces. Daniel Trilling's *Lights in the Distance: Exile and Refuge on the Borders of Europe* follows some dozen refugees, highlighting the strength they have needed simply to stay alive in the dangerous years they typically spend trying to find any safe haven in Europe. Despite the racism they encountered and the deaths or imprisonments of fellow migrants they witnessed, Trilling reports that each of the refugees he interviewed still hoped simply to be allowed to contribute to the new societies they were attempting to reach and find shelter in.[19]

There are currently many significant initiatives designed to encourage and nourish stories from all displaced people, such as the Stories in Transit project, created and managed by Marina Warner in London and Valentina Castagna in Palermo. The goal is to construct what the Palestinian poet Mahmoud Darwish described as 'a country of words' that can help strengthen the rights, identities, and resilience of people on the move.[20]

Tragically, however, many asylum seekers continue to experience discrimination and abandonment once they do finally arrive in the countries they have endured so much to reach. In England, for example, an extraordinary 200 asylum-seeking children recently went missing after being placed in hotels run by the Home Office. As people had warned, the lack of adequate supervision or care for these children made them easy prey for criminal networks who would spirit them away into lives of exploitation and abuse. Meanwhile, 150,000 asylum seekers in the UK are currently stranded, unable to work, waiting for their claims to be assessed by the Home Office. Worse, they often encounter organized abuse and hostility in whatever dismal accommodation they are being held. Reactionary anti-immigrant forces are encouraged by government talk of a migrant 'invasion', a shameful description of people in need of asylum. Meanwhile, the UK has taken in the lowest number of asylum seekers in Europe, only about a third that of Germany.

Of course, the official hostility towards and neglect of those on the move globally is not confined to Europe and America. My own birthplace, Australia, was ahead of the game with its disgraceful asylum strategy. Australia's prolonged offshore imprisonment of refugees trying to enter Australia in the notorious Manus Island detention centre in Papua New Guinea has been exposed in the powerful writing of the Kurdish-Iranian journalist Behrouz Boochani. Fleeing persecution in Iran for publicizing the mistreatment of its Kurdish population, Boochani was imprisoned on Manus Island from 2013 until its closure in 2017. He was never granted refugee status in Australia, despite winning two literary prizes in that country for his book *No Friend but the Mountains: Writing from Manus Prison*. Denied pencils or paper on Manus, Boochani composed his memoir in fragments sent to friends from the phones he had to keep hidden between their (repeated) confiscations. As Boochani would later comment, 'the toilets were our sole sanctuary for freedom', the only place in the camp where there were no CCTV cameras.

After his long ordeal in Australia's offshore jails, Boochani somehow surmounted the many hurdles placed in his way and flew to Auckland for a writing conference at the close of 2019. Once there, he was granted refugee status and was soon warmly welcomed by most New Zealanders. Since then, Boochani has continued to speak out on the violation of the human rights of refugees. As he explained to the German writer Jina Khayyer, over several interviews in 2021 and 2022, his dream is to help empower marginalized people throughout the world – 'to rehumanize the dehumanized'. Boochani also spoke of his theatre work with Aboriginal peoples in Australia, emphasizing that the fortunes of refugees and Indigenous peoples are connected to each other. As a writer, Boochani's ambition is to persuade more people that humans have no sanctuary except in mutual warmth and support.[21]

Extending the Politics of Compassion

This warmth and support we are prepared to offer one another, and hope to receive, is what this book is all about. It chimes with a sentiment more frequently expressed today, the belief that since neglect and greed got us into our current mess, only care and generosity can get us out of it. Once we acknowledge and accept our mutual interdependence, the significance of friendships and expansive solidarity is obvious in helping us to build a more equal, kinder world. However, getting there is not just an interpersonal affair. It will also surely require the harnessing of resources that only local authorities, national governments, and regional and global networks can ensure, or try to ensure, facilitating our ability to understand, relate to, and support one another.

Placing care and kindness at the heart of our politics is an indispensable step for achieving any caring future, for compassion breeds compassion, just as hate breeds hate. But is compassion sufficient to achieve that genuinely egalitarian world where we can all try to protect and share the earth's resources? My friend, the socialist feminist historian Barbara Taylor, who first resurrected those Owenite feminists for us forty years ago, looks at the history of compassion in her contribution to a recent anthology on the politics of compassion. There she reminds us just 'how tough good people can be when they need to be' in support of 'the things they value'. It is certainly true that to produce real change we surely need to be strong, as well as caring and kind.

Historically, Taylor notes, drawing on philosophers such as David Hume and Jean-Jacques Rousseau, compassion meant feeling *with* people, rather than any detached sentiment of pity. Moreover, she concludes, in the light of our current 'compassion emergency', 'If there ever was a time when such tough-minded compassion was called for – when a hard-hitting politics of compassion is desperately wanted – then now is surely such a time.'

Coming to exactly that conclusion, the mainstream philosopher Anthony Grayling comments in the same anthology: 'If there were a single injunction that, if obeyed, would make the world a better place, it would be, "Be compassionate".' However, the tough struggle to make the world a better place, which is not elaborated on by either writer, means persuading people to broaden their compassion to value all the ties that bind us, near and far, and to fight for the social and economic policies which might provide good lives for all on a habitable planet.

Yet another contributor, the inspiring feminist lawyer and activist Pragna Patel, agrees on the importance of compassion, but with significant cautions. Patel was one of the founders and till recently the charismatic director of Southall Black Sisters. She knows all about the desperate need for compassion in public and political discourse, describing its frequent degeneration into right-wing populism and a general lack of trust in public life. Such erosion is evident, of course, in our government's appalling treatment of asylum seekers, including their targeted attacks on immigration lawyers for defending migrant rights.

Government actions, she writes, have normalized an inflammatory racism throughout the public sphere, illustrated not long ago by a knife attack at one law firm. Yet, as Patel rightly adds, racism and xenophobia were already deeply embedded in Britain, shaping the unequal allocation of resources and life chances across all our institutions. Thus, while she urges greater compassion in politics, cherishing all the many spaces of kindness, courage, resistance, and solidarity that now exist, even in this bleak historical moment, Patel insists that compassion must also connect with a vision of and struggle for comprehensive social justice. It is only by pushing that agenda that we have a chance 'to unsettle power, change hearts and minds and re-imagine a political culture that works in the interests of [all] the people'.[22]

Thus, the insistence on greater compassion in politics and the prioritizing of care at every level of political and social life is essential. But where can we find or support those with the power to build something better? It's going to be a long, slow process, so all I can do is point to ways of observing and even, when possible, contributing to that process.

As we've seen many times over, supportive grassroots activities regularly emerge in times of unexpected crisis. Seeing this as one crucial resource for hope, the North American writer and activist Rebecca Solnit has for years been chronicling communities that arise in response to sudden, desperate situations, following earthquakes, hurricanes, or other natural disasters. The historical research deployed in *A Paradise Built in Hell* confirms that amid fear and loss, new networks of community support and mutual aid invariably arise, transcending the routine divisions that isolate people and creating new affinities among survivors.

However, as we know, these networks tend to disappear when the emergency recedes and established institutions of governance and social behaviour return. Yet Solnit discovers that some people remain irrevocably changed, suggesting that these temporary caring networks can teach us a great deal about how to organize lasting, sustainable communities. This is all the more necessary given the relentless disasters and calamities we are learning to expect, with the climate emergency looming above them all.[23]

Cultivating Hope

Nevertheless, many of my old political friends and collaborators of every stripe remain deeply depressed by the state of the left, in Britain and globally. Many who, like me, were inspired by the progressive manifestos of the Corbyn/McDonnell–led Labour Party as they faced the electorate in 2017 and 2019 have been devastated both by the continuing Conservative mismanagement of everything, and by the rightward shift under the new Labour leader, Keir Starmer.

Yet, as Mike Phipps, among others, insists in his recent book *Don't Stop Thinking about Tomorrow*, it is surely wrong to believe that the burst of energy, imagination, and hope that animated all those inspired by the Corbyn project has entirely evaporated. It lives on in the resilience of new radical media outlets for political education, and the ongoing support for any and all forms of resistance to our mounting crises.[24] The annual festival 'The World Transformed' (TWT), launched in 2016 to coincide with the first Labour Party conference when Jeremy Corbyn was party leader, has continued to grow in strength. From the beginning its goal has been to build the left's presence in and around the Labour Party, as well as in progressive movements and community activism, encouraging exchanges between party and movement politics. It has always included speakers and audiences of all ages, from teenagers to septuagenarians like me, at each of its annual events.

Other ongoing left educational outlets flourishing in the UK include the near-daily podcasts and articles from Novara Media, set up over a decade ago by Aaron Bastani and James Butler during student protests against increases in university tuition fees, soon joined by Ash Sarkar and others. An ongoing radical left culture was also evident with the relaunch and survival of *Tribune* (2018) shortly after the establishment of *Salvage* (2015), together with a diversity of weekly podcasts from other well-known radicals, such as Owen Jones. These newer media outlets join more veteran left productions, such as *Red Pepper* magazine, associated from its inception in 1995 with the socialist feminist Hilary Wainwright, my co-writer from *Beyond the Fragments* over forty years ago.

The year 2023 also kicked off with a continuing upsurge of union militancy across the UK. The calm and canny Mick Lynch, general secretary of the National Union of Rail, Maritime and Transport Workers (RMT), has become a sort of media star, with his articulate condemnations of the deepening inequities of life in the UK and cogent defence of strike action. Along with what remains of the Labour left, Lynch backs the militancy of other workers, too, mostly those providing essential services, now fighting to maintain wages which have been falling for decades.

A parallel trajectory has been evident in the US. First of all, the left fought hard to promote the two attempts by Vermont senator Bernie Sanders to become the presidential candidate of the Democratic Party in 2016 and again in 2020. He finished second each time, though many thought that only a progressive politics such as his might have stood a chance of beating Trump's reactionary populism in 2016. Other left Democrats supported Sanders, with Alexandria Ocasio-Cortez and the 'Squad' merely the best known.

Trade union membership and militancy have also exploded in the United States. In 2022, Chris Smalls helped coordinate a successful campaign at an Amazon warehouse in Staten Island, New York, and since then more than fifty other Amazon warehouses have begun establishing unions of their own. Starbucks workers are now trying to unionize, with some successes for the very first time, demanding improved pay and working conditions. There has similarly been an expansion of radical media outlets and podcasts. One of them, *Jacobin*, launched by Bhaskar Sunkara at the end of 2010, has been steadily multiplying its readership, international ties, and high-profile contributors ever since.

However, it is the growth of the so-called pink tide washing across Latin America that has most significantly increased hopes of the left coming to power at national levels. The presidential win of Gustavo Petro in Colombia and then, with even greater fanfare, the (admittedly narrow) victory of Luiz Inácio Lula da Silva in Brazil suggest that left forces are making headway against the harsh neoliberal regimes favoured by the United States and global capital – as testified by recent electoral victories in Mexico, Argentina, Bolivia, Chile, and, briefly, Peru. This emboldened left direction came to the fore when several Latin American leaders stayed away from the Summit of the Americas in June 2022, which was organized by President Biden to exclude Cuba, Nicaragua, and Venezuela. Medea Benjamin, one of the founders of the US-based international Women for Peace group CODEPINK, noted that countries that did attend spoke up to demand the US respect the sovereignty of the region, knowing all too well the dark tradition of US intervention in Latin America.[25]

A similarly progressive confidence was in evidence at the largest global climate summit COP27, in 2022, where after three decades of constant advocacy, Indigenous and other voices from the Global South finally succeeded in their call for a loss and damage fund: compensation from richer nations to help poorer ones deal with the destructive impacts of climate change. Now there remains the hugely tough job of pushing the wealthier countries to make good on their promises and cough up, which would mean finally getting serious about transitioning in the face of unremitting environmental devastation.

I don't travel much nowadays, in fact I never did, but I wish I could have attended Lula da Silva's third inauguration as president of Brazil, on New Year's Day 2023, as he stood flanked by Indigenous and other habitually exploited Brazilian minorities. For I would have heard something unique, a national leader using the language of care – a language absent from the repertoire of most male politicians, who recoil from 'care' as too 'soft' and 'feminine'. Lula's speech closed with these words on his political goals:

> When I say govern, I mean take care. More than govern, I will take care of the country and of the Brazilian people, with affection ... I reassert my commitment to take care of all Brazilians, especially those who need it most. To put an end to hunger in this country again. From taking the poor person out of the bone queue [for leftover bones] to putting that person back in the Budget.[26]

Nevertheless, confronting the continuous setbacks of the 2020s requires high levels of optimism and the most diverse patterns of resistance, wherever we are. On top of the cost-of-living crisis generated by extreme levels of inequality to the climate emergency, global health threats, and persistent violence against women and other vulnerable groups, we now see the grotesque violence of the war in Ukraine, while the civil wars or unrest in Sudan, Yemen, Myanmar, and elsewhere continue. Moreover, we still have the existence of far-right, proto-fascist voices in the US, committed to white supremacy and supporting Trump's America First movement, while aggressively attacking women's rights. In many parts of Europe, we have also seen the formidable rise of a nationalistic-conservative right, especially in reaction to the perceived 'threat' of migration. Apparent across Europe, it is most successfully ensconced in Hungary and Poland.

Meanwhile India remains in the grip of the extreme authoritarian Hindu nationalism of Narendra Modi, with verbal and physical assaults on Muslims and the sanctioned destruction of Muslim homes and properties. Turkish progressives live with the continuing repression of Erdoğan's war on any form of Kurdish resistance, with around 50,000 Kurds killed over the last four decades, and hundreds of those calling for an end to the violence imprisoned. The recent election of the most extreme form of anti-Palestinian settler nationalism in

Netanyahu's latest coalition in Israel is also a devastating setback for efforts towards peace and justice in the Middle East.

Despite all of this, however, the preservation of hope – sometimes hope over experience – remains a type of duty for any of us determined to assert the value and connection of all human life. It means refusing to abandon our concern for others or for our planetary future. That hope means facing up to the horrors of the moment, while also believing that our actions matter, in however minimal a way, as we try to resist or speak out against brutal displays of power, along with the overarching lack of care for so many in need, or for the world that sustains us.

Our actions matter, and never more so than when we express our concern and care for others. For as David Graeber, that much-missed anthropologist and anarchist activist, said so well, the work of care is all about enabling the freedom of others. Moreover, and as I have been arguing throughout this book, Graeber also professed that not only do we all need to be cared for, but we have an even greater psychological need to care for others, or at least to care for something.[27]

However, in preserving hope in our abilities to give and receive care, we cannot do without the support of others every step of the way. Some sense of public engagement is necessary, both to sustain our confidence individually and to preserve community life and belonging generally. Greater inclusiveness and openness to others helps us to enjoy diverse forms of hospitality and cosmopolitanism rather than fear them. I am surely far from alone in finding that taking an interest in and where possible supporting others, ready to welcome rather than fear the 'stranger', whether they come from near or far, usually helps to assuage our own inner terrors and loneliness, enabling us to feel more alive.

At the best of times, as I illustrated in my book *Radical Happiness*, we revel in some sense of shared exuberance, however transitory, whenever we collectively resist injustice or harms towards others, or when we step forwards to support those fighting to improve their lives – on picket lines or in other common spaces.[28]

The Return of the Feminist Left

For me, today, there is also the pleasure of seeing a revitalized left feminism, which another friend, Jo Littler, celebrates in her new collection *Left Feminisms: Conversations on the Personal and the Political*.[29] What left feminists all agree on is the contradictory, often oppressive, ways in which this current capitalist formation relates to and engulfs women, at odds with everything feminists once fought for. It's true that a minority of women have found career success, sometimes joining the managerial elite. But this has been against a background of growing immiseration for the majority of women, above all through the slashing and outsourcing of welfare and near-total lack of support for the work of care in all its forms. Today, that work is routinely performed by an underpaid, often migrant workforce, cementing new forms of racialized sexism, while leaving most of us without the time or resources to care adequately for each other, or for our communities.

It is dissatisfaction with this state of affairs that stimulates the recent exuberant growth of female militancy around the world, with calls for broad-based, inclusive coalitions against attacks on women's rights, aware that attempts to defend traditional masculinity have been feeding reactionary formations of every stripe. Hence feminist and gender justice movements have become prime drivers of many new global struggles. Moreover, these feminist mobilizations have re-centred the need for an anti-racist outlook within political organizing. Finally, as the Kenyan feminist Awino Okech argues in all her writing, it is the issue of care that features most prominently in all of this feminist organizing. Whether in Pakistan, Nigeria, Brazil, India,

Argentina, or Lebanon, care and well-being lie at the heart of building and sustaining feminist resistance.

Once we recognize care as the key to the comprehensive changes we need for any sustainable future, it's clear that we have to build a new collective imaginary capable of reversing the underpinnings of the world as we know it. Contesting the emphasis on unspecified 'growth' still endorsed by almost every current national leader, in power or in opposition, left feminists agree that we must begin instead with significant investment in the social infrastructures that sustain us all.

So, there will be growth, but it will be strictly sustainable, caring growth. The accent on care also requires us to prioritize commitments to shorter working time for everyone, not just a shorter working week, but shorter working days for those who need them. This would enable a sharing of the work of caring, while hopefully breaking the link between work and consumption. At present it is our absurd culture of overwork that fuels people's need to escape into compensatory consumerism, because they are either uninspired by their ultimately futile jobs or worn out by the pointless bureaucracy that routinely accompanies vitally useful work, especially in the public sector.

Underpinning these changes there would need to be a new social contract that promises certain universal entitlements, including some form of minimal income guarantee, for people in or out of work, and above all access to essential universal care to meet personal welfare needs and create sustainable communities. These measures are affordable once governments commit to a fairer tax system: we know that the absurd profits being made by the very few today are barely taxed at all.

To begin with, we should impose hefty windfall taxes on the fossil fuel corporations, with their ever mounting profits, although with the ultimate goal of phasing them out. We could implement the so-called Tobin tax on all financial transactions, a move supported by most EU countries and which would generate significant new revenue. We also need to reduce the sums wasted on the military, as on Britain's pointless nuclear deterrent. Indeed, while the UK spends less on welfare benefits than the rest of Western European countries, it spends more than any of them on defence.[30] So, while these transformations may sound utopian, they are plainly realizable were we to commit to them.

For instance, despite our excessive work culture, there has recently been an interesting pilot project in the UK called the 4 Day Week Campaign that has involved seventy companies, representing over 3,000 workers, experimenting with a four-day, thirty-two-hour week with no loss of pay. The reported results are impressive with regard to productivity, well-being, and dealing with the cost-of-living crisis. Almost half of the workers reported less stress, better sleep patterns, and greater ability to cope with home life, while taking fewer days off sick and being happier to remain in their jobs.[31] Similar schemes are now being developed elsewhere.

Projects encouraging companies to implement shorter hours are also being piloted in other European countries, according to a recent report on working time from the International Labour Organization based in Geneva. These include a four-day week in parts of Spain, currently meeting with success, and another project rolled out by the Icelandic government in 2018 and 2019, suggesting that work-week reduction in general increased people's well-being, creating greater harmony between work and home life.[32]

Such schemes constitute modest beginnings. More radically, as some feminists have been arguing for decades, what we need is to ditch the idea of work for its own sake and make 'part-time' paid work the norm, accompanying a living wage for all. The obvious gains are uncoupling work from growth as well as leaving time for more caring work, at all levels. Of course, we know that this remains completely contrary to the ongoing thrust of the global corporate world, which makes it all the more important.[33]

Building Collectivities on Every Front

A living wage for all is hardly the mindset in the UK at present, where we remain committed to the brutal policy of reducing taxation and shrinking the welfare state. As James Meadway, one of Britain's leading left economists, wrote at the start of 2022: 'Britain is uniquely stacked with institutions seemingly designed to generate the worst, most short-term and stupid solutions to any given economic problem – witness, for instance, a decade spent cutting the pay of nurses in response to the bankers' financial crisis.'[34] It certainly challenges that duty of hope I have been suggesting we need to embrace.

Yet even Meadway sees two positive portents. The first is the triumphant rise of union militancy in the UK, with many current union leaders moving well beyond traditional labourism to proclaim the need for progressive politics and values at every level, in what boils down to genuine socialist perspectives. The second, uniting a vast range of progressive people from the liberal centre to the far left, is the ever growing awareness of climate change, which makes a mockery of the idea that corporate greed can continue unregulated and unchecked.

Indeed, some British union leaders, and not only Mick Lynch, have begun linking their struggle for a fair wage to that of securing a better, sustainable world. They point out that if more of our essential utilities were to be brought into public ownership and democratized, it could significantly help offset the climate emergency. This could happen sector by sector, were we to commit to a radical democratization of all our resources. As Jeremy Gilbert and Alex Williams point out at the close of their useful book *Hegemony Now*, 'The number and range of social constituencies with a direct objective interest in advancing the cause of socialism is growing, not shrinking.'[35] Much the same has been suggested in the United States, where an unexpected support for socialism has also been growing, driven by Black Americans and women, according to recent polls.[36]

However, to even approach any such goal will require the broadest possible coalition-building, forming alliances between all progressive people working for change. Many will be busy at the grassroots where seminal actions often begin, but they can link up with others working within and across institutions, from community networks, feminist organizations, and trade unions to forward-thinking people across political parties, fostering maximum solidarity between them. This would be especially important in the UK, whose first-past-the-post electoral system denies a voice to minority parties. We need to see the strengthening of ties between everyone committed to environmental goals – aiming at comprehensive decarbonization – and any alliances or parties working to reduce social inequality and to promote well-being overall.

Necessary as these alliances are for human survival, no one can doubt the prolonged battle required to achieve meaningful results. On the way, there is so much to keep fighting for, starting with rebuilding our social infrastructures, investing properly in social care, building and transitioning to eco-friendly homes, as well as switching to green technology generally. We have seen the beginnings of such attempts at creating new infrastructures for radical care, but they remain dispersed.

It is in Barcelona, following the election of the radical Barcelona en Comú council in 2015, that we can find the best examples of what a radically caring municipalism would look like. This authority began investing in childcare centres as a way of providing greater neighbourhood care and education. It also supports the local cooperative for migrant women, Mujeres Pa'lante, which has many domestic workers as members. Between 2015 and 2021, the BComú budget for social care, including social services, health, and education, increased by 39.7 per cent.[37]

We have yet to see that matched elsewhere, although many local councils in the UK have made moves towards setting up community wealth funds to further local investment, while attempting – against enormous financial constraints and the damaging effects of the privatization of public resources – to address how they might find resources to improve care services. There are a few small-scale examples of what new, cooperative caring practices could look like, as the British radical economist and activist Christine Berry reports. These include a parent-led nursery in Deptford, London, known as Caring Families, and a cooperative platform based in Halifax, in the north of England, the Equal Care Co-op, which supports a group of cooperatively based care workers. Both these initiatives not only exemplify what caring practices could be, free from profit extraction and with some local backing, but they also seek to break down the barriers between professional carers and the parents, friends, and relatives who are providing unpaid care.[38]

Despite the carelessness still so prevalent today, calls for a more caring future grow louder all the time, voicing the realization that we cannot fix what is wrong with care within the confines of present structures. It means our collective demands and imagination must continue to insist upon and work towards the total transformations some of us have been fighting for all our lives.

I called this book *Lean on Me* as my way of affirming our interdependence and the recognition, care, and support we all need from each other, and owe to others, everywhere. Our human condition should mean knowing that our bodies will often fail us, just as our desires will frequently end up rejected or dismissed. Yet that hardly excuses us from paying heed to the lives of others. Quite the contrary.

I am myself becoming just a little more fragile nowadays, even as I continue to seek out new intergenerational encounters that sustain radical action and personal pleasure and well-being. None of us can survive well without the care and kindness of friends, acquaintances, even strangers. The difficulties so many people face in mobilizing or sustaining such caring intimacies in our driven times are what lie behind the soaring levels of clinical depression now afflicting almost all ages. This tells me that for most of us, most of the time, it is the sustenance of connectedness that serves best to provide meaning and satisfaction in our lives. It is why we all need to work to create more compassionate communities, both in our daily interactions and in our institutions across all scales of life.

Being able to admit the interconnected vulnerability of human existence ought to be sufficient to cement our ties to others, near and far. It means disregarding the drumbeat of market-driven rhetoric that works to thwart such recognition, with its illusory assurances of individual gratification. Surely, it is past time for us to respond to the persistent perils of the present and fatalistic forebodings of the future by deepening our commitment to a compassionate, inclusive sociality, placing care at the heart of our lives and politics. As the eminent theologian and poet Rowan Williams affirms: 'In a fragile world, we must turn to our fellow humans.'

Let's do it, together.

Notes

Introduction: The Kindness of Strangers

1 Martin Evans, 'Critic Reveals She Was the True Inspiration behind Blanche DuBois', *Telegraph*, 27 July 2014.

2 Quoted in Nina Auerbach, *Ellen Terry: Player in Her Time*, New York: Norton, 1987, p. 126.

3 Eric Fromm, *To Have or to Be?* London, New York: Continuum, 1977, p. 87.

4 John Locke, *Two Treatises of Government*, 1690, 'Of the State of Nature', Chapter 2, Section 4, line 1.

5 Immanuel Kant, 'An Answer to the Question: What Is Enlightenment?' (1784), in *Practical Philosophy: The Cambridge Edition of the Works of Immanuel Kant*, trans. and ed. Mary J., Gregor, New York: Cambridge University Press, 1999.

6 Adriana Cavarero, *Inclinations: A Critique of Rectitude*, trans. Amanda Minervini and Adam Sitze, Stanford: Stanford University Press, 2016, pp. 2, 3, 15.

7 Cyril Connolly, *The Enemies of Promise*, London: Andre Deutsch, 1938, p. 110.

8 Cavarero, *Inclinations*, p. 131.

9 Judith Butler, *Precarious Life*, London: Verso, 2004, pp. xiv, 42–3.

10 Emmanuel Levinas, *Totality and Infinity: An Essay on Exteriority*, Pittsburg: Duquesne University Press, 1969, p. 51.

11 Sigmund Freud, 'A Difficulty in the Path of Psycho-analysis', in *The Standard Edition of the Complete Works of Sigmund Freud*, vol. 17 [1917], London: Vintage, 2001, p. 142.

12 Jean Laplanche, *Life and Death in Psychoanalysis*, trans. J. Mehlman, Annapolis, MD: Johns Hopkins University Press, 1976, p. 129.

13 Sarah Benton, 'Dependence', *Soundings: A Journal of Politics and Culture*, 70, Winter 2018, pp. 61, 62.

14 The Health Foundation, *What Geographic Inequalities in COVID-19 Mortality Rates and Health Can Tell Us about Levelling Up*, 17 July 2021.

15 Future Care Capital, *The Marmot Review: Longevity and a Call to Action*, 18 February 2020.
16 Jonathan Freedland, 'Coronavirus Crisis Has Transformed Our View of What's Important', *Guardian*, 8 April 2020.
17 There have been many exposures of government corruption in court cases won by the Good Law Project. See 'BREAKING: High Court Finds Government PPE "VIP" Lane for Politically Connected Suppliers "Unlawful"', 12 January 2022, goodlawproject.org.
18 The Health Foundation, 'Unequal Pandemic, Fairer Recovery', July 2021, health.org.uk.
19 The World Bank, 'COVID-19 and Rising Inequality', 25 January 2022, live.worldbank.org.
20 Women's Budget Group, 'Creating a Caring Economy: A Call to Action', 30 September 2020.
21 The Leap, *The Leap Manifesto: Caring for the Earth and One Another*, September 2015, theleap.org.
22 Foundation for European Progressive Studies (FEPS), *Towards a Fairer, Care-Focused Europe* (FEPS and Friedrich-Ebert-Stiftung, 2020), feps-europe.eu.
23 FEMNET, *The Care Manifesto: Towards a Caring Economy, as Envisioned by Women*, June 2021, p. 1, femnet.org.
24 Joan C. Tronto, *Caring Democracy: Markets, Equality, and Justice*, New York: New York University Press, 2013, p. 94.
25 Nancy Fraser, 'Contradictions of Capital and Care', *New Left Review*, 100, July–August 2016; Laura Briggs, *How All Politics Became Reproductive Politics: From Welfare Reform to Foreclosure to Trump*, Oakland: University of California Press, 2017.
26 Ellie Benton and Anne Power, 'Community Responses to the Coronavirus Pandemic: How Mutual Aid Can Help', *LSE Public Policy Review*, 1 (3), 2021.
27 Susanna Rustin, 'Beyond Radical Neighbourliness: The Case for Micro-Democracy', *Soundings* blog, 10 June 2020, lwbooks.co.uk.
28 These attempts at radical municipalism are described in the Care Collective, 'Caring Communities', in *The Care Manifesto*, London: Verso, 2020, Chapter 3.
29 Jia Tolentino, 'Can I Help You?: What Mutual Aid Can Do during a Pandemic', *New Yorker*, 11 May 2020.
30 Miranda Bryant, 'Coronation's Big Help Out Volunteering Project at Risk of Lack of Participants', theguardian.com, 16 April 2023.
31 Rebecca Solnit, '"The Way We Get through This Is Together": The Rise of Mutual Aid under Coronavirus', theguardian.com, 14 May 2020.
32 Dean Spade, *Mutual Aid: Building Solidarity during This Crisis (and the Next)*, London: Verso, 2020, p. 148.

33 Malte Klar and Tim Kasser, 'Some Benefits of Being an Activist: Measuring Activism and Its Role in Psychological Well-Being', *Political Psychology*, 30 (5), October 2009, pp. 755–77.

1. Call That a Mother?

1 Ellen Ross, *Love and Toil: Motherhood in Outcast London, 1870–1918*, Oxford: Oxford University Press, 1993.

2 Mary Wollstonecraft, *A Vindication of the Rights of Woman*, London: Everyman, 1922 [1792], p. 7.

3 Charlotte Perkins Gilman, 'Moving the Mountain', 1911, in *Charlotte Perkins Gilman: Her Progress toward Utopia with Selected Writings*, ed. Carol Farley Kessler, Liverpool: Liverpool University Press, 1995.

4 Ada Nield Chew, quoted in Ann Oakley, 'Feminism, Motherhood and Medicine', in *What Is Feminism?*, ed. Juliet Mitchell and Ann Oakley, Oxford: Blackwell, 1983, p. 131.

5 Mrs Bertrand Russell, *The Right to Be Happy*, New York: Garden City Publishing, 1927, p. 185.

6 Simone de Beauvoir, *The Prime of Life*, London: Andre Deutsch and Weildenfeld & Nicolson, 1962, p. 292.

7 Christopher M. Callahan and German Berrios, *Reinventing Depression: A History of the Treatment of Depression in Primary Care, 1940–2004*, Oxford: Oxford University Press, 2005, p. 107; Jonathan Metzl, ' "Mother's Little Helper": The Crisis of Psychoanalysis and the Miltown Resolution', *Gender and History*, 15 (2), 2003, pp. 240–67, 240.

8 R. D. Laing, *Politics of the Family*, Toronto: CBC Massey Lectures, 1969, p. 35.

9 Adam Phillips, 'Unforgiven', *London Review of Books*, 7 March 2019.

10 Simone de Beauvoir, *The Second Sex*, trans. H. M. Parshley, London: Vintage Classics, 1997, p. 528.

11 Rochelle (Sheli) P. Wortis, 'Child-Rearing and Women's Liberation', in Michelene Wandor, *The Body Politic: Writings from the Women's Liberation in Britain*, London: Stage 1, 1969–1972, p. 129.

12 Alix Kates Shulman, *A Marriage Agreement and Other Essays: Four Decades of Feminist Writing*, New York: Open Road, 2012.

13 Jan Williams, Hazel Twort, and Ann Bachelli, 'Women and the Family', in *Once a Feminist*, ed. Michelene Wandor, London: Virago, 1990, p. 228.

14 Ann Oakley, *Housewife*, London: Allen Lane, 1974, p. 236.

15 Institute of Employment Studies, *Women in the Labour Market: Two Decades of Change and Continuity*, 1994.

16 Sarah Crook, 'The Women's Liberation Movement: Activism and Therapy at the Grassroots, 1968–1985', *Women's History Review*, 27 (7), 2018, pp. 1152–68.

17 Sheila Rowbotham, *A Century of Women: The History of Women in Britain and the United States*, London: Viking, p. 425.

18 Lynne Segal, ed., *What Is to Be Done about the Family?*, Harmonds-worth: Penguin, 1983; Michèle Barrett and Mary McIntosh, *The Anti-Social Family*, London: Verso, 1982.

19 Adrienne Rich, *Of Woman Born: Motherhood as Experience and Institution*, New York: Norton & Company Inc., 1976, pp. 285–6.

20 Nancy Chodorow, *The Reproduction of Mothering: Psychoanalysis and the Sociology of Gender*, Oakland: University of California Press, 1978.

21 Carol Gilligan, *In a Different Voice: Psychological Theory and Women's Development*, Cambridge, MA: Harvard University Press, 1982; Sara Ruddick, *Maternal Thinking: Toward a Politics of Peace*, Boston: Beacon Press, 1989.

22 Oakley, 'Feminism, Motherhood and Medicine', p. 140.

23 Alice Walker, *In Search of Our Mothers' Gardens: Womanist Prose*, New York: Harcourt Brace Jovanovich, 1983; Toni Morrison, 'Rootedness: The Ancestor as Foundation', in *Black Women Writers (1950–1980): A Critical Evaluation*, ed. Mari Evans, New York: Doubleday, 1988, pp. 342–3.

24 bell hooks, *Feminist Theory: From Margin to Center*, New York: Routledge, 1984, p. 133.

25 Maureen Freely, *What about Us? An Open Letter to the Mothers Feminism Forgot*, London: Bloomsbury, 1995; Madeleine Bunting, *Labours of Love*, London: Granta, 2020, p. 28.

26 Pew Research Center, *Motherhood Today – A Tougher Job, Less Ably Done*, 9 May 1997.

27 Marianne Levy, *Don't Forget to Scream: Unspoken Truths about Motherhood*, London: Phoenix, 2022; Tami Amit, 'Depleted Mother Syndrome', *Counselling BC*, 4 October 2014.

28 Anne Enright, *Making Babies: Stumbling into Motherhood*, London: Jonathan Cape, 2004, p. 136.

29 See Roberta Garrett, 'Novels and Children: "Mum's Lit" and the Public Mother/Author', *Studies in the Maternal*, 5 (2), 2013, pp. 1–28.

30 Angela McRobbie, 'Feminism, the Family and the New "Mediated" Maternalism', *New Formations*, 80, 2013, pp. 119–37.

31 Catherine Rottenberg, *The Rise of Neoliberal Feminism*, Oxford: Oxford University Press, 2018.

32 Human Rights Council, *Report of the Special Rapporteur on Extreme Poverty and Human Rights*, April 2019.

33 Shani Orgad, *Heading Home: Motherhood, Work, and the Failed Promise of Equality*, New York: Columbia University Press, 2018, pp. 192, 255.

34 Jo Littler, 'Mothers Behaving Badly: Chaotic Hedonism and the Crisis of Neoliberal Social Reproduction', *Cultural Studies*, 33 (4), 2020, pp. 499–520.

35 Brigid Shulte, ' "The Second Shift" at 25: Q & A with Arlie Hochschild', *Washington Post*, 6 August 2014.

36 See, for example, Tine Rostgaard, *Family Policies in Scandinavia*, Berlin: Friedrich-Ebert-Stiftung, 2014.

37 Jemima Olchawski, *Parents, Work and Care: Striking the Balance*, Fawcett Society, May 2016; Giselle Cory and Alfie Stirling, *Pay and Parenthood: An Analysis of Wage Inequality between Mums and Dads*, TUC, March 2016.

38 Eliane Glaser, 'Parent Trap: Why the Cult of the Perfect Mother Has to End', *Guardian*, 18 May 2021.

39 Adam Phillips, 'Unforgiven', review of *Down Girl: The Logic of Misogyny*, *London Review of Books*, March 2019, emphasis added.

40 Jacqueline Rose, *Mothers: An Essay on Love and Cruelty*, London: Faber & Faber, 2018.

41 Helen Penn, 'Policy Rationales for Early Childhood Services', *International Journal of Child Care and Education Policy*, 5, 2011, pp. 1–16.

42 Maddy Savage, 'How Covid-19 Is Changing Women's Lives', BBC Worklife, 30 June 2020, bbc.com.

43 Maude Perrier, *Childcare Struggles, Maternal Workers and Social Reproduction*, Bristol: Bristol University Press, 2022.

44 Dani McClain, *We Live for the We: The Political Power of Black Motherhood*, New York: Bold Type Books, 2019.

45 Angela Garbes, *Essential Labor: Mothering as Social Change*, New York: Harper Wave, 2022, pp. 9, 14.

46 Jia Tolentino, 'Can Motherhood Be a Mode of Rebellion?', *New Yorker*, 8 May 2022.

47 Laura Briggs, *How All Politics Became Reproductive Politics*, Oakland: University of California Press, 2017; Lynne Layton, 'Irrational Exuberance: Neoliberal Subjectivity and the Perversion of Truth', *Subjectivity*, 3, 2010, p. 308.

48 Sarah Knott, *Mother: An Unconventional History*, London: Viking, 2019, p. 258.

2. Valuing Education

1 Martha C. Nussbaum, 'Compassion and Terror', *Daedalus*, 132 (1), 2003, p. 24.
2 Paulo Freire, *Pedagogy of the Oppressed*, London: Penguin, 1996 [1968].
3 bell hooks, *Teaching to Transgress: Education as the Practice of Freedom*, New York: Routledge, 1994, p. 207.
4 Stuart Hall, 'Absolute Beginners: Reflections on the Secondary Modern Generation', in Paul Gilroy and Ruth Wilson Gilmore, *Selected Writings on Race and Difference*, Durham, NC: Duke University Press, 2021, pp. 29, 25.
5 Bernard Coard, *How the West Indian Child Is Made Educationally Sub-normal in the British School System*, London: New Beacon Books, 1971.
6 See interviews in Selina Todd, *The People: The Rise and Fall of the Working Class 1910–2010*, London: John Murray, 2015.
7 Diane Ravitch, *The Death and Life of the Great American School System: How Testing and Choice Are Undermining Education*, New York: Basic Books, 2010.
8 Department for Education, *Participation Rates in Higher Education Academic Years 2006–2018*, National Statistics, 26 December 2019, gov.uk.
9 Stefan Collini, *What Are Universities For?* London: Penguin, 2012, p. 243. See also Raewyn Connell, *The Good University: What Universities Actually Do and Why It's Time for Radical Change*, London: Zed Books, 2019; Joe Berry, *Reclaiming the Ivory Tower: Organizing Adjuncts to Change Higher Education*, New York: Monthly Review Press, 2005; Christopher Newfield, *The Great Mistake: How We Wrecked Public Universities and How We Can Fix Them*, Baltimore, MD: Johns Hopkins University Press, 2016; Wendy Brown, *Undoing the Demos: Neoliberalism's Stealth Revolution*, Brooklyn: Zone Books, 2015.
10 Rosalind Gill, 'Girl Interrupted', from 'How We Got Here', unpublished collection of essays in which women reflect on education, work, and social mobility since the 1950s.
11 Les Back, *Academic Diary*, London: Goldsmiths Press, 2016, p. 214.
12 Jo Littler, 'Universities', from 'How We Got Here'.
13 See Ludwig Wittgenstein, *Philosophical Investigations*, Oxford: Basil Blackwell, 1968, II, xiv, p. 232.
14 Solomon Asch, *Social Psychology*, Englewood Cliffs, NJ: Prentice Hall, 1962; Michael Argyle, *The Psychology of Interpersonal*

Behaviour, Harmondsworth: Penguin, 1967; *Gaze and Mutual Gaze*, Cambridge: Cambridge University Press, 1976.

15 George Brown and Tirril Harris, *Social Origins of Depression*, London: Tavistock, 1978.

16 See Michael Billig, *Social Psychology and Intergroup Relations*, London: Academic Press, 1976.

17 Ian Taylor, Paul Walton, and Jock Young, *The New Criminology: For a Social Theory of Deviance*, London: Routledge, 1973.

18 Littler, 'Universities'.

19 Sheila Rowbotham, Lynne Segal, and Hilary Wainwright, *Beyond the Fragments: Feminism and the Making of Socialism*, London: Merlin, 1980.

20 These early publications included *Is the Future Female? Troubled Thoughts on Contemporary Feminism*, London: Virago, 1987; *Slow Motion: Changing Masculinities, Changing Men*, London: Virago, 1990; *Straight Sex: The Politics of Pleasure*, London: Virago, 1994; *Why Feminism?: Gender, Psychology, Politics*, Cambridge: Polity Press, 1999.

21 Judith Butler, *Gender Trouble: Feminism and the Subversion of Identity*, London: Routledge, pp. 147, 148.

22 Stefan Collini, *Speaking of Universities*, London: Verso, 2017, p. 154.

23 Will Davies, *Contextualising the Assault on Universities*, Goldsmiths Political Economy and Research Centre, 5 August 2020, perc.org.uk.

24 Nathan M. Greenfield, 'The Unkindest Cut? – Behind the Paring of the Humanities', *University World News*, 13 August 2022, universityworldnews.com.

25 Marina Warner, 'Why I Quit', *London Review of Books*, 36 (17), 11 September 2014.

26 John Williams, 'Rowan Williams on Higher Education's "Inhuman and Divisive" Jargon', *THE*, 29 January 2015.

27 Anisa Purbasari Horton, 'Why Australia Is Doubling Fees for Arts Degrees', BBC Worklife, 29 July 2020, bbc.com.

28 Joy Connolly, 'The Assault on the Humanities and Social Sciences', *ACLS*, 6 April 2021.

29 The British Academy, *Qualified for the Future*, London: British Academy, May 2020.

30 Liz Morris, 'Pressure Vessels: The Epidemic of Poor Mental Health among Higher Education Staff', HEPI (Higher Education Policy Institute) Occasional Paper, 23 May 2019.

31 Nussbaum, 'Compassion and Terror'.

3. A Feminist Life

1 From the song 'We Don't Need the Men', words and music by Malvina Reynolds, copyright 1959, Schroder Music Co. (ASCAP). All rights reserved. I am very grateful to Ruth Pohlman for arranging the copyright permission.

2 Barbara Taylor, *Eve and the New Jerusalem: Socialism and Feminism in the Nineteenth Century*, London: Virago, 1983, pp. xi, xiv.

3 Edward Aveling and Eleanor Marx, 'The Woman Question: From a Socialist Point of View', *Westminster Review*, 125, January 1886.

4 E. Sylvia Pankhurst and Kathryn Dodd, *A Sylvia Pankhurst Reader*, Manchester: Manchester University Press, 1993, pp. 141–9.

5 Simone de Beauvoir, *The Second Sex*, trans. H. M. Parshley, Harmondsworth: Penguin, 1972 [1949], p. 1.

6 Sheila Rowbotham, *Daring to Hope: My Life in the 1970s*, London: Verso, 2021, p. 2.

7 Valerie Charlton, 'The Patter of Tiny Contradictions', *Red Rag*, 5, 1973.

8 Reported in Mary Holland, 'Hell-Bent on Women's Liberation', *Observer*, 1 March 1970; Audrey Wise, 'Equal Pay Is Not Enough', *Black Dwarf*, 10 January 1969.

9 See Audrey Wise, Women and the Struggle for Workers' Control, Spokesman Pamphlet, no. 33, London: The Bertrand Russell Foundation, 1973.

10 Swasti Mitter, *Common Fate, Common Bond: Women in the Global Economy*, London: Pluto Press, 1986, p. 163.

11 This description of Derrick Day appeared in Phil Cohen and Carl Gardner, eds, *It Ain't Half Racist, Mum: Fighting Racism in the Media*, London: Comedia/CARM, 1982; the contribution is available online in ' "The Only Black and the Only Woman Reporter …": Hackney Gazette in the 1970s', The Radical History of Hackney, 29 January 2022, hackneyhistory.wordpress.com/tag/derrick-day.

12 Sally Belfridge, 'Nine Years Together', *Spare Rib*, April 1978, reprinted in *Spare Rib Reader: 100 Issues of Women's Liberation*, ed. Marsha Rowe, Harmondsworth: Penguin, 1982, p. 569.

13 Eleanor Stephens, 'The Moon within Your Reach: A Feminist Approach to Female Orgasm', *Spare Rib*, December 1975, p. 15.

14 As reported by Rowe in *Spare Rib Reader*, p. 440.

15 Barbara Ehrenreich, 'What Is Socialist Feminism?', Working Papers on Socialism and Feminism published by the New American Movement (NAM) in 1976, available at marxists.org.

16 Kimberlé Crenshaw, 'Demarginalizing the Intersection of Race and Sex: A Black Feminist Critique of Antidiscrimination Doctrine,

Feminist Theory and Antiracist Politics', *University of Chicago Legal Forum*, 140, 1989, pp. 139–67; Patricia Hill Collins, *Black Feminist Thought: Knowledge, Consciousness, and the Politics of Empowerment*, New York and London: Routledge, 1990.

17 Herbert Marcuse, 'On the Need for an Open Marxist Mind', *The Listener*, 9 February 1978, p. 171; André Gorz, *Farewell to the Working Class*, London: Pluto Press, pp. 85–6.

18 Ellen Willis, 'Radical Feminism and Feminist Radicalism', in *The 60s without Apology*, ed. S. Sayrers et al., Minneapolis: Minneapolis University Press, 1984, p. 93.

19 Ann Rossiter, 'Risking Gossip and Disgrace: Asian Women Strike', *Spare Rib*, 18 January 1977.

20 Angela Carter, *The Sadeian Woman: An Exercise in Cultural History*, London: Virago, 1979, p. 9.

21 Barbara Ehrenreich, 'Life without Father', *Socialist Review*, 14 (1), January–February 1984, p. 49.

22 Michael Ann Mullin, 'Why Socialist Feminism? Gatherings in Paris and Amsterdam', in Rowe, *Spare Rib Reader*, pp. 387–8.

23 Catharine A. MacKinnon, 'Feminism, Marxism, Method, and the State: An Agenda for Theory', *Signs*, 7 (3), Spring 1982, pp. 515–44.

24 See Lynne Segal, *Straight Sex: Rethinking the Politics of Pleasure*, London: Verso, p. 62.

25 Ronald Butt, 'Mrs Thatcher: The First Two Years: Interview for *Sunday Times*', *Sunday Times*, 3 May 1981.

26 Anne Phillips, *Hidden Hands: Women and Economic Policies*, London: Pluto, 1987.

27 Sasha Roseneil, 'Queering Home and Family in the 1980s: The Greenham Common Women's Peace Camp', talk given at Queer Homes, Queer Families: A History and Policy Debate, British Library, 17 December 2012.

28 Beverley Bryan, Stella Dadzie, and Suzanne Scafe, *Heart of the Race: Black Women's Lives in Britain*, London: Virago Press, 1985; Shabnam Grewal et al., eds, *Charting the Journey: Writings by Black and Third World Women*, London: Sheba Press, 1988.

29 The Management Committee, 'Activism Is the Rent We Pay to Live on This Planet – Our Tribute to Pragna Patel', Southall Black Sisters, 17 November 2021, southallblacksisters.org.uk.

30 Melissa Benn, 'Trailblazer of Feminism', *Guardian*, 22 July 2000.

31 Polly Toynbee, 'Fay Plays the Fool', *Guardian*, 1 July 1998; Libby Brooks, 'Time for a Good Scrap on What Our Feminism Really Is', *Guardian*, 23 July 2009.

32 Libby Brooks, 'No Turning Back on Questions about Feminism's Future: Reviewing Lynne Segal's *Why Feminism? Gender, Psychology, Politics*', *Guardian*, 13 November 1999.

33 Juliet Mitchell, 'Reflections on Twenty Years of Feminism', in *What Is Feminism?*, ed. J. Mitchell and A. Oakley, Oxford: Blackwell, 1986, pp. 45–8.

34 Nancy Fraser, *Fortunes of Feminism*, London: Verso, 2013.

35 Angela McRobbie, *The Aftermath of Feminism: Gender, Culture and Social Change*, London: Sage, 2008.

36 Sheryl Sandberg, *Lean In: Women, Work, and the Will to Lead*, New York: Alfred A. Knopf, 2013, pp. 8, 9.

37 Kate Losse, 'Feminism's Tipping Point: Who Wins from Leaning In?', *Dissent*, 26 March 2013.

38 Dawn Foster, *Lean Out*, London: Repeater Books, 2016, p. 56.

39 Catherine Rottenberg, *The Rise of Neoliberal Feminism*, Oxford: Oxford University Press, 2018.

40 See Jia Tolentino, 'Barbara Ehrenreich Is Not an Optimist but She Has Hope for the Future', *New Yorker*, 21 March 2020.

41 See Julie Turkewitz, 'How Colombian Feminists Decriminalized Abortion – With Help from Their Neighbours', *New York Times*, 23 February 2022.

42 Verónica Gago, *Feminist International: How to Change Everything*, London: Verso, 2020, pp. 1, 4.

43 Ewa Majewska, *Feminist Antifascism: Counterpublics of the Common*, London: Verso, 2021.

44 Rosa Campbell, 'Global Feminisms', *History Workshop*, 4 March 2022, historyworkshop.org.uk.

45 Sandra E. Garcia, 'The Woman Who Created #MeToo Long before Hashtags', *New York Times*, 20 October 2017.

46 See Jessica Ringrose and Emma Reynold, 'Slut-Shaming, Girl Power and "Sexualisation": Thinking Through the Politics of the International SlutWalks with Teen Girls', *Gender and Education*, 24 (3), 4 May 2012, pp. 333–43.

47 Sally Hines, 'Trans and Feminist Rights Have Been Falsely Cast in Opposition', *Economist*, 28 April 2019.

48 Selma James, *Sex, Race, and Class – The Perspective of Winning: A Selection of Writings 1952–2011*, London: PM Press, 2012. See also Becky Gardiner, 'A Life in Writing: Selma James', *Guardian*, 8 June 2012.

49 Silvia Federici, with Arlen Austin, *Wages for Housework: The New York Committee 1972–1977: History, Theory, Documents*, Brooklyn: Autonomedia, 2017.

50 Sara Jaffe, 'The Factory in the Family: The Radical Vision of Wages for Housework', *Nation*, 14 March 2018.

51 Joke Swiebel, 'Unpaid Work and Policy-Making towards a Broader Perspective of Work and Employment', United Nations, DESA Discussion Paper Series, no. 4, February 1999.

52 Mike Maciag, 'The Fastest-Growing Jobs and Where They're Most Common', *Governing: The States and Localities*, 7 November 2017.

4. Admitting Vulnerability

1 Barbara Taylor, 'No Island Is an Island: Covid and the Deadliness of Willed Isolation', Solitudes – Past and Present blog, 16 November 2021, solitudes.qmul.ac.uk.

2 Sigmund Freud, 'Thoughts for the Time of War and Death', *The Standard Edition of the Complete Psychological Works of Sigmund Freud*, London: Vintage, 2001 [1915], pp. 273–301.

3 Walt Whitman, 1841, originally published from 'We All Shall Rest at Last' in the *Long Island Democrat*, 14 July 1840.

4 Liz Crow, 'Including All of Our Lives: Renewing the Social Model of Disability', in *Encounters with Strangers: Feminism and Disability*, ed. Jenny Morris, London: Women's Press, 1996. See also Jenny Morris, *Pride against Prejudice: Transforming Attitudes to Disability*, London: Women's Press, 1991; Michael Oliver, *The Politics of Disablement*, London: Macmillan, 1990.

5 Lois Keith, *Take Up Thy Bed and Walk: Death, Disability and Cure in Classic Fiction for Girls*, London: Taylor & Francis, 2001.

6 Jenny Morris, 'Impairment and Disability: Constructing an Ethics of Care that Promotes Human Rights', *Hypatia*, 16 (4), 'Feminism and Disability', Autumn 2001, pp. 2, 15.

7 See Maggie Sullivan, *Boss Ladies of CLE: Stories from 20 Leading Women in Their Own Words*, Cleveland: Media Lady Press, 2020.

8 Margrit Shildrick, *Dangerous Discourses of Disability, Subjectivity, and Sexuality*, London: Palgrave Macmillan, 2009.

9 Tim Dartington, *Managing Vulnerability: The Underlying Dynamics of Systems of Care*, London: Routledge, 2010, pp. 149, 141.

10 Department for Work and Pensions, *Equality Impact Assessment – Response to the Work Capability Assessment Independent Review*, 23 November 2010, gov.uk.

11 Department for Work and Pensions, 'Mortality Statistics: ESA, IB and SDA Claimants', official statistics, 27 August 2015, gov.uk.

12 Jenny Morris, 'Shocking Survey Results Show "Yawning Gap" between Care Act and Real Life', *Disability News*, 16 October 2015, disabilitynewsservice.com.

13 'Scrapping Work Capability Assessments Could Lead to Even More Broken Benefits System', Mind, 16 March 2023, mind.org.uk.

14 Eileen Clifford, *The War on Disabled People: Capitalism, Welfare and the Making of a Human Catastrophe*, London: Zed Books, 2020.

15 Frances Ryan, *Crippled: Austerity and the Demonization of Disabled People*, London: Verso, 2019; Stef Benstead, *Second Class Citizens: The Treatment of Disabled People in Austerity Britain*, Sheffield: Centre for Welfare Reform, 2019.

16 Office for National Statistics (ONS), 'Updated Estimates of Coronavirus (Covid-19) Related Deaths by Disability Status, England: 24 January to 20 November 2020', 11 February 2021, ons.gov.uk.

17 Rebecca Vallas, '7 Facts about the Economic Crisis Facing People with Disabilities in the United States', The Century Foundation, 21 April 2022, tcf.org.

18 Jenny Morris, 'Fulfilling Potential or Potential Unfulfilled?', blog, 6 March 2012, jennymorrisnet.blogspot.com.

19 Luke Beesley, 'From Cuts, to Resistance, to Where? The State and Non-state Actors in the Strategy of Disabled People against Cuts', Beyond the Manifesto, *New Socialist*, 30 May 2019.

20 China Mills, 'For as Long as the DWP Has Been Killing People, Disabled Activists Have Been Fighting Back', Novara Media, 26 November 2021, novaramedia.com.

21 Robert McRuer and Anna Mollow, eds, *Sex and Disability*, Durham, NC: Duke University Press, 2012.

22 Alice Wong, *Year of the Tiger: An Activist's Life*, New York: Vintage, 2022, pp. 70–1.

23 Riva Lehrer, *Golem Girl: A Memoir*, London: Virago, 2020, pp. 155, 353.

24 Frances Ryan, 'Living in a Woman's Body: This Body Is a Genetic Mistake – But It Is Sex, Laughter and Beauty Too', *Guardian*, 9 February 2022.

25 NSPCC, ' "We Have the Right to Be Safe": Keeping Disabled Children and Young People Safe from Abuse', letterfromsanta.nspcc. org.uk; Joseph Shapiro, 'The Sexual Assault Epidemic No One Talks About', National Public Radio, 8 January 2018, npr.org.

26 Stephanie Wright, 'Between Vulnerability and Sexual Agency', *History Workshop*, (Un)Silenced: Institutional Sexual Violence, 10 February 2022, historyworkshop.org.uk.

27 Tom Shakespeare, 'We Are All Frail', *Aeon*, 16 November 2021, aeon.co.

28 Anne Boyer, *The Undying: A Meditation on Modern Illness*, London: Penguin, 2019, pp. 141, 53, 109.

29 Eva Feder Kittay, *Love's Labor: Essays on Women, Equality, and Dependency*, New York: Routledge, 1999, pp. xii–xiii.

30 Shakespeare, 'We Are All Frail'.

31 Grace Paley, 'Upstaging Time', in *Just as I Thought*, London: Virago, 1999 [1989], p. 294.

32 Olga Tokarczuk, *Drive Your Plow over the Bones of the Dead*, London: Fitzcarraldo Editions, 2018.

33 William Ian Miller, *Losing It*, New Haven: Yale University Press, 2012, p. 3.

34 Scott A. Small, *Forgetting: The Benefits of Not Remembering*, New York: Crown, 2023.

35 Age UK, *All the Lonely People: Loneliness in Later Life*, 1 September 2018, ageuk.org.uk.

36 For example, Christina R. Victor et al., 'Loneliness in Mid-life and Older Adults from Ethnic Minority Communities in England and Wales', *European Journal of Ageing*, 18 (1), March 2021, pp. 5–16.

37 Kerstin Gerst-Emerson and Jayani Jayawardhana, 'Loneliness as a Public Health Issue: The Impact of Loneliness on Health Care Utilization among Older Adults', *American Journal of Public Health*, May 2015; K. F. Ferraro and T. P. Shippee, 'Aging and Cumulative Inequality: How Does Inequality Get under the Skin?', *Gerontologist*, 49, 2009.

38 Campaign to End Loneliness, 'Preventing and Alleviating Loneliness for Older Women', January 2023, campaigntoendloneliness. org.

39 Margaret Atwood, 'Torching the Dusties', in *Stone Mattress: Nine Tales*, London: Bloomsbury, 2014, pp. 245, 265, 256–7.

40 Margaret Morganroth Gullette, *American Eldercide: How It Happened, How to Prevent It Next Time*, in press.

41 Helen Hogan et al., 'Preventable Deaths Due to Problems in Care in English Acute Hospitals: A Retrospective Case Record Review Study', *BMJ Quality and Safety*, 21 (9), September 2012, quality safety.bmj.com.

42 Dartington, *Managing Vulnerability*, p. 50.

43 Beverley Skeggs, 'A Crisis in Humanity: What Everyone with Parents Is Likely to Face in the Future', *Sociological Review Magazine*, 18 January 2017, thesociologicalreview.org.

44 Michael Marmot et al., *Health Equity in England: The Marmot Review 10 Years On*, London: The Health Foundation, February 2020.

45 Susan Douglas, *In Our Prime: How Older Women Are Reinventing the Road Ahead*, New York: W. W. Norton & Company, 2020.

46 OECD, *Promoting an Age-Inclusive Workforce: Living, Learning and Earning Longer*, Paris: OECD Publishing, 16 December 2020, oecd-library.org.

47 Ursula Le Guin, *The Wave in the Mind: Talks and Essays on the Writer, the Reader, and the Imagination*, Boston: Shambhala Publications, 2004, p. 142.

48 Jane Miller, *In My Own Time: Thoughts and Afterthoughts*, London: Virago, 2016, p. 1.

49 One of the most comprehensive and useful is the report from the Centre for Ageing Better, *Reframing Ageing: Public Perceptions of Ageing, Older Age and Demographic Change*, London: Centre for Ageing Better, July 2021.

50 Barbara Ehrenreich, quoted in Stassa Edwards, 'Barbara Ehrenreich Isn't Afraid to Die', *Jezebel*, 1 May 2018, jezebel.com.

51 Ashton Appleton, *This Chair Rocks: A Manifesto against Ageism*, New York: Celadon Books, 2019.

52 Leah Thorn, 'Older Women Rock', leahthorn.com, January 2023.

53 Ajit Shah et al., 'Suicide Rates in Five-Year Age-Bands after the Age of 60 Years: The International Landscape', *Aging and Mental Health*, 20 (2), 2016, pp. 131–8; Diego De Leo, 'Late-Life Suicide in an Aging World', *Nature Aging*, 2 (1), 2022, pp. 7–12.

54 See, for example, Benjamin Cornwell, 'Independence through Social Networks: Bridging Potential among Older Women and Men', *Journal of Gerontology Series B*, 66 (6), November 2011, pp. 782–94.

55 Kylie King et al., '"Is Life Worth Living?": The Role of Masculinity in the Way Men Aged over 80 Talk about Living, Dying, and Suicide', *American Journal of Men's Health*, 14 (5), September–October 2020.

56 Maria T. Brown and Brian R. Grossman, 'Same-Sex Sexual Relationships in the National Social Life, Health and Aging Project: Making a Case for Data Collection', *Journal of Gerontological Social Work*, 57 (2–4), 2014, pp. 108–29; Amy Chandler, 'Boys Don't Cry? Critical Phenomenology, Self-Harm and Suicide', *Sociological Review*, 67 (6), 2019, pp. 1350–66.

57 Anne Karpf, 'The Liberation of Growing Old', *New York Times*, 3 January 2015.

58 Sara Alhatou, 'The Generational Digital Divide', 1 October 2021, storymaps.arcgis.com.

59 Elana D. Buch, *Inequalities of Aging: Paradoxes of Independence in American Home Care*, New York: NYU Press, 2018, pp. 2–3, 7.

60 The King's Fund, 'Staffing Shortfall of 100,000 Could Reach Quarter of a Million by End of Next Decade', 15 November 2018, kingsfund.org.uk.

61 Joan Tronto, 'Democratic Care Politics in an Age of Limits', in *Global Variations in the Political and Social Economy of Care: Worlds Apart*, ed. Shahra Razavi and Silke Staab, London and New York: Routledge, 2012, pp. 29–42.

5. Repairing the Planet

1   Amitav Ghosh, 'European Colonialism Helped Create a Planet in Crisis', *Guardian*, 14 January 2022.

2   Anne Karpf, *How Women Can Save the Planet*, London: Hurst, 2021.

3   See 'John Keats Letter to Benjamin Bailey, 8 October 1817', *English History*, 24 February 2015, englishhistory.net.

4   Ralph Waldo Emerson, 'Nature' (1936), in *Nature and Selected Essays*, New York: Penguin Classics, 2003; Henry David Thoreau, *Walden, or Life in the Woods*, New York: Dover, 1996 [1854].

5   Walt Whitman, *Leaves of Grass*, Brooklyn: 1855, p. vi; *Leaves of Grass*, Philadelphia: David McKay, 1891–2, p. 319, Walt Whitman Archive, whitmanarchive.org.

6   Robert MacFarlane, *Landmarks*, London: Penguin, 2016; Richard Muir, *Landscape Encyclopaedia: A Reference to the Historic Landscape*, Oxford: Windgather Press, 2004; Roger Deakins, *Wildwood: A Journey through Trees*, London: Unbound, 2007.

7   Katharine Norbury, ed., *Women on Nature*, London: Unbound, 2021, p. 8.

8   Kathleen Jamie, *Sightlines*, London: Sort of Books, 2012, p. 242.

9   Penelope Lively, 'The Gardening Eye', in *In the Garden: Essays on Nature and Growing*, ed. Jamaica Kincaid, London: Daunt Books, 2021, pp. 12–13.

10 Kirsty Nutt, 'Nature Prescriptions Helping Hundreds of Patients in Edinburgh', Royal Society for the Protection of Birds, 17 January 2022, rspb.org.uk.

11 Victoria Forster, 'Canadian Physicians Can Now Prescribe Nature to Patients', Forbes Healthcare, 28 February 2022.

12 See Lynne Segal, *Radical Happiness: Moments of Collective Joy*, London: Verso, 2017.

13 Barbara Taylor, *Eve and the New Jerusalem: Socialism and Feminism in the Nineteenth Century*, London: Virago, 1983.

14 John Bellamy Foster, *Marx's Ecology: Materialism and Nature*, New York: Monthly Review Press, 2000; Paul Burkett, *Marxism and Ecological Economics: Toward a Red and Green Political Economy*, Chicago: Haymarket Books, 2009.

15 Karl Marx, *Capital: A Critique of Political Economy*, New York: International Publishers, 1967 [1867], pp. 505–7.

16 Friedrich Engels, *The Origin of the Family, Private Property, and the State*, London: Penguin Classics, 2010 [1884], pp. 260–1.

17 William Morris, 'How We Live and How We Might Live', published online by Cambridge University Press, August 2013 [1884], available at marxists.org.

18 William Morris, *News from Nowhere*, in *News from Nowhere and Other Writings*, London: Penguin Classics, revised edn, 1993 [1890].

19 Edward Carpenter, *Towards Democracy*, 1922, p. 240, available at edwardcarpenter.net.

20 John Ruskin, *The Storm-Cloud of the Nineteenth Century*, New York: J. Wiley, 1884, available at Project Gutenberg, gutenberg.org.

21 See for instance, Marquita K. Hill, *Understanding Environmental Pollution*, Cambridge: Cambridge University Press, 2012; Monica Crippa et al., 'Forty Years of Improvements in European Air Quality: Regional Policy–Industry Interactions with Global Impacts', *Atmospheric Chemistry and Physics*, 16 (6), 2016, pp. 3825–41.

22 Royal College of Physicians, 'Doctors Say 40,000 Deaths a Year Linked to Air Pollution', news release, 23 February 2016, rcplondon. ac.uk.

23 See, for instance, Jocelyn Timperley, 'Who Is Really to Blame for Climate Change?', BBC Future, Climate Emotions, 19 June 2020, bbc.com.

24 Naomi Oreskes and Erik M. Conway, *Merchants of Doubt: How a Handful of Scientists Obscured the Truth on Issues from Tobacco Smoke to Global Warming*, London: Bloomsbury Paperbacks, 2012.

25 Neela Banerjee et al., *Exxon: The Road Not Taken*, London: Create-Space Independent Publishing Platform, 2015.

26 Fiona Harvey, 'Enormous Emissions Gap between Top 1% and Poorest', *Guardian*, 1 November 2022.

27 Yannick Oswald, Anne Owen, and Julia K. Steinberger, 'Large Inequality in International and Intranational Energy Footprints between Income Groups and across Consumption Categories', *Nature Energy*, 5, 2020, pp. 231–9.

28 Peter Stott, *Hot Air: The Inside Story of the Battle against Climate Change Denial*, London: Atlantic Books, 2021.

29 George Monbiot, 'From the Amazon to Australia, Why Is Your Money Funding Earth's Destruction?', *Guardian*, 30 November 2022.

30 See Bill McKibben, 'In a World on Fire, Stop Burning Things', *New Yorker*, 18 March 1922.

31 Rachel Carson, *Silent Spring*, London: Penguin Classics, 2000 [1962].

32 Natural Resources Defense Council, 'The Story of *Silent Spring*', 13 August 2015, nrdc.org.

33 Susan Griffin, *Woman and Nature: The Roaring Inside Her*, New York: Harper, 1978, pp. 5, 26.

34 Barbara Tannenbaum, 'Hear Her Roar: Ecofeminist Author Susan Griffin Isn't Going Away', *California* (Cal Alumni Association magazine), 29 March 2017, alumni.berkeley.edu.

35 Françoise d'Eaubonne, *Feminism or Death*, trans. Ruth Hottell, London: Verso, 2022 [1974].

36 Vandana Shiva, *Staying Alive: Women, Ecology and Development*, London: Zed Press, 1989 [1988]; Vandana Shiva, *Reclaiming the Commons: Biodiversity, Traditional Knowledge, and the Rights of Mother Earth*, Santa Fe, NM: Synergetic Press, 2020.

37 Val Plumwood, *Feminism and the Mastery of Nature*, London and New York: Routledge, 1993. The Norwegian sociologist Agnes Bolsø has written an excellent overview of Plumwood's work, 'Val Plumwood: Organizing for the Future', in *Morality, Ethics and Responsibility in Organization and Management*, ed. Robert McMurray and Alison Pullen, London: Routledge, 2020.

38 Kim TallBear, 'Caretaking Relations, Not American Dreaming', *Kalfou*, 6 (1), 2019.

39 Robin Gomes, 'Myanmar Military's Offensive against Karen People', *Vatican News*, 7 April 2021.

40 Dev Kumar Sunuwar, 'Victoria Tauli-Corpuz Reflects on Her Six-Year Tenure as Special Rapporteur on the Rights of Indigenous Peoples', *Cultural Survival*, 23 April 2020.

41 Front Line Defenders, *Global Analysis 2019*, Dublin, Ireland, February 2020.

42 Ashish Ghadiali, 'Editorial: Planetary Imagination', *Soundings*, 78, 2021, p. 6.

43 Quoted in Donna Lu, 'Extremes of 40C above Normal: What's Causing "Extraordinary" Heating in Polar Regions?', *Guardian*, 21 March 2022.

44 United Nations Climate Change, 'What Is the Kyoto Protocol?', unfccc.int.

45 Richard Partington, 'UK Green Economy Has Failed to Grow since 2014, According to Official Data', *Guardian*, 17 February 2022.

46 Andreas Malm, *How to Blow Up a Pipeline*, London: Verso, 2021, p. 3.

47 Andreas Malm, quoted in George Eaton, 'Andreas Malm: "The Likely Future Is Escalating Catastrophe" ', *New Statesman*, 14 October 2020.

48 See, for example, Lourdes Sanchez, 'Five Missed Opportunities to Support the Energy Transition in COVID-19', *IISD-SDG Knowledge Hub Recovery*, 14 October 2021.

49 Ann Pettifor, *The Case for the Green New Deal*, London: Verso, 2019; Naomi Klein, *On Fire*, London and New York: Allen Lane, 2019.

50 Rebecca Solnit, 'Every Protest Shifts the World's Balance', *Guardian Review*, 1 June 2019.

51 George Monbiot, *Out of the Wreckage: A New Politics for an Age of Crisis*, London: Verso, 2016.

52 Jason Hickel, *Less Is More: How Degrowth Will Save the World*, London: Windmill Books, 2021.

53 Mark Z. Jacobson et al., 'Low-Cost Solution to the Grid Reliability Problem with 100% Penetration of Intermittent Wind, Water, and Solar for All Purposes', *PNAS*, 112 (49), 8 December 2015.

54 See McKibben, 'In a World on Fire'.

55 Molly S. Castelloe, 'Coming to Terms with Ecoanxiety: Growing an Awareness of Climate Change', *Psychologist*, 9 January 2018.

56 Susan Kassouf, 'Thinking Catastrophic Thoughts: A Traumatized Sensibility on a Hotter Planet', *American Journal of Psychoanalysis*, 82 (1), March 2022, pp. 60–79.

57 Stuart Capstick, 'Climate Change: Greener Lifestyles Linked to Greater Happiness – In Both Rich and Poor Countries', *The Conversation*, 4 April 2022.

58 Matt McGrath, 'Climate Change: IPCC Scientists Say It's "Now or Never" to Limit Warming', BBC Science, 4 April 2022, bbc.com.

59 Stuart Capstick et al., 'The Connection between Subjective Well-being and Pro-environmental Behaviour: Individual and Cross-National Characteristics in a Seven-Country Study', *Environmental Science and Policy*, 133, 2022, pp. 63–73.

60 Bristol Energy Cooperative, *Community Benefit 2020*, October 2020, bristolenergy.coop.

61 Justine Calma, 'The Places Paving the Way to 100 Percent Renewable Energy', *Verge*, 25 May 2021.

62 See, for example, Mathew Lawrence and Laurie Laybourn-Langton, *Planet on Fire: A Manifesto for the Age of Environmental Breakdown*, London: Verso, 2021.

63 Kate Soper, *Post-growth Living: For an Alternative Hedonism*, London: Verso, 2020.

64 Extinction Rebellion, *This Is Not a Drill: An Extinction Rebellion Handbook*, London: Penguin, 2019.

65 Rowan Williams, afterword in ibid., pp. 181, 184.

66 Donna Haraway, *Staying with the Trouble: Making Kin in the Chthulucene*, London and Durham, NC: Duke University Press, 2016, p. 1.

6. Caring Futures

1 Beverley Skeggs, 'Care with Bev Skeggs', *Sociological Review*, 22 April 2022, thesociologicalreview.org.

2 Kamila Shamsie, 'A Hostile Environment Baton Passed from Theresa May to Priti Patel – And a Decade of Cruelty', *Guardian*, 23 June 2022.

3 Thomas Piketty, *Capital in the Twenty-First Century*, Cambridge, MA: Harvard University Press, 2014; Oxfam America, 'Poverty in the USA', January 2023, oxfamamerica.org.

4 United Nations High Commissioner for Refugees, *Global Trends: Forced Displacement in 2021*, Copenhagen: UNHCR, 2022, unhcr. org.

5 W. H. Auden, 'September 1, 1939', available at poets.org.

6 Subcomandante Marcos, 'Why We Need Independent Media', Zapatista address to the Freeing the Media Teach-In, 31 January– 1 February 1997, New York, available at subsol.c3.hu.

7 Sindre Bangstad and Torbjørn Tumyr Nilsen, 'Thoughts on the Planetary: An Interview with Achille Mbembe', *New Frame*, 5 September 2019, newframe.com.

8 Los Angeles County Alternatives to Incarceration Work Group, *Care First, Jails Last*, final report, October 2020, ceo.lacounty.gov.

9 Clément Petitjean and Ruth Wilson Gilmore, 'Prisons and Class Warfare: An Interview with Ruth Wilson Gilmore', Verso blog, 2 August 2018, versobooks.com.

10 Movement for Black Lives (M4BL), 'Vision for Black Lives', Policy Platforms, January 2023, m4bl.org.

11 Keir Monteith et al., *Racial Bias and the Bench: A Response to the Judicial Diversity and Inclusions Strategy (2020–2025)*, Manchester: University of Manchester, November 2022, manchester.ac.uk.

12 Adam Elliott-Cooper, *Black Resistance to British Policing (Racism, Resistance and Social Change)*, Manchester: Manchester University Press, 2021.

13 Cradle Community, *Brick by Brick: How We Build a World without Prisons*, London: Hajar Press, 2021.

14 Joe Sim, *Punishment and Prisons: Power and the Carceral State*, London: Sage, 2009.

15 Forensic Oceanography, 'The Left-to-Die Boat', 11 April 2012, forensic-architecture.org.

16 Amnesty International UK, 'Safe and Legal Routes to the UK', briefing, January 2021, amnesty.org.uk.

17 Sue Clayton, *The New Internationalists: Activist Volunteers in the European Refugee Crisis*, London: Goldsmiths Press, 2020.

18 Tess Berry-Hart, 'People to People: The Volunteer Phenomenon', *Refugee History*, 19 June 2018, refugeehistory.org.

19 Daniel Trilling, *Lights in the Distance: Exile and Refuge on the Borders of Europe*, London: Picador, 2018.

20 Marina Warner, 'Stories in Transit: Words on the Move', January 2023, storiesintransit.org.

21 Behrouz Boochani, interview by Jina Khayyer, *Fantastic Man*, 34, Autumn and Winter 2021/22, fantasticman.com/features/behrouz.

22 Barbara Taylor, 'The History of Compassion'; Anthony Grayling, 'The Philosophy of Compassion'; Pragna Patel, 'Justice', in *How Compassion Can Transform Our Politics, Economy and Society*, ed. Matt Hawkins and Jennifer Nadel, Abingdon: Routledge, 2022.

23 Rebecca Solnit, *A Paradise Built in Hell: The Extraordinary Communities that Arise in Disaster*, New York: Viking Press, 2009.

24 Mike Phipps, *Don't Stop Thinking about Tomorrow*, London: Or Books, 2022.

25 Medea Benjamin, 'A World of Possibilities: 10 Surprisingly Good Things that Happened in 2022', *Salon*, 31 December 2022, salon.com.

26 Lula da Silva's inauguration speech, 1 January 2023, as translated by my friend João Manuel de Oliveira.

27 David Graeber, 'From Managerial Feudalism to the Revolt of the Caring Classes', talk given to 36th Chaos Communication Congress, 27 December 2019, transcript available at opentranscripts.org.

28 Lynne Segal, *Radical Happiness: Moments of Collective Joy*, London: Verso, 2017.

29 Jo Littler, ed., *Left Feminisms: Conversations on the Personal and Political*, London: Lawrence and Wishart, 2023.

30 IPR, 'How Generous Is the British Welfare State?', University of Bath, 28 October 2022, blogs.bath.ac.uk; Statista, 'Healthcare and Military Expenditure as a Percentage of GDP in Select Countries Worldwide in 2020', 12 December 2022, statista.com.

31 Heather Stewart, 'Four-Day Week: "Major Breakthrough" as Most UK Firms in Trial Extend Changes', *Guardian*, 21 February 2023.

32 International Labour Organization, *Working Time and Work-Life Balance around the World*, Geneva: International Labour Office, 6 January 2023, ilo.org.

33 See, for example, Maeve Cohen and Sherilyn MacGregor, *Towards a Feminist Green New Deal for the UK*, London: Women's Environmental Network, Women's Budget Group, 2020, genderclimatetracker.org.

34 James Meadway, 'If You Thought 2022 Was Bad for Your Bank Balance, Just Wait for the Sequel. Still, There Are Reasons for Hope', Novara Media, 31 December 2022, novaramedia.com.

35 Jeremy Gilbert and Alex Williams, *Hegemony Now: How Big Tech and Wall Street Won the World (and How We Win It Back)*, London and New York: Verso, 2022, p. 252.

36 Laura Wronski, Axios-Momentive Poll: 'Capitalism and Socialism', surveymonkey.com.

37 Angelina Kussy et al., 'The Caring City? A Critical Reflection on Barcelona's Municipal Experiments in Care and the Commons', *Urban Studies*, 8 December 2022.

38 Christine Berry, 'Challenging the Asset Economy: Ownership in the Care Sector', Autonomy think tank, 22 December 2021, autonomy. work.

Index

INDEX

Norbury, Katharine 158–9
Northern Ireland 99
Norway 40–1
Novara Media 203
nuclear weapons 210
Nussbaum, Martha 48, 75

Oakley, Anne 27–8, 32, 35, 60
Obama, Michelle 111
Ocasio-Cortez, Alexandria 15, 177, 204
Off Our Backs (magazine) 27
Ohio 14
Okech, Awino 208
Older Women Rock 148
Oliver, Mike 124
Orbach, Susie 92
Oreskes, Naomi 165
Orgad, Shani 39
Organisation of Women of African and Asian Descent 106–7
Ova 89
overwork, culture of 40
Owen, Robert and the Owenite movement 79–80, 161

Palestinian struggle 188–9
Paley, Grace 137, 145
Pankhurst, Christabel 82
Pankhurst, Emmeline 80, 82
Pankhurst, Sylvia 80, 82–4
Paris Agreement, 2015 174–5, 177
Patel, Pragna 107, 201–2
patriarchy 95
Pearson, Karl 81
Peckham Rye Women's Group 26–7
Perrier, Maude 43
Personal Independence Payment 8
pessimism, moving beyond 186–91
Pettifor, Ann 178
Phillips, Adam 24, 42
Phillips, Anne 104
Phipps, Mike 203
Piketty, Thomas 187
pink tide, the 205
Plumwood, Val 170, 171
Poland 114–15
police and policing 16, 67, 97, 114, 193–4
political activism, well-being and 17
political culture 202
political sociology 60
Politics of Sexuality conference 68
pollution paradox, the 167
populism 204
pornography 68, 98, 100, 101
postmodernism 68
post-natal depression 23–4, 27

poverty 129–30, 186–7, 192
Power, Anne 13
prejudice 59
Preston model 13–14
prison abolition movement 15, 191–5
private property 3
privatization 213
productivity 146
profiteering 10
protests 11
psychoanalysis 5–6
psychology 56–7
public engagement 207
public schools 49
Push, the 77

race deterioration 21
race and racism 51, 59, 82, 90, 92, 132, 192, 193–4, 201
radical feminists 100
rape 116–17
Rathbone, Eleanor 22, 84
Ravitch, David 53
Raworth, Kate 183
Reagan, Ronald 102–3, 126
Red Rag (magazine) 97–8
redistributive neighbourliness 13
Refugee History posts 197
refugees 187, 195–200
    Australian policy 199–200
    children 196–7
    hostile environment policy 186
    invasion rhetoric 198–9
    left-to-die policy 196
    Rwanda deportation policy 196
    Stories in Transit project 198
    suffering 196–7
    volunteer activists 196–7
religious fundamentalism 107
reproductive rights 85–6, 113
resources, democratization of 211–12
responsibility 5, 191
revolutionary feminism 100–1
Reynolds, Malvina 78
Rich, Adrienne 33–4
rich, the 7
Rights of Indigenous Peoples 173
Robbins Report (1963) 62, 64
Roberts, Michèle 31
Rock against Racism concert 61
Roehampton University 72
Rose, Jacqueline 42
Roseneil, Sasha 106
Ross, Ellen 21
Rottenberg, Catherine 38, 112
Rousseau, Jean-Jacques 48, 200–1
Rowbotham, Sheila 30, 65, 85–6, 93, 97–8, 101–2, 105, 107–8

243